A STRANGER IN THE LAND

* * * * * *

A STRANGER IN THE LAND

* * * * * *

Jewish Identity Beyond Nationalism

DANIEL CIL BRECHER

Translated by BARBARA HARSHAV

Other Press • New York

Production Editor: Mira S. Park

Book design by Jeremy Diamond

This book was set in 10.5 pt. Janson Text by Alpha Graphics of Pittsfield, NH.

10 9 8 7 6 5 4 3 2 1

 Printed in the United States of America on acid-free paper. For information write to Other Press LLC, 2 Park Avenue, 24th Floor, New York, NY 10016. Or visit our Web site: www.otherpress.com.

Library of Congress Cataloging-in-Publication Data

Brecher, Daniel Cil, 1951-
[Fremd in Zion. English]
A stranger in the land : Jewish identity beyond nationalism / Daniel Cil Brecher ; translated by Barbara Harshav.
p. cm.
Includes bibliographical references.
ISBN-13: 978-1-59051-211-1
ISBN-10: 1-59051-211-1
1. Arab-Israeli conflict. 2. Zionism–History. 3. Jews–Germany–Identity.
I. Title.
DS119.7.R713513 2007
956.04—dc22

2006018919

As a mother lays her infant to her breast
without waking it, so, for a long time
does life treat the still tender memories of childhood.

—WALTER BENJAMIN, *Berlin Childhood around 1900*

You shall leave everything most dearly loved:
This is the first one of the arrows which
The bow of exile is prepared to shoot.
You shall discover how salty is the savor
Of someone else's bread, and how hard the way
To come down and climb up another's stairs.

—DANTE, *Paradise Lost* XVII

* CONTENTS *

* * * * * *

* PREFACE *

This book is both a personal account and a political reflection on Israel, Zionism, and Jewish identity. The personal parts of the book present my experiences as an immigrant in Israel and as an historian in the education corps of the Israel Defense Force, as a regular soldier and later as a reservist between 1979 and 1984. The education system of the Israeli army is responsible for training, indoctrinating, and entertaining the troops and converts the political and ideological guidelines set by the government into concrete programs. It was no accident that the military history projects I undertook in the department of "Battle Heritage" put me on a collision course with my superiors. My work on the rival pre-state Jewish underground armies formed to combat the British Mandatory forces and the Arab militias, and on Jewish armed resistance to the Nazis during World War II, related directly to specific historical myths about the emergence of the State of Israel, the Holocaust, and the link between the two. These myths have played a significant role in Zionist thought and have been crucial in shaping Israeli public opinion. Thus, for me, conflicts about these research projects became a confrontation with contemporary political problems of the Middle East conflict.

These years were a period of inner change for me, culminating during the war in Lebanon. My report begins with my experiences in the first year of war and ends with an evening in February 1984, when I refused to cross the Lebanese border to reinforce troop morale. In between, I describe my confrontation with the political reality of Israel, the basic ideas of Zionism, and Jewish nationalism in the Diaspora. Personal reports and observations alternate with historical retrospectives and analyses of attitudes and myths in Jewish and Israeli society. With the adventure in Lebanon as a background, I investigate the peculiar dynamic of the Jewish-Palestinian conflict and re-examine the fate of the Palestinians in 1948. In a critical reconsideration of the forces that shaped my Jewish identity in postwar Europe, I revisit that special setting of the re-emerging Jewish communities in postwar Germany, where the ideas of Zionism spread unchecked as a reaction to the years of persecution and to an environment perceived as hostile.

It was not easy to combine the historical retrospectives and personal accounts of this book, and I often wondered if I shouldn't have chosen one or the other. Critical considerations of the basic political and social constellations in the State of Israel and the behaviors and ideas I include under the rubric of "Jewish nationalism" could easily fill this book. And so could the descriptions of my adventures in the Israeli army, my initiation as a new citizen of the State, and the review of my youth in postwar Germany. But while Zionism as an ideology and a political movement is well defined, Jewish nationalism, after flowing into Zionism as an intellectual current in the late nineteenth century, now consists of a loose conglomeration of attitudes and convictions among Jews referring to Jewish history, Jewish uniqueness, and relations to non-Jews. These views and behaviors are much harder to grasp, are easy to misunderstand, and can best be described from one's own experience. But the real motive lies deeper.

I grew up at a time and in a milieu in which the victory of Zionism and the creation of Israel were considered the culmination of an extraordinary, even mythical development—as the triumph of the tormented and almost exterminated Jewish people over their foes, as a judgment of history that finally compensated for the suffering caused by centuries of anti-Semitism and the Holocaust. These ideas were deeply ingrained in my Jewish identity and made all later debates with Israel and Zionism into a process of self-understanding. I have tried to explain this internal process here. Thus, this book is also a chronicle of the abandonment of a monolithic, exclusive Jewish identity founded in nationalism for a heterogeneous, multicultural one, in which Jews appear as bearers of both Jewish and non-Jewish cultural traditions.

The political and personal conflicts discussed in this book originate in the broadest sense from my double origin. During World War II, my parents were stripped of their rights, robbed, locked up, and abused as slaves by the Nazis and their henchmen. Their survival was a matter of luck. After the liberation, they went first to Israel, and then to Germany. Thus, I was first initiated into the heritage of a Jewish nationalism that had changed during my parents' lifetime from a movement of cultural renewal and emancipation to a radical and militant state ideology propagating the principle of an ethnically pure society. Then, influenced by the enlightened thinking prevalent in postwar West Germany, I came to a humanism, pacifism, and anti-nationalism that found an especially eager disciple and champion in me, the scion of a minority group harmed by nationalism.

My story was also experienced by others, not with the same details but with the same outline: as a member of a generation of postwar Jewish youth in the West, who heeded the call to the banner of Israel and Zionism, and joined the struggle to ensure the security of the state and to help build the new society in some way. Thus, I invite the reader to discover the contours of this generation behind the narrator, who stands inevitably in the foreground. The basic subject of this book, the search for a group identity beyond nationalism, has preoccupied many of us, wherever we come from.

The debate with Zionism has a long tradition within Jewish communities. Until the end of World War II, supporters of Zionism represented a small minority, while most Jewish organizations and the Jewish "establishment" considered themselves explicitly anti-Zionist. Critics accused Zionism of challenging or endangering the emancipation and integration of Jews in their homelands, and even supporting the anti-Semitic thesis that the coexistence of Jews and non-Jews was undesirable or harmful. Even within the Zionism movement, the main goal—the creation of a state under colonial conditions—was controversial. "This side of the issue," wrote the German-Jewish historian and Zionist Gershom Scholem, "until Hitler's annihilation of the Jews, had for me and many others played only a secondary or even very small role."

The Holocaust revolutionized not only Jewish attitudes toward Zionism. Public opinion in the Christian countries of Europe and America now also supported the plan for a state for Jews and made Israel a joint project of the West, in which the Jewish settlers in Palestine initially only played the role of junior partner. Today, the overwhelming majority of Jews can be defined as pro-Zionist. But this means little more than solidarity with the Jews of Israel and support of the State in its conflict with the Arabs. The issues of the prewar internal Jewish discussion have lost their foundations—with one exception. Even in the 1930s, critics both inside and outside the Zionist movement indicated an essential structural defect in Zionist thought—that the land claimed by Zionism was inhabited by others. With the territorial expansions of 1948–1949 and after 1967, this issue has assumed a new dimension. The modern settlement of Jews, the creation of the State, and its expansion were acts of colonialism that have led to the displacement of the original Arab population, to a bloody conflict with neighboring countries, and to the destruction of the Arab society of Palestine. This congenital defect of Israel, its tragic consequences for the Arab and Jewish population of the region, and the justifications and myths that have arisen around the history and behavior of the State, form the focus of this book.

The creation of no other state in the twentieth century has stirred so much sensation, found so much consent and rejection, and produced so much violence. An author who dives into these quarrels runs a greater risk that his arguments will be misunderstood and misused. Among both Jews and non-Jews, Israelis and Arabs, far too many seek justifications for their nationalistic prejudices and goals, for hatred and acts of violence. This book will offer them no encouragement, for it contains a clear demand: to cast off the cloak of national myths and take responsibility for one's own acts. The process leading to rapprochement, understanding, and peace in the Middle East can be concluded only by acknowledging one's own responsibility and guilt for the suffering of others. In our time, when the border fences of national identities are once again rising to the sky, the only way to get there is through dialogue.

My work on this book was supported by several friends and colleagues, who read and judged parts of the manuscript in various stages. Thanks to Frederik Bogin, Ulrich Borsdorf, Stefanie Hoster, Peter Lataster, Petra Lataster-Csisch, Eckhard Roelcke, and Kristian Wachinger for their help, criticism, and encouragement; to my editor Julia Hoffmann at DVA for her patient and expert revision of the German text; and to my magnificent English translator, Barbara Harshav. Special thanks to Jacqueline Ebskamp and Bluma Brecher, who bravely put up with my moods during the many months of work.

* PART 1 *

1

* WAR *
By Way of Introduction

* 1 *

On the night before my reserve duty, I couldn't get to sleep. My thoughts were trained anxiously on the future, but the memory of the past years kept me awake, too. The search for rest, pursued initially with desperate energy, soon turned into an effort that brought me no closer to sleep. My call-up had caught me by surprise. Why was our unit mobilized? What could a handful of non-belligerent historians accomplish in Lebanon? What would I have to do? My reserve mobilization was based on a special war order and was unlimited in terms of time. A dark abyss gaped before me. I was scared.

In the dark of my bedroom, I started talking to Colonel Wechsler. Walking for hours at headquarters, I had fought with that head of the "battle heritage" unit about assignments and texts, often comma by comma, about ideological lines, proper wording. My job consisted of writing training manuals for education officers in the field who instructed the common soldiers on the history of the Israeli army, training manuals on wars, battles, heroic acts, on "battle heritage," its official title. This unit played an important role in the historical and political indoctrination of the troops. This was the source of my conflicts, for I had to insist on defending the independence of my judgment and the integrity of my profession. Now that I'd completed my regular military service, I still served in the reserves, but had meanwhile taken to delivering innocuous lectures on more remote chapters of Jewish history.

Colonel Wechsler was also under pressure. He had to keep his eye on the general scheme of things, the ideological lines formulated by the general staff, to be translated into programs by the education division. Above all, he had to consider the opinion of his new superior, an infantry general appointed by Menachem Begin's first government to rid the education division of Labor Party influence. I only had to worry about saving my own soul, about the conscience of a scrupulous opportunist, who could no longer support the Zionist consensus and its corresponding versions of history but who didn't have the courage to refuse orders and simply leave.

Wechsler had only a little hair left. The skin in the middle of his scalp, a perfectly round hole like a tonsure, was almost decimated by the sun. When we walked in the intense heat on the dusty paths of headquarters, I worried about that, too. The two of us preferred to discuss our differences outside, as if a conversation in the office would have hardened our views and restricted our scope. Why had he let us be mobilized now? Why had he even accepted me into the unit back then? Why had he played a game of cat and mouse with me for years?

At the beginning of the week, my wife and I, who had been separated for a while, had gotten divorced at the Jerusalem rabbinate. I was neither religious nor for a long time had I been a Zionist, and it was growing harder for me to negotiate the ever widening gap between me and my environment. My life in Israel increasingly seemed a failure—too many compromises, too little happiness. Only professionally was I doing well. A few months before, the director of my institute, who was about to retire, revealed that he wanted to propose me to the board as his successor. My other work, doing research at the Hebrew University, also meant a lot to me. That's what kept me from leaving Israel. And there was also the question of where would I go.

At dawn, I got up and tried to eat something. Then I packed my things. My uniform, seldom worn, had lain at the back of the closet for years. When I took it out, the smell of the army hit me: the cheap scent of the central laundry detergent, traces of sweat, lubricating oil, and the Lysol I had used in the last phase of basic training to clean the latrines of the base all summer because I had refused all other duties. The rest of my gear was still tied up for the field in small plastic-wrapped packages. I spread everything out on the kitchen table to check the contents and get used once again to the objects: hair and clothing brushes, shaving gear, washcloths, shoe-shine and sewing kits, field cutlery that always made food taste like metal, the underwear, socks, and belt—everything in olive green or army beige.

My flat was on the top floor of an apartment house constructed hastily and badly in the early 1950s for the big waves of immigration from Europe and North Africa, on a hill at the edge of downtown Jerusalem. The gloomy mood of the entrance, stairs, and corridors vanished as soon as you opened the door of my flat and entered the light of the Jerusalem sky falling through the big windows. There was hardly a visitor who didn't rush first to one of the windows or to the balcony to be amazed at the magnificent sky, the mountain chain around the city, and the Disneyland architecture of the government and university buildings below. Every table and chair in the flat was aligned with this panorama. No matter how bad my mood was when I sat down at the kitchen table in the morning, it could usually be improved by the clear outlines of the Judean Mountains, the brilliant light beaming from the whitewashed walls of the Monastery of the Cross, and the ever-fascinating spectacle of the Jerusalem traffic jams. But this morning, nothing helped.

I laid the contents of the uniform pockets on the kitchen table—the requisite items and what I was used to carrying as talismans and consolations. Most of the contents were prescribed, but it was something private that could remain secret even in inspections. On the right—or left for those who were left-handed—in the big side pocket of the pants went the two spare magazines for the weapon. Some soldiers tied the magazines together with the openings at opposite ends, others at an angle of 180 degrees. As soon as one magazine was emptied and pulled out, it could be replaced with a twist of the wrist. Even if there were practical reasons for either of the solutions, I thought such practices looked like magic acts still necessary in a time of mechanized weapons to confer to the individual strength, courage, and a sense of invulnerability. In the other pants pockets went dressings, pressure bandages, wound powder, and an odd-looking package containing a morphine injection, which terrified me the most.

In the left shirt pocket, I had to carry a small, curious document—the prisoner-of-war card. The first page said: "Israel Defense Forces. ID (art. 17, Geneva Convention relative to the treatment of prisoners of war, August 12, 1949)." Inside were details about the bearer: first name and last name, date of birth, civilian and military ID numbers, father's first name, blood type, and any chronic illnesses or afflictions worth mentioning to the enemy. Together with the list of inoculations I had received in the army on the back of the page, this card was a testimony of sorts to the army's concern for its soldiers.

The shirt pocket offered just enough room for a little book. During the months of my basic infantry training, all I wanted to do was read a book, but I had to make an outward show of an obedient student fascinated by the instructor's lecture. Just carrying a book around openly would have subjected me to unnecessary discussions. So I had to find books that could be hidden not only in the shirt pocket, but also in hand. As a graduate of a classical Gymnasium and a German university, I had a suitable format—books from the Universal Library of Reclam, a traditional Leipzig publisher of classical texts, whose small size seemed made expressly for the pockets of the Israeli uniform. Even the demanding reading material turned out to be ideal. Lighter reading could not have provided as effective an escape from army life. It was only the color of the Reclam books, a bright yellow, which seemed unsuitable for military use.

The last article that went in the shirt pocket was the pocket knife. My father-in-law had given me this knife, that red Swiss Army knife, when I started basic training. He was the only one around who was proud of this moment, and I supposed he himself would have liked to serve in this army. He had spent his youth in World War II fleeing the Nazis in Holland, and perhaps he saw my military service as something he would like to have done then. I was his proxy. Sometimes he drove me to the most remote bases, as a way of making a small contribution to the defense of the country.

What else should I take? I didn't know how soon I'd get a weekend pass, so I packed everything I considered absolutely necessary for a long absence. Like all reservists, I could ride free on public transportation to the base, but I usually waived that privilege to preserve a little individuality and mobility. Now, too, I wanted to drive my own car to army headquarters on the coast.

* 2 *

The war had broken out on a Sunday morning. For days, there had been shooting on both sides of the Lebanese border, but when the clock radio woke me on Sunday with the news that the war had begun, I was surprised. The escalation had started on Wednesday. After dinner, the Israeli ambassador in London was standing in front of the Dorchester Hotel at Hyde Park, when a member of the Abu Nidal group popped up in front of him and shot him in the head with a machine gun. The man was wounded so badly that his death was imminent. The Israeli government, which had gritted its teeth for eleven months and maintained a U.S.-imposed truce, used the attack as an opportunity to launch an air raid against the PLO in Lebanon. In response, the PLO poured Katyusha rockets onto the houses and fields of the northern kibbutzim. The Israeli air force retaliated, the PLO fired more Katyushas into Israel, and thus the Israeli and Lebanese inhabitants of the border region spent the following days in air-raid shelters that hadn't been used in eleven months and couldn't be cleaned fast enough.

As on almost every other Saturday, I had also spent this Saturday of June 5, 1982, with friends in the Arab part of Jerusalem to get away from the crushing Sabbath rest in the Jewish part of the city; we shopped in the souk and had dinner in an Arab restaurant. In the empty streets of the Jewish new city, we passed Orthodox families hurrying to prayers in broad phalanxes, girls in white socks, women in velvet dresses, men in dark suits and wide-brimmed hats. Where a wall had divided Jerusalem until 1967, we passed into another world. East Jerusalem was an occupied territory, but crossing the old border still meant changing from a modern, nervous, tense Israel into the reserved, patient, and traditional lifestyle of captured Palestine. The scene changed completely. Poorly dressed farmers from the surrounding villages came toward us, leading their heavily laden mules to market; here we encountered the exhaust of the colorfully painted trucks, with talismans dangling on their windshields. Past and present blended, not always harmoniously. Beggars lay in the gutters holding out their bowls to passersby. The coming and going of the rulers, fashions, and cultures that had left their traces in the city for the last fifty years could be studied in the colorful medley of their old secondhand shoes picked up in the bazaar. In the devastated, dusty square in front of Damascus Gate, Arab day laborers congregated in packs, smoking and waiting for a Jewish employer to offer them a few hours of hard, badly paid work.

How calm and peaceful the atmosphere was on this spring day in East Jerusalem can hardly be imagined today. There had not yet been any Madrid, Oslo, Camp David, Wyet or Taba—not yet any hopes and defeats in the struggle for peace, not yet any first and second Intifada, and the occupation of Lebanon had not yet begun, which was to last until May 2000 and infect the Middle East repeatedly like a gaping, suppurating wound. The scenery of the Old City, which seemed unchanged for centuries, still offered consolation and escape from my tense West Jerusalem life. Maybe it was this soothing scene on that Saturday that helped make us still expect a good outcome of the Israeli-Palestinian conflict, even if not immediately.

I was convinced that the immediate problem was for the adversaries to find their own way back to a truce. Recent years had shown that this duel over the Lebanese border was futile. The guerilla force of the PLO in southern Lebanon could not reconquer the lost Palestine; the air raids of the Israeli government could not liberate Lebanon from the PLO or the Palestinian refugees. Yet, both sides were still willing to use extreme force. Thus, a kind of equilibrium was reached. Despite the great discrepancy in military strength, a stalemate resulted, an effective mutual deterrence providing both sides with reasons for restraint.

Only one small detail made me sit up and take notice, one single note in the otherwise familiar canon of justifications the Israeli government trotted out for its policy toward the Palestinians. The government spokesman had said that a ceasefire in the war against terror wasn't possible. Then he had been provoked into a rhetorical question by a journalist's comment. Can Israel be expected, he asked, to accept a ceasefire in the war against the butchers of the Jews? A ceasefire with Hitler?

This hackneyed phrase was new, even if the ban on comparisons with the Nazis had begun to falter under the Begin government. If the government spokesman pulled Hitler out of the bag, more modest arguments must have seemed ineffective. Pressure to justify government policy existed only vis-à-vis the outside world. A former general and commander of the education corps had once explained that in case of an external threat, the population gladly accepted all government explanations: "Israelis buy everything the government says, even the cheapest promises, if only they are packaged expensively enough." Thus, the rhetorical appearance of Hitler signaled a really big campaign.

According to my journal, we ate that Saturday in one of the most beautiful restaurants in the city. German Foreign Minister Genscher had paid the government and Jerusalem a brief visit to mediate on behalf of the Europeans, and a rearguard of German journalists had remained in Jerusalem for the weekend. Some of them had joined us. The conversation revolved inevitably around the political situation. Most of them showed an understanding for Israel's situation and saw the need to halt the PLO's constantly expanding military operations in Lebanon. The consensus was that no country could let itself be shot at or threatened from the territory of a neighboring country for long. Since the Lebanese government was either unable or unwilling to take care of the threat itself, Israel had the right to interfere. I expressed my fear that the Begin government's violent policy toward the PLO would now come up with a new opportunity to use the army to solve a problem that really demanded negotiations and compromise from Israel. The state within a state, which the Palestinians had set up in Lebanon, was ultimately only a substitute for the state they were deprived of by the current Israeli government and all its predecessors. Only a political solution to this fundamental problem could bring peace to Israel. As far as I could see, another round of violence and retaliation made this goal even more remote.

When I returned to Israel in 1976, I still supported the basic Zionist consensus—that the Jews had a right to settle in their ancient biblical homeland; that the Arab and Palestinian resistance to the Zionist undertaking was not justified; that Israel acted out of self-defense. Five years of living and working in Israel had completely changed my ideas. I thought that the Palestinians had suffered a great injustice—by the settlement of Jews in Palestine forced on them since the 1920s, by the violent creation and "ethnic cleansing" of the state in 1948, by the permanent settlement of the territories occupied in 1967. Meanwhile, I also came to a different view of the ethnic dominance of the Jews in the country, the Zionist sine qua non of Israel. How could I, as a German Jew, accept such a nationalistic principle of nation and nationality? And what annoyed me particularly was that this was presented as compensation for the persecution of Jews in Christian countries and as the only conceivable consequence of the Holocaust. I thought Israel had to be a state for all her citizens and had to give up Zionism. This view determined my judgment in most questions and made me forgive the errors of the other side more easily than those of my own.

These opinions were anathema to many of my friends and colleagues and to most Israelis. The great majority assumed that it was the Jews who had suffered grave injustice, from Arab hostility to the Zionist enterprise, and that it was Israel that continued to be victimized by Arab terror and violence; that the political immaturity and intolerance, even anti-Semitism of the other side made a peaceful solution impossible; that only a policy based on military might could guarantee Israel's survival. In short, "they," the Palestinians, "understand only one language: violence."

These different positions vis-à-vis the basis of the Israeli-Palestinian conflict meant not only political differences. There was a deep rift here dividing Jews and Arabs in Israel and friend and foe within Jewish society. Only now did I begin to sense the depth of that rift as my wavering political position began to solidify under the pressure of the war. Here, different interpretations of Jewish history confronted one another, different versions of the origins of the Middle East conflict; here myths and legends formed a muddled, almost impenetrable labyrinth. Changing sides had far-reaching consequences.

One of the myths and legends was the story of David and Goliath. I don't know who first came up with this idea, but the inventor deserves the Israel Prize. It wouldn't surprise me if this stroke of genius had been hatched in the Israeli Foreign Ministry, where so many well-known arguments have come into being. The struggle between David and Goliath as an analogy for the Middle East conflict first emerged in 1967, during the Six Day War, in discussions and political caricatures—the little Israeli David in his short pants, rolled-up sleeves, and typical dunce cap; and the boorish Goliath, wrapped in a biblical bear hide and armed with a club, a get-up that brands him as a violent but ultimately ineffective bungler. Thus the impression that small and weak Israel, with four million Jewish inhabitants, had to defend itself against a superior, united Arab nation of over 100 million people was anchored solidly in the consciousness of world public opinion. This image, which belongs in the realm of political fantasy and propaganda, still determines the thinking of a large part of the Israeli population. As I saw it, on the other hand, Israel was a modern Western industrial country with a big well-equipped army. Goliath consisted of several developing countries that couldn't even manage to feed their own populations adequately.

Like all propaganda, this image had a special message aimed exclusively at its own population. While the danger and weakness of the country was emphasized abroad, its own population had to be convinced of the opposite. The story of David and Goliath was suited to that. According to tradition, little David's victory over the superior Philistine was achieved by the wondrous strength granted him by God. It was not a matter of muscles, said the internal message, but rather the force of faith.

In reality, Israel was the only major power in the region, and the balance of power between Jews and Arabs within Israel and in the occupied territories was even more one-sided. Nevertheless, Israeli governments kept representing the Palestinians as the dangerous aggressors, who were not only resolved to drive all the Jews into the sea but also had the forces necessary to do that. Their own population, on the other hand, stood there as the innocent victim. The violent methods of the PLO and the groups represented in it made it easy to shape public opinion. Airplane hijackings, bombings, the indiscriminate killing of civilians, the rocket attacks on villages and cities from Lebanon, all the injustice committed by Palestinians, served to soothe our own conscience and dismiss the justified demands of the Palestinians along with the methods they used to advance them. What concerned me most of all was that Jewish society was fixated on the atrocities of the others, which made them blind to their own. The modern myth of the Jews as perpetual victims of persecution and injustice, who always had right on their side, played an important role here. Wasn't the hostility of the Palestinians a new variant of the old hatred of the Jews? The often violent, sometimes anti-Semitic speeches on the Arab side seemed to confirm that. Israeli governments never tired of emphasizing that in their public relations. Actually, these concepts of the enemy were only a side-effect of a conflict whose causes lay elsewhere. Arab regimes and elites used anti-Semitic stereotypes to keep their own population loyal and ready for hatred and war; Jewish Israelis were full of dehumanizing, racist prejudices against Arab society that enabled them to despise the people on the other side, trample on their human rights, and kill them, if need be. Because the myth of the permanent victim status of the Jews was so closely linked with the creation of Israel, anyone who expressed doubt about the moral superiority of the Zionist enterprise was practically equated with those who deny the persecution and murder of the Jews.

All this led most Israelis to a thoroughly one-sided and unrealistic view of the conflict and its causes. If your own side can hardly be guilty of anything, the hostility of the Palestinians could be based only on cultural and religious differences—on the alleged intolerance of Islam toward other religions, on the political immaturity of Arab society that does not tolerate any minorities, and so on. But an incorrect diagnosis leads to an incorrect therapy, and a painful prognosis.

The restaurant where we gathered that evening was in the cellar of a pilgrim hotel, an exuberant late-nineteenth-century building in the Roman Catholic gingerbread style, at the edge of the Old City in the former no-man's-land. It was crowned with an enormous statue of the Madonna that towered so far over the flat houses around it that it seemed to dash over the roofs of the Old City. The regular customers of the restaurant could have served as a model of the region—Italian priests in tailored suits, Israeli businessmen in jeans and sneakers, old-school British Palestinian gentlemen in tweed jackets, upper-middle-class Jewish ladies whose knitwear came from Frankfurt or Leipzig. Moslems, Jews, Christians, Palestinians, and Israelis came together peacefully here and left their rancor, their resentments, and their prejudices in the coatroom. On that evening, my friends and I parted in hopes that reason and goodwill could prevent an expansion of the shooting and that Menachem Begin's government could once again be restrained.

But, out of consideration for God or the religious parties, the Israeli government had waited only for the end of the Sabbath. The next morning, Sunday, June 6, 1982, a bloody and destructive campaign began that cost the lives of almost twenty thousand people. With the entrance of Israeli troops into Lebanon, a period of hopes for peace that had begun with Sadat's visit to Jerusalem in November 1977 also came to an end.

* 3 *

That Sunday morning, the first workday of the Israeli week, I went as usual to the Institute. On my desk was a message from an historian friend, a lieutenant colonel, in command of a reserve battalion of paratroopers. He had called and cancelled our appointment for that morning. His unit had been mobilized and he was probably already somewhere in Lebanon. Work was inconceivable anyway. In the offices, the transistor radios hummed, the staff ran or sat around nervously and stood in line at the table with the coffee machine. The first news showed clearly that the so-called "Peace for the Galilee" invasion was a comprehensive military campaign. The government blamed the PLO and called the attack in London a violation of the cease-fire agreement. That was an original interpretation. That the Israeli government saw the agreement as extending to terrorist acts against Israeli targets in Israel and elsewhere, could be understood. But what was bizarre was that the assault had been carried out by the Abu-Nidal group in violent opposition to the Palestinian leadership, which was thus made the partner of the agreement in retrospect.

The government and the army claimed that preparations for the invasion began only on Thursday, the day after the London attack. My military knowledge came mainly from my brief, brutal training in the infantry, but in the military historical projects I had been assigned on reserve duty, I had learned a little more. Even if complete plans for all conceivable cases were prepared by the general staff, pulling together the necessary ground troops, air force, and navy units for war required a lot of time. In the 1973 war, the only one in which the Israeli army was unprepared, it took several days just to move the slow-track vehicles—tanks, armored personnel carriers, and artillery—to the front. In the first moments, the current attack on Lebanon seemed in fact only to protect the northern part of the country. The entire Jewish population of Israel could identify with this goal. It took a few weeks until it dawned on us that the issue was quite different, that this was about settling accounts with the PLO militias and Syrian troops in Lebanon, and had been planned well in advance. In the words of Ariel Sharon, the minister of defense, the PLO was a "cloud hanging over Israel" and had to be driven out.

I still remember precisely the confusing mood that morning. Conflicting loyalties and feelings tugged at me, pulled me first in one direction and then in another. First I felt carried away by the powerful wave of solidarity with the soldiers and their families who now had to wait anxiously at home for news of their men. Like probably all Jews in Israel at that moment, I felt part of a community that was in difficult straits and appealed to the solidarity of the individual. Members of the community did not have to agree with all measures, nor did they have to show any enthusiasm, as long as they preserved the basic consensus, stuck together, and took responsibility for each other. Then I was revolted, felt alienation and disgust at the harsh and merciless Israeli society that saw nothing, heard nothing, and felt nothing beyond the narrow confines of their community. I imagined the helpless people in the Palestinian refugee camps who now had to save themselves from Israeli bombs, the dead, the civilians and soldiers maimed in mind and body that would be produced by this war. At lunchtime, I went home, too outraged and depressed to be able to concentrate on work.

At home, I found a note on the door containing instructions specifying the time and place to report to my unit. We had practiced this mobilization at least once a year. For me, this had been a special waste of time, both ridiculous and advantageous. I had to copy the note, get in my car, and drive to four or five other members of the unit in my neighborhood, whose names and addresses I carried on a list with me for this purpose. They also had their own lists. This chain enabled the whole unit to be mobilized quietly within a few hours. This procedure was advantageous because those two hours deducted a whole day from my annual reserve duty. It was ridiculous because we weren't fighters, but a group of lecturers and scholars, armed with briefcases and sandwiches, who gave talks, collected educational material, or organized conferences. If the army was depending on us, the country must have been in really bad shape.

I had to report to my unit at army headquarters in Tel Aviv the next morning at eight. The usual data about the length of this mobilization was lacking. The call-up order was a shock and I began to worry about everything possible. What did the army want from me? I couldn't imagine being useful in any way. How long would the call-up last? Where would I be sent? Should I inform my parents? It was not only my physical well-being that seemed endangered. It was also immediately clear to me that this time, I couldn't suppress the political and moral problems I had previously avoided. Informing my parents, who lived in Germany, was especially tricky. They didn't know that I served in the army. In the years since my first call-up, basic training, military service, and reserve duty, I had managed to keep them in the dark about the real reason for my absences. I didn't want to worry them. Unlike many other Zionist families, they would have felt no pride that their son was serving in the Israeli army, but only fear.

This secrecy had led to strange situations. Once my mother had showed up in Israel unexpectedly just when I returned to Jerusalem from a four-week training program. I made a mad dash to the airport to pick her up. I had very short hair, a dreadful crew cut I had been given in the training camp. I had slept very little for four weeks and had eaten very little, nothing but special power bars that I ate instead of the disgusting army grub. I was emaciated, looked as if I had suffered a serious illness, and now had to count on my secret being discovered. As my mother came toward me in the airport reception room, she hesitated a moment. She examined me critically from head to foot, and I expected her to make the usual remarks about sons obviously lacking sleep and food as soon as they dared leave their mothers. But this time, the old ritual took another turn. She beamed at me and congratulated me on my new haircut. "Short hair looks much better on you, my boy. I always told you so." Given the uncertainty of the situation, should I now tell my parents the truth?

I spent the rest of this Sunday talking to myself and trying in vain to phone my unit in Tel Aviv to find out more details about the impending mobilization. Then I went back to the city. My journal indicates that, late that Sunday afternoon, I found time for one of the most important measures an education officer can take in case of war: I went to the barber.

* 4 *

After a sleepless night, I set off early to avoid the morning traffic jam. At the foot of the Monastery of the Cross, I had to stop. My legs were shaking and my stomach was cramped. While furious drivers kept honking behind me, I pulled over to the curb, gripped by fear.

All radio stations had interrupted normal programming. News of the first clashes with the Syrian army, in control of parts of Lebanon, poured from the car radio. The news was delivered in that quick nervous tone that itself prepared the public for something horrible. The intonation was one of the many small, often imperceptible signals that send people into the mode of collective acts and feelings in moments of danger. This transformation had often amazed me. Israeli society is a more colorful mixture than most others, wide gaps separate opinions and temperaments; but whenever conflict with the Palestinians or an external threat is involved, an uncritical conformity spreads. Every official expression, every report of acts of enemy horror, no matter how propagandistic they may seem to others, is taken at face value. Even I couldn't always escape this internal synchronization, and the prejudices and myths that had crept into my thinking were often no longer apparent to me.

The details reported on the radio were coming through to me less and less the closer I got to my destination on the coast. Israeli tanks and infantry were clearly there, advancing deep into Lebanon—along the coast toward Beirut and over the mountain passes toward the Chouf Mountains and the Biqa Valley, where the Syrian army was. That the Israeli army was waging war, that I was wearing a uniform and was on my way to my unit, suddenly seemed something that had no direct connection to me.

In my right shirt pocket, I carried a small transistor radio that had served me well during my basic training. The radio could only pick up middle waves but that was enough, because I only wanted to hear foreign stations anyway. On night marches, during guard duty, or while cleaning latrines, I stuck the button in my ear and let myself go off to another world. The French-speaking Radio Monte Carlo aimed at Lebanon came in clearest. The station played popular music round the clock and interrupted it only seldom with brief news bulletins. I tuned into Monte Carlo for light moods. I especially loved the commercials that transplanted me in a flash from the stony hill I was toiling up, or the lonely post I was guarding, to the shiny clean kitchen of a Beirut family or the richly decked table of an elegant Parisian dinner party. After a while, I had memorized the jingles extolling French merchandise and food and, when the situation around me threatened to become especially unbearable, I could amaze my fellow soldiers with "La vache qui rit, la vache qui rit." Even if I didn't like the soft cheese, the laughing cow became a close companion.

The other station was the BBC World Service. I tuned in to the BBC so often every day that I could sometimes recite the text of the news along with the announcer. It gave me the comfortable effect of an easy chair, a glass of wine, and the daily paper. Regularly listening to the news, I became the citizen of a universe of enlightened, reasonable people, who seemed to shake their collective head over the unpredictably dumb world. It was enough for me to get the latest reports from the Middle East and the most recent oddities of Israeli politics a few hours later, after a detour through London. This distance of a few thousand kilometers made everything much more bearable, and it was this imaginary distance I particularly enjoyed.

On this morning, the country was in a state of controlled panic. In front of me on the freeway, a driver suddenly slammed on his brakes for no obvious reason. The driver behind him, and I behind him, rushed apart to avoid a collision. A car in front of me went into a skid. For a few seconds, I was scared to death, then the car recovered and we drove on. Even in the best of times, traffic on this stretch of road was lethal, but now all caution was clearly superfluous. In the Ayalon Valley, where the freeway emerges from the Judean Mountains onto the Coastal Plain and speed increases most, I had already seen two accidents. I had a sad memory. On Yom Kippur, 1973, when the surprise attack of Egypt and Syria abruptly interrupted the repose of the holiest day, a frighteningly high number of fatal traffic accidents had occurred among reservists hurrying to their units. Was that going to happen now to me too? What was really in store for me? My fear, repressed for half an hour, had come back.

* 5 *

At army headquarters, everything seemed calm. Only when I tried to park my car in one of the side streets did I notice that it wasn't a normal Monday. How intently I could concentrate on ridiculous trifles, when big things were so hard to accept! Since yesterday, I had worried about parking the car. As a reservist, I had no permission to drive into the grounds of headquarters and had to find a parking place outside. How many parking vouchers should I leave on the dashboard? Wouldn't it be better to describe the situation in a note on the window and hope for the patriotism of the parking cop? Didn't I thus indicate to a thief that I'd return to my car only days or maybe weeks later? The problem now seemed thoroughly insoluble.

At that time, the education section of the army was not yet an independent corps but a division in the general staff, and was housed in a row of green barracks on grounds that also accommodated the Defense Ministry and a few other government offices. The grounds were on the edge of downtown Tel Aviv in an area that indicated Israel's stormy emergence and growth. The small houses of Sarona were still there. That was an agricultural settlement established in 1871 by members of a Pietist Protestant sect from Württemberg, and would have fit nicely into a German landscape. Now some of the cabins of the Templars were dilapidated and boarded up. In the 1970s, the first high-rise buildings of Tel Aviv were erected here, already showing signs of decay ten years later. The presence of government offices in this place went back to the situation of 1947–1948. At that time, Tel Aviv was the only "Jewish" town, while Jerusalem—because of the international status assigned to it in the U.N. Partition Plan—was not eligible as the capital. The government had been installed in Sarona because the German inhabitants had been evacuated during World War II and the houses were empty. After the War of 1948, which invalidated the Partition Plan, most of the ministries and the parliament moved to Jerusalem. But the new capital had also become a front-line city, and so the Defense Ministry and army headquarters remained in Tel Aviv.

The impression of permanent temporariness, of incurable makeshift, that could be found all over the State even thirty years after it was founded, was also seen in the government grounds. Relics of earlier, rapidly obsolete plans for the future stood or lay around, long useless but not yet removed. It was here of all places that I felt most intensely that the resolution of the Jewish settlers of the country demonstrated so bravely to the outside secretly lacked the necessary permanence, and that the experiment of the Jewish State could still be abandoned.

I still remember my amazement the first time I entered the barracks of my unit. The education section was responsible for the civic education of the soldiers, for training officers, educating and indoctrinating troops. The section supervised a few boarding schools, a radio station, a publishing house, a newspaper, a film production unit, and not least, the military history unit where I served. All these complex functions were carried out with a minimum of expenditure and personnel. The offices were small and poorly equipped. The director of the departments and the commanding general himself ruled their empire from offices that reminded me of photos of the Russian civil war—two simple tables placed perpendicularly, formed a T. The commander sat at the head, the staff on the sides. Working conditions, comfort, and individuality were not considered, in accordance with general military traditions. The warm climate in Israel made it possible to produce accommodations simply and cheaply. In many places, troops were lodged all year in tents, a tin roof on four posts giving shade was enough for training or assemblies, and instead of windows in bathrooms and latrines there were big openings in the external walls for light and ventilation. It seemed to me that this parsimoniousness in the Israeli army had another meaning. Many national movements promote qualities like modesty, humility, and simplicity as exercises in self-sacrifice, and here too, renunciation of small things symbolically seemed to include renunciation of big things. The young soldier certainly couldn't give his life every day, but here he might sacrifice his comfort and individual needs to the cause.

My unit dealt with the historical documentation and description of Israeli army battles. For a year and a half, I had performed my military service there, and now my reserve duty as a lecturer as well. I knew many of the officers, tasks, and procedures. Nevertheless, the purpose and reason for my mobilization was a riddle to me. And, it turned out, I wasn't alone. As I entered, a group of colleagues were trying to get information about our call-up. The problem was to find even one officer of our unit. The desks were empty. That could be a sign of normality, for like all other people, the professional Israeli officer tended to report for duty as late as possible in the morning and to go home as early as possible in the afternoon. These strict professional ethics seemed to be valid in time of war as well, for it was after eight o'clock and normal service hadn't yet started. So we went to the canteen.

Whenever grown men in Israel put on a uniform and report for reserve duty, an amazing change takes place. They become comrades. In the canteen, my colleagues, who otherwise had little to do with one another, began acting as if they had played together in sandboxes—and still did. Even though I had also practiced this rule of behavior since my sandbox days, I felt excluded. The reserve unit, a squad or a company, is a group of people with whom the soldier spends most of his time, with whom he shares happiness and suffering, sleeping space, mosquitoes and food. In the reserve unit, good and bad news is taken with the same composure, effects of the outside world are cushioned and muted. A few jokes, putting events in relation to specific parts of the body, are usually enough. This tendency to trivialize outside events is undoubtedly an advantage in the military, but this time it got on my nerves. A while later, we were tracked down by officers of our unit and called to a discussion of the assignment.

A first lieutenant we didn't know explained our function. He was obviously regular army. He spoke in the military substantive style, a row of finished verbal bricks that indicate that the speaker is not speaking for himself but is the mouthpiece of a higher power. He was almost incomprehensible because he attempted to use a complex syntax for us, which he wasn't used to. Our mission was to take place on the grounds of headquarters and sounded so bizarre that it took us a while to grasp the news. Somebody had come up with the idea of assigning our unit to guard duty at headquarters.

I still remember my mixed feelings. On the one hand I was disappointed: for a moment I longed for adventure and manly acts and thought we deserved a more interesting and demanding function. On the other hand, this assignment would not entail encounters with the enemy or political conflicts. My colleagues, on the contrary, felt degraded.

The man from the guard battalion led us to a small windowless structure on the grounds that looked like the garage of a private house. I had also heard rumors of underground leadership bunkers accessible through camouflaged entrances, and began again to hope for an adventure. But behind the heavy steel door hid a single room with neither trapdoors nor elevators, but rather a dozen bunks and a latrine. The officer of the guard battalion explained the tactics. Here, in this hole, we were to stay for forty-eight hours, hidden as a secret strike force, and burst out of the bunker and surprise the enemy in the event of an alarm. Some of us had to laugh, others seemed to be in shock. The first lieutenant looked at us disgusted. He couldn't work with the human material that had been given him.

This high point was followed by a wait. I tried to get used to the idea of having to commute between the hole and my flat in Jerusalem every two days. During reserve duty, I was freed from my civilian work, but, if circumstances allowed, I wanted to go by the institute as often as possible. Thinking of the coming weeks, I was terrified of the nights in the bunker, the forced intimacy and the lack of private space. But it was clear to me that, compared with other possible assignments in this war, service in a bunker in the middle of Tel Aviv could be considered paradise.

We sat around for quite a few hours. Nowhere else is the individual so badly informed as in the military, and nowhere else is there so much speculation. We began discussing the meaning of the wait. Was it the normal sloppiness, the usual negligence and dilly-dallying of the authorities, which had to issue weapons to us and register us administratively, or was something special going on? Clueless, we headed for another high point of the day.

After a few hours of sitting around—it was now late afternoon—we were finally called back to the office of our unit. There, Colonel Wechsler informed us laconically that the planned transfer to the guard battalion was off. He didn't know the precise reasons. The commanding general had obviously wanted to prove the usefulness of his academic unit in wartime and assigned us to the guard service, but because of the bad "human material," the guard battalion resisted. Since we were now mobilized, other uses would be sought for us. This would certainly take another day. And thus we were dismissed.

* 6 *

I wished that back then, on the second day of the Lebanese war, this episode had seemed as funny as it does now. In fact, the excitement of the last twenty-four hours, the lack of sleep, the fearful tension and the waiting had thoroughly frazzled my nerves. I went back to Jerusalem in a daze and spent the rest of the evening dozing on the sofa. The next morning at eight, I reported again to my unit in Tel Aviv. There, somebody had come up with a new use for me: I was to take over the research project of a colleague who studied military history as a professional officer, but who had been assigned to a combat unit in Lebanon. His subject was "The Military Doctrine of David Ben Gurion." It was the first time I heard of this project. In my service, I had specialized in pre-state military history and had studied and written on the underground work of the Jewish militias and the predecessor of the Mossad. In the project now turned over to me, I was to work through the dispatches and personal letters Ben Gurion had sent to the commanders in the field during the campaigns of 1948 and 1949, and examine their content for basic strategic and tactical ideas. To me, the whole thing smacked of the cult of personality devoted to the first Israeli prime minister.

Ben Gurion's political figure was so equivocal and ambiguous that it could serve as a reflection of a national movement combining such diverse elements as the religious humanism of a Martin Buber and the vision of the settlers of a Greater Israel empire purged of non-Jews. Ben Gurion came from the Palestinian-Jewish Labor movement, a broad coalition of social democrats and socialists that dominated the Jewish community as the largest political force during the British Mandate period and built the democratic and socialist institutions that formed the kernel of the State established in 1948. With regard to the political demands of the Palestinians, the Labor movement represented a moderate Zionism aimed at compromise, and embraced at times both the British concept of two separate states and the idea of a shared, binational state of Palestinians and Jews.

What was the political background of my assignment? Ben Gurion was the undisputed architect of the Jewish victory of 1948–

1949. But for a few years, an historical revisionism had been spreading in my department that questioned other contributions of the Zionist Labor movement to the construction of the state. This initiative came from the first rightist government led by Herut since the establishment of the State. Between 1945 and 1948, the Revisionist movement engaged in a power struggle with the Labor party, which threatened at times to erupt into civil war. In this period, Ben Gurion built the military strength of the Yishuv and secretly set in motion a comprehensive armament plan crucial for Israel's victory in 1948, and which excluded the rightist Zionist militias. It was Ben Gurion who accepted the hardly viable boundaries projected by the U.N. for the Jewish state, forced his party to accept it, and violently suppressed the strong dissent of the right-wing Zionists—with the help of the British. So where was the real thrust of the project I was now given? Was it a vehicle of conventional glorification of this politician, or was a shadow to fall on the father of the fatherland?

Personality cult is an obvious tool in army departments promoting pride in military traditions. Myths of larger-than-life commanders or stories of the simple but brave lieutenant who sacrifices himself for his men are used everywhere as material to enhance esprit de corps. These myths were especially important for the Israeli army, which had existed for only three decades and also had an integrative function as a central institution of an ideologically synchronized but culturally diverse society. I liked the assignment. Clearly the subject was not to be taken seriously scientifically, nor was it especially difficult, and the archive that housed the letters was in a part of Tel Aviv with a lot of small cafes and restaurants where I could recover nicely from Ben Gurion's ideas.

While I was still studying the material of my colleague who was now fighting in Lebanon and trying to discover the political subtext, the plan was suddenly scuttled again. One of the administrative staff of the unit had discovered a note in my personal dossier that I did not have the necessary security clearance for a certain secret part of the archive containing material about the War of 1948. This note was the result of a tactical maneuver I had undertaken myself at the beginning of my basic military service in order to spare myself ticklish situations. At that time, because of my studies and my knowledge of languages, the personnel office proposed me for service in military intelligence. That didn't please me and I really did not want a security clearance, but the planned assignment could not be prevented. In the endless security examinations preceding employment in military intelligence, I had to give detailed facts about all phases and activities of my life, as well as organizations I had ever belonged to. This offered me the suitable tool. As a student in Germany, I had participated in the work of a leftist group that belonged to the unparliamentary opposition. I had always been a "sympathizer" and had never become a member, but this fine distinction now seemed unimportant. I gladly gave information about my activity in GIM, the Group of International Marxists, which was part of the Trotskyite Internationale. That was enough. At the end of the examinations, I was informed without explanation that I could not have access to the higher security classification and my assignment to military intelligence came to naught.

So, on this third day of the war, Colonel Wechsler had to dismiss me again, and I could resume my civilian life in Jerusalem. A while later, a new assignment was found for me. The campaign in Lebanon had now taken an unexpected turn. Israeli troops were in Beirut, the allied Christian militias had carried out a massacre among the Palestinians under the eyes and with the protection of the Israeli troops, and troop morale had sunk dangerously low. My reserve unit of non-belligerent lecturers was assigned a delicate mission not in Tel Aviv, but in Lebanon itself.

2

* A GOOD FENCE *

Israel, Lebanon, and the Palestinians

* 1 *

Lebanon was the only neighboring country Israelis used to be romantic about. When I returned to Israel on Christmas Eve 1976 and took a taxi from the port of Haifa up to Mount Carmel at night, my driver, who had commented profusely on all the invisible sights along the way, also praised the location of my new flat. From here, on the northern edge of the Carmel Mountains, was the best view of the bay and the suburbs. "If you're lucky," he said as we parted, "you can even see beautiful Lebanon from your window."

The windows of my flat faced in other directions, and there was no splendid panorama. But my landlady had a remedy. She sent me to the toilet with a small window high up under the ceiling and, standing on tiptoe, over the edge of the window, I managed to make out a chain of hills on the horizon. So that was Lebanon.

Among Zionists right at the beginning of the Yishuv, enthusiasm for the "Orient," that romantic and yet derogatory European idea, shattered on the reality of an environment hostile to Zionist colonization and was quickly replaced by an unambiguously negative image of Arab society and culture. But Israelis saw Lebanon as different—a Christian country shaped by European culture, where the Arabs were a minority. The Christian majority seemed to have a great deal in common with the Jews in Israel. Both groups were oriented toward the West and maintained a liberal economic system; both had to fight for a place in a region dominated by Islam and Arab culture, and both formed islands in an overwhelmingly hostile environment. That was the image that prevailed in Israel until 1967.

Israel and Lebanon are both unhistorical entities formed after World War I from the colonial legacy of the Ottoman Empire by European powers that struggled for hegemony in the Middle East and used willing local minorities to do so. As states, both emerged hastily after the end of World War II, when the original power strategies had suddenly become invalid. The problems of both countries were and still are partly the consequences of this failed process of de-colonialization. In Lebanon, the protecting power, France, connected the settlement areas of two antagonistic population groups—the Moslems and Druse oriented to the Arab world, and the Western-oriented Christians, some of whom didn't even define themselves as Arabs. Under the French, the Christians enjoyed an advantageous position, which was constitutionally locked in place after the establishment of the state in 1946 much to the dislike of the ever growing Moslem population. In Palestine, Great Britain, the Mandatory power, tried to settle Jewish immigrants from Europe and create a homeland for them, at the expense and against the will of the Arab majority.

Back in the 1920s, Zionists and Lebanese Christians recognized common interests and established friendly relations. Even though Lebanon took part in the Arab-Jewish civil war of 1947–1948 and officially in the Israeli-Arab conflict that followed the establishment of Israel in 1948, the Lebanese state was restrained. But during the fighting, about a hundred thousand Arabs fled to Lebanon from Haifa, the villages of the coastal plain, and the Galilee. The upper and middle class refugees settled in Beirut and the cities along the coast, and most were able to build a new life. But the majority of people who had fled the new Israeli state, supported now by international organizations, had to eke out a living in refugee camps. After the arrival of the Palestinians, the demographic key at the base of the Lebanese governmental system corresponded even less to the real ratios. Thus, the second, tragic phase of relations between Israel and Lebanon began, linked by the fate of the Palestinians.

In 1949, a cease-fire was signed between Israel and Lebanon. In the postwar years, you could often hear a phrase in Israel that summarized the relationship to Lebanon at that time: "The Lebanese border? It can be defended by the army orchestra." Another statement, expression of the same blend of megalomania and ignorance, was: "We don't know which Arab country will make peace with us first. The second is Lebanon." There were times when this wishful thinking seemed justified. For twenty years, the Israeli-Lebanese border remained calm, until the Arab defeat in the 1967 war pushed the unsolved question of the Palestinian refugees and their failed state into the foreground.

Soon after I came back, I met a friend from Munich who had immigrated to Israel before me. He had just finished his military service and told me of his experiences. As an engineer he had wound up in the artillery where immigrants with technical professions were often assigned. For maneuvers, he said, his unit moved to the Lebanese border. There, they had simply shot artillery shells into the country as an exercise. As he told me about that, his eyes examined me, as if he himself wasn't clear about the meaning of his report and wanted to get my reaction. "What does it mean, 'simply shot'?" I asked. "Simply. Without any special reason." "Was it aimed at specific targets?" I asked. "Naturally we got coordinates, but as far as I know, there weren't any special targets." I simply didn't understand what he meant. Given the twenty- to thirty-kilometer range of the howitzers used by the Israeli army, you had to know what was in the target area. "Was the area abandoned? Weren't there any villages, people in the fields, on the roads?" He looked at me with a tormented expression and was silent. Clearly, these questions had preoccupied him, too, but he hadn't asked them. What had happened in the meantime at the Israeli-Lebanese border?

In the 1967 war, the Lebanese government had refused to provide troops for the fight against Israel. This angered not only the Moslem parts of the population that identified with the Arab issue. Neighboring Syria, which had lost the Golan Heights in that war, also felt left in the lurch. In that same year, the Syrian government began to send Palestinian militias under its control on terrorist missions into the north of Israel. Since Syria no longer had a direct border with Israel, its path led through Lebanon.

The ensuing development, which was also a long-term consequence of the expulsion and flight of the Palestinians, shattered the peace on the Israeli-Lebanese border altogether. The direct reason was the conflict between the government and the PLO in Jordan, culminating in "Black September" in 1970, and forcing the PLO to move its base from Jordan to Lebanon.

* 2 *

Like Lebanon, Jordan had also taken refugees from Israel in 1948. Some three hundred thousand people from the villages and towns of the coastal plain, the Judean Mountains, and West Jerusalem fled to western Jordan, an area included in the U.N. Partition Plan in a Palestinian state, but which was annexed in 1948 by the kingdom of Jordan. About a hundred thousand refugees settled across the Jordan River, in eastern Jordan. When Israel conquered the West Bank and East Jerusalem in 1967, most of the refugees of 1948 fled again to the camps east of the Jordan. The Palestinians now constituted the majority in Jordan. King Hussein's government, like all post-colonial regimes in the region, maintained control with an adroit distribution of power, and was supported mainly by the local Arab tribes, who felt threatened by the immigrants, creating a tension that still prevails.

The almost total Arab defeat of 1967 radicalized the political climate on both the Israeli and the Arab side. In Israel, the Labor government pursued a double, contradictory strategy. On the one hand, a willingness for peace and negotiation was indicated with the prospect of returning the occupied areas to their Arab neighbors. On the other hand, the resettlement of Jews began almost immediately in East Jerusalem and a small area along the Bethlehem-Hebron Road, where Jewish inhabitants had been expelled in 1948. Thus, Israel exercised the right of return for the small number of Jewish refugees of 1948, while denying it to the more than seven hundred thousand Arab refugees of 1948. Resettlement was followed by a massive new settlement. Jewish colonies emerged first in the relatively thinly settled areas of the Golan Heights and the Jordan Valley, then in the densely populated Palestinian areas and cities of the West Bank and the annexed suburbs of Jerusalem.

About half the Palestinians lived in what was now Israeli-occupied Palestine, and half of them in exile. For them, the defeat of 1967 and the helplessness of the Arab states vis-à-vis Israeli expansion in the rest of Palestine was particularly oppressive. The only representation, the Palestinian Liberation Organization, the PLO, arising in 1964, represented primarily the traditional leadership class of big Palestinian landowners. In the crucial situation of 1947–1948 this elite had failed completely because of political inexperience, rivalries between the most influential families, and corruption. Dissatisfaction with the traditional representatives smoldered particularly among the young generation of exiled Palestinian bourgeoisie. In Beirut, Cairo, and Damascus, the most important cities of the Palestinian Diaspora, a group of young activists now appeared, whose militant strategies gave a new turn to the Middle East conflict. In the Arab universities, they established radical Palestinian organizations based on Marxist ideas and modeled on liberation movements in Latin America and Africa. In the early 1960s, some organizations carried out the first guerilla operations against Israeli targets. The leadership crisis after the defeat of 1967 created a favorable moment for these forces, and seven of the new organizations joined the PLO. The two biggest ones, Al-Fatah and the Popular Front for the Liberation of Palestine (PFLP), were allotted half the seats in the Palestinian National Congress, and a year later, the leader of the Fatah movement, Yassir Arafat, was elected chairman of the PLO. Armed groups, the Feddayin, operating under the umbrella of the PLO, took control of the refugee camps in Jordan, and the PLO began increasing its power in the country.

In November 1968, led by George Habbash, a Palestinian pediatrician living in Beirut, the PFLP carried out the first of a series of sensational airplane hijackings. Terrorists seized an El Al plane on a flight from Rome to Tel Aviv and forced it to land in Algiers. A few weeks later, the same group hit an Israeli plane at Athens airport. In retaliation, the Israeli government sent a commando unit to Beirut International Airport, where thirteen planes of Middle East Airlines were destroyed on the ground. The Lebanese army did not intervene.

The presence of the proverbial Israeli army orchestra irrevocably came to an end on September 6, 1970, when the Popular Front for the Liberation of Palestine began the most spectacular series of airplane hijackings the world had ever seen. A Swissair passenger plane and a TWA flight were hijacked to Jordan at the same time. A PanAm Boeing jet was forced to land in Cairo and was blown up before the cameras. Another group of hijackers tried to take control of an El Al plane in flight. The flight landed at London's Heathrow Airport, where the hijackers, including Leila Chalid, were captured. To free the hijackers, a BOAC plane was taken. All three hijacked planes and some three hundred hostages were held at a former British airstrip in the Jordanian desert. Since the governments of Great Britain, Germany, and Switzerland did not agree to the demands of the PFLP to free the prisoners, the hijackers blew up the three commercial planes on September 12, six days after the beginning of the hijackings. Images of the explosion were broadcast around the world.

Provoked by the unhindered operation of the PLO on its own territory, the Jordanian government faced a difficult decision, whether to act harshly against the Palestinian militias and thus trigger a civil war, whose outcome was uncertain; or to put up with the hegemony of the PLO. King Hussein's government decided to act. Two days after the planes were blown up, the Jordanian army attacked. PLO strongholds in Amman and Sarka and the refugee camps came under artillery fire, which cost thousands of lives. After a few days of inconclusive fighting, the civil war threatened to escalate into a new Mideast war. Armored units of the Syrian army and the Palestinian Liberation Army (PLA) supported by Syria penetrated Jordan from the north and threatened Amman. Yassir Arafat, who called the Jordanian army attack a "genocide," declared the northern part of Jordan a liberated area.

The next step, the inclusion of Israel by Hussein's government, a maneuver that decided the civil war in Jordan's favor, was shrouded in legends for decades. Among many Palestinians, the prevailing opinion was that the Jordanian government, in secret contacts dating back before the 1948 war, had conspired with Israel against the Palestinians and that this conspiracy was responsible for the defeat of the PLO. Since January 2001, when British cabinet minutes were released after thirty years, it has been known that, in fact, the Jordanian government pressed Israel to intervene through the British and American governments. King Hussein asked Israel to carry out an air raid on advancing Syrian troops. However, a direct military intervention by Israel was no longer necessary. The threat of Israel and a mobilization of units were enough to serve as a deterrent. Syrian troops withdrew and the Jordanian army asserted itself with the PLO.

Within a few months, tens of thousands of Palestinian militia left Jordan for Lebanon, followed by an even larger number of refugees who no longer felt safe there. The number of armed Palestinians operating against Israel from Lebanon grew from some four thousand to more than twenty thousand, thus making the PLO the biggest military power in Lebanon. The influx of the second group of Palestinian refugees since 1948 threw the political and ethnic structure of Lebanon completely out of balance. The weakness of the central government and the anarchy of the civil war triggered by the arrival of the Palestinians enabled the PLO to carry on a war against Israel from Lebanon for more than ten years, a war that included not only Lebanon and Israel but also Israeli and Jewish establishments throughout the world.

* 3 *

Driven out of Jordan and on the way to the new center of exile in Beirut, the PLO leadership met in Damascus in the summer of 1971. The movement had reached the nadir of its brief history. How could Palestinian resistance against the Israeli occupation be maintained? On the agenda was a plan to revive a campaign of terror by all factions. Some PLO leaders were against a strategy of terror, but the hour and the dynamic of the movement worked against them. Yassir Arafat, who voted neither for nor against the plan, worried that the attacks were to be carried out in the name of the PLO and pleaded to find another name. Thus Black September was born.

The first attack came at the end of November 1971, a little more than a year after the events of Black September 1970. The victim was the Jordanian prime minister, Wasfi Tel, leader of the campaign against the PLO militias, a former officer in the British army and the only one on the Arab side who had outlined an adequate strategy against Israel in the 1948 war. His death on a Cairo street was followed by an attack on the Jordanian ambassador in London and on a West German and a Dutch energy supply plant. Black September had outlined the scope of the campaign—all those whom they considered complicit in the fate of the Palestinians were to be targets. The ensuing ten months developed into one of the most violent periods in the war between Palestinians and Jews. Palestinian groups and their aides hijacked a plane, and with the help of the Japanese "Red Army," they perpetrated an attack on tourists in the arrival lounge at the Tel Aviv airport, on a refinery in Italy, and on settlements in northern Israel. The Israeli army responded with air raids on PLO military bases and with ground offensives in southern Lebanon.

In September 1972, the second anniversary of Black September, a group of terrorists attacked the quarters of the Israeli participants in the Munich Olympics. Two athletes were killed in the attack, nine more died in the police rescue operation, along with five terrorists and a policeman. Three Palestinians, who had survived the gunfight, were later freed by the hijacking of a Lufthansa jet. The Munich attack damaged the PLO's reputation more than nearly any other.

In March 1973, the last attack in the name of Black September was committed. A group of eight terrorists attacked a party in the house of the Saudi Arabian ambassador in Khartoum and posed the usual demands for the release of hostages. After the negotiations failed, the attackers shot the American ambassador in Sudan, his deputy, and a Belgian diplomat. Israelis and Americans, who eavesdropped on radio communications between the hostage-takers and Beirut during the negotiations, later stated that Arafat himself had given the orders. Involving Saudi Arabia and Sudan, two states that had supported the PLO financially and diplomatically, now threatened to damage the reputation of the PLO in the Arab world as well.

The declared objective of the terror campaign was to attract world attention to the plight of the Palestinians, but internal motives were equally important. The groups united in the PLO, which had carried out independent attacks against Israel since the early 1960s, wanted to demonstrate both their will to fight and their striking force—to the Palestinian population, the Arab governments, and, not least, the other organizations within the PLO. The area of operations was the whole world. By cooperating with other revolutionary underground groups—the Red Army faction in Germany, the Red Army in Japan—the war against Israel could now be presented as part of the global struggle against colonialism and imperialism. PLO terror groups adopted the tactics of guerrilla warfare—to neutralize the enemy's superiority in conventional means by selecting unconventional targets and methods. Jewish institutions were not spared either. One effect of the attacks was to reinforce identity. Because of the destruction of its urban centers in 1948, Palestinian society had been dispersed to an archipelago of non-contiguous places of exile and refugee camps, which could hardly offer political and cultural cohesion. A militant nationalism, enhanced by spectacular attacks and Israel's equally spectacular reactions, was to fill this vacuum.

In the early 1970s, the Israeli government must have been aware of the deterrent example of the failed U.S. intervention in

Vietnam. To avoid the mistake of a conventional war against an unconventional opponent, the Israeli government also reached into the arsenal of guerilla warfare and assigned the secret service to find and liquidate those responsible for the attack in Munich and those who were behind Black September. In April 1973, an Israeli commando unit led by Ehud Barak, later chief of staff and prime minister, murdered three prominent PLO representatives in their beds in Beirut. In subsequent years, the Mossad campaign claimed at least a dozen victims.

The Israeli attack on the PLO leadership in Beirut led to a governmental crisis in Lebanon. The prime minister, a Moslem, according to the traditional division of power, accused the commander of the Lebanese army, a Christian, of ignoring the order to defend against the Israeli attack and demanded his dismissal. The president, a Christian, supported the commander of the army. He remained, the prime minister retreated, and the Moslem groups saw the confirmation of their thesis that the Lebanese Christians and the Israelis were hand in glove. What had already been a tense relationship between the PLO and the Lebanese army worsened, and the central government lost more ground to special ethnic and religious interests. The well-armed Lebanese factions prepared for a new round in the civil war.

At the end of April 1973, the first armed confrontations occurred, culminating in a shelling of the Beirut airport by PLO militias and an air raid by the Lebanese army on a Beirut refugee camp. The neighboring Arab states, which had been secretly preparing an attack on Israel for the coming October, were not interested in expanding the conflict and forced the parties to negotiate. The result was a legalization of the PLO militias and the sanctioning of attacks against Israel from Lebanese territory. For all intents and purposes, this meant acknowledging an armed autonomy of the Palestinians in their camps and residential areas, and led directly to the Lebanese civil war, which was merely delayed for more than a year by the new Middle East war in October.

* 4 *

With the Black September campaign and Israel's countermeasures, the Israeli-Palestinian conflict spread over the whole world. A cycle of attack and counterattack, revenge and retaliation was set in motion. The goals of the bloodshed became increasingly more intangible: influence over international public opinion, governments, or parliaments; mobilization of one's own population for a greater willingness to sacrifice; or simply the demonstration of "strength." Since punishing terrorist acts only led to new ones, and propagandistic effects were hard to measure, a cost-benefit analysis at the base of conventional military actions was hardly feasible. The relationship between Israel and the PLO drifted into a zone of political irrationality, where it remains to this day.

The terror and counterterror campaigns contributed a great deal to the militarization of both societies. On both sides, the entire population is involved—as potential fighters and as potential targets. The boundaries between civilian and combatant have disappeared, and the conflict and its accompanying nationalist ideologies have penetrated deep into all areas of life. The unbridled nature of terror and counterterror also led to the brutalization and dehumanization of the conflict. The sweeping ruthlessness of the attacks indicated not only lack of respect for your opponent's humanity, but also undermined your own humanity. One reflection of this process is the status accorded to the victims or "martyrs" of the conflict.

In Israel it has always been customary for the media to report in detail on the personality and life of every military and civilian victim. Friends and relations tell about the dead person and show their grief. Newspapers and television regularly display pictures of despairing, weeping people. On the radio, there are minutes of sobbing at an open microphone. This public ritual serves to emphasize the humanity and individuality of the dead person, the goodness, warmth, and humanity of your own society, and the harshness and inhumanity of the opponent. Along with feelings of solidarity and sympathy, aggression and the urge for revenge are also fanned. But above all, such rituals contain the hidden message that the opponent does not deserve any human treatment or consideration.

It is a deeply rooted conviction in Israel that Jewish society has a much higher level of morality than the opponent, that the loss of human life weighs much heavier here, and that, on the other hand, human life is less valuable in Arab society. This racist stereotype, reminiscent of European colonialism, is apparently confirmed by the fact that the victims of our own violence are uncounted, unnamed, and faceless. Israeli citizens usually hear a very clipped, formal communiqué about army attacks, which speak simply of the action against "terrorists," that our own troops suffered no losses. That is the most important information. If you want information about the victims, you have to turn to foreign news media.

On the Palestinian side, a nationalist death cult has emerged that has a comparable effect. Here it is the "martyrs" fallen in the struggle against the occupier whom young people emulate and whose model inspires and radicalizes politics. The solitary progress of the warrior and his inevitable death in the struggle against a superior opponent are archaic motifs that mask the delusion of the attacker, his useless death, and the devastating effect of a bomb filled with nails. His picture appears on posters and videos, his name is immortalized in military and civilian institutions, myths and legends circulate about him. The dehumanization of the enemy, just all Israelis, or more briefly "Jews," makes it possible to represent and minimize the killing of unarmed and defenseless civilians, often including children, as a courageous strike and a glorious act of heroism. Arab criticism of the brutal terrorist strategy of the Palestinian leadership, which has contributed considerably to aggravate and prolong Palestinian suffering, is seldom to be found except in foreign media.

In Israeli society, the conventional glorification and masking of violence that can be described as "heroism" hardly plays a role. The self-image of the Israeli soldier is a pacifist forced into battle. Especially conspicuous in this self-view is the "suffering," the subjective innocence and affliction of the individual, who "shoots and weeps," in the words of a well-known Israeli idiom. This view corresponds to the basic tenor of Israeli apologetics, the idea of the just but reluctant self-defense against an apparently unjustified Arab aggression, an historic myth emphasizing one's own passivity in the causes and dynamic of the conflict. This self-identification as victim is just as mystifying and morally numbing as the glorification of violence.

Whenever the idea of self-defense, a grossly inflated sense of your own humanity and of the inhumanity of your opponent prevails so absolutely, a particularly warped sense of proportion manifests itself. One Palestinian missile fired from Lebanon onto the field of an Israeli kibbutz was quite often considered as justification for an overwhelming counterattack with many dead and wounded, mostly civilians. Thus, the idea of the "cheapness" of Arab life was converted into horrible reality. Attacks on Israeli army patrols in occupied southern Lebanon, in which soldiers were wounded, but no vital Israeli security interest was at stake, triggered counterattacks forcing tens of thousands of civilians to flee. Responsibility for these devastating and exaggerated countermeasures was laid at the door of the organizations that had carried out the original attack.

* 5 *

In the first year after my return, a relative invited me to visit him during his reserve duty at a place that would certainly be interesting to a newcomer—an Israeli military post in Lebanon. It was 1977 and a few things had changed on the Lebanese border. Syria's intervention during the first phase of the Lebanese civil war ended in 1976 with a ceasefire agreement stipulating the disarmament of the PLO militias in the south. The presence of Syrian troops, advantageous as it may be in this regard even for Israel, also meant the danger of clashes between the two armies on the long, unfortified border with Lebanon. Rabin's government and after 1977, Begin's government, too, tried to solve this dilemma in two ways. The first was the policy of the "Red Line." The "Red Line" meant that Israel placed a limit on Syria's military potential in Lebanon and tolerated no Syrian troops on this side of a line parallel to the border on the Litani River. This created a buffer zone, in which the Syrian army could not keep the PLO in check. The solution for this problem consisted of a local Lebanese Christian militia armed and financed by Israel. The task of this troop of about three thousand men commanded by former Lebanese army major Saad Haddad, was to protect the Israeli border against PLO attacks from within the buffer zone. Shortly after, many Christian inhabitants somewhat hastily called this area in southern Lebanon controlled by Israel "Free Lebanon"—a name that sounded good to politicians in Jerusalem. To guarantee the functioning of Haddad's "Free Lebanese Army" and to bind the population even closer to Israel, a second policy was formulated—the "Good Fence."

So, one day I set out to visit the Good Fence. Right before the border, on a short connecting road between the civilian world of Israel and the empire of the army, I drove along a military road closed to civilian vehicles, mined to the right and left, and controlled by jeeps. Even though I advanced into the blocked zone in my unmilitary-looking orange-colored car, nobody stopped me. The road passed by watch towers on the mined fence, studded with electronic sensors and topped with barbed wire, marking the international border. The ever brilliant Israeli propagandists of the Foreign Ministry had dubbed these monstrous border fortifications a "Good Fence" because the Christian population of the Lebanese buffer zone could get to the other side of the fence in a few places for a couple of hours a day.

My host had given me precise instructions. The border strip climbed behind a curve to a hill that was visible in the distance. There, at one of the gates, I was to register. The soldier on duty had clearly been informed of my arrival and let me through without anymore questions, as if the appearance of a civilian at this spot was the most normal thing in the world. I was in Lebanon.

The post I now reached on a dirt road dominated the area from its high position. A few soldiers commanded by my cousin had set up a truly cozy makeshift bunker under primitive conditions. That was customary among reserve units, and here too I had the impression that the non-regulation equipment, the imaginative costume, and the general disorder must have served as an antidote to the military gravity of the assignment. Even my invitation was to be considered an attempt to hold onto the conventions of civilian life by deliberately violating the rules. But the very visible presence of my car seemed to go too far. Fearing not the enemy so much as his superiors, my host had me drive the car back to the border fence and then brought me back to camp in a jeep.

The reservists, who have to plunge into the parallel world of the army for a few weeks a year, took my arrival as an opportunity to stop working and serve the usual refreshments. In view of the long night duty, the major effort seemed to be devoted to keeping your eyes open during the day. One of the troop's assignments was to supervise the coming and going of Lebanese civilians, who came by foot in the morning, registered at the border fence, were examined and then taken to their destinations in Israel in buses or trucks. In the evening, the procedure was repeated in reverse. The army only helped. Relations with Major Haddad's "army" and the Lebanese population were in the hands of Israeli civilians, known as "secret service people," but nobody knew anything more precise about them. What the Lebanese did during the day in Israel was a subject of constant speculation. Did they go to work, shopping, training? This policy of the open door to the Arab world, which was really only a crack, had to be confusing for everybody, not only Israelis.

In retrospect, what amazes me most is still the great relaxation and calm that prevailed in this Israeli-controlled area. Meanwhile, Lebanon may have become the home base of the PLO and suffered under the back-and-forth of Palestinian attack and Israeli retaliation, not to mention the lethal civil war of the local factions, but here in the south, the "security zone" remained secure for a while—not much longer than a year, but for local relations, that was a small eternity.

* 6 *

After the Likud victory in the 1977 election and a new round in the Lebanese civil war the following year, the situation grew worse. The random shelling of Lebanese territory by Israeli artillery, reported to me by my friend from Munich, dated from this time, and was part of the so-called "preventive measures." This particularly inhuman method had been introduced by the Begin government at the urging of the newly appointed Chief-of-Staff Raphael Eytan. They, too, were based on the tactic of guerilla war—leaving the time and place of the operation not to the initiative of the enemy, tying up enemy forces in a defensive position with the element of surprise and unpredictability, and thus preventing attacks. These unconventional methods only had conventional consequences: even more victims and further escalation.

The 1977 triumph of Menachem Begin and the Likud party was the first time since the establishment of the State that a political movement had come to power that was fundamentally opposed to the policy of the dominant Labor movement. As in many other areas, Likud also sought a new beginning with regard to Lebanon. Shortly after Begin came into office, secret contacts with the Christian Marronite groups, abandoned since the Syrian intervention in the civil war, were resumed and intensified. The Israeli secret service and the Marronite militias resumed a mutually advantageous cooperation, consisting of weapons supply and training courses for one side and information about the PLO for the other. What was new were the geopolitical visions that Begin, who liked to think in historical dimensions, brought with him into this cooperation, and the intensity of the contacts. The target of all efforts was the unsolved problem of the Palestinians.

Begin and his colleagues were seeking a way to hold onto the territories of the West Bank, including East Jerusalem, conquered in the 1967 war, for the long term. In terms of international law, the situation did not look bad for them. The area was to have been part of the Palestinian state not realized in 1948, but had been annexed by Jordan. The annexation had not been granted international recognition, and thus the territory conquered by Israel belonged to no sovereign state to whom it could be returned. Israeli governments circumvented the issue of the international legal status of the West Bank by defining the area as "disputed territory," that is, neither Israeli territory nor the occupied territory of another country, where the Geneva Convention for the protection of the civilian population applied. The Israeli position was indirectly supported by the fact that, on the other side, Jordan and the PLO debated about the right to representation and succession, a conflict settled only in 1988 when the kingdom of Jordan ceded all territorial claims against Israel to the Palestinians.

Into this vacuum of international law, Israeli governments—both on the left and the right—placed their faits accomplis of building settlements and expanding Jerusalem. A permanent guarantee of these "facts" was, nevertheless, possible only with the agreement of Jordan and the political representatives of the Palestinians. Their right of self-determination, included in the 1947 Partition Plan, was considered confirmed in the U.N. Resolutions after 1967, which, however, had left the borders of a future state open. Because of the rather inconsistent nature of the resolutions, the Palestinians virtually had only a right of veto against annexation, a right that could become effective only in case of a final settlement. All Israeli governments used this political weakness of the Palestinians to great effect in the international arena to strengthen Israel's position in the occupied areas.

In their settlement policy, Labor governments mainly sought a large-scale improvement of the borders of 1948. Their aims were both strategic and demographic. Territorial buffers were to settle the strategic weaknesses in the coastal plain and along the Jerusalem corridor; and settlements on the heights of the West Bank and the Golan and on the Jordanian border in the Jordan Valley were to serve as defensive outposts. At the same time, the number of Arab residents added by the territorial expansion was to be kept as small as possible. The settlement strategy of the Labor party also aimed, as before 1948, at destroying the contiguity of Palestinian population centers, a strategy considered advantageous in later border negotiations.

After 1977, Likud governments had another vision of the future—the greatest possible expansion of the State in order to guarantee unlimited Jewish immigration and settlement. But what was to happen with the Palestinians in those territories? To grant so many non-Jews citizenship would mean the end of the Zionist dream of the state for Jews. Moreover, the consent of the Palestinians was hardly likely.

In 1977, Menachem Begin and his colleagues faced the same problem in the occupied territories as David Ben Gurion and his generation had in the 1930s: How to get rid of an undesired and recalcitrant population without provoking the resistance of powers whose support Israel was dependent on? For both situations, there was a vague formula—"peaceful" or "voluntary" transfer, a slogan that was now revived. This sinister term concealed the most diverse ideas. It meant mainly that, in case of a peace agreement, there would be a contractual population exchange. Since at no stage of the conflict had an Arab partner ever supported such an idea, the real meaning of this formula was purely propagandistic. One's own followers had to get an answer for the most important, largely open questions of Zionism, and the protecting powers had to get the promise of a solution free of violence. As a practical measure, "voluntary transfer" meant wearing down the undesired fellow residents with the goal of moving them to emigrate or flee, as the Jewish leadership had succeeded in driving over a half million Palestinians out of Israeli territory between December 1947 and June 1948.

This was how the solution was presented thirty years later, too. The occupation had to lead to the gradual displacement of the Arab population—through the daily harassment of closing roads, identity checks, searches, blocking exits; through suppressing political and cultural life; through building Jewish settlements, diverting water, blocking economic growth, preventing any development at all. The Palestinians who remained in the occupied territories, who hadn't yet emigrated after decades of brutal occupation, were to be offered communal self-government and cultural autonomy within a Greater Israel, if necessary even the kind of second-class citizenship enjoyed by Palestinians living in Israel itself.

For all this to work, the PLO had first to be eliminated as a political and military power. Then the fate of the Palestinians remaining in Israel and the occupied territories—some 1.8 million in 1978—had to be separated from the refugees living in Diaspora—about 2.6 million. After thirty years, most of these refugees were not yet integrated, and Israeli governments had to fear being forced to take them back in case of peace. But the impoverished, radicalized population in the refugee camps was politically weak and dependent on their host countries. After the failure of the Arab intervention in the war of October 1973 and the peace initiative of Egyptian President Sadat, the Israeli government could assume that the neighboring countries were finally ready to settle the conflict between the states. Even more important, in negotiations with Egypt, the most powerful Arab country, the Begin government learned that the neighbors were also willing to drop the issue of the Palestinians. It must have appeared to Israeli strategists that the PLO was now the only obstacle to a solution. The practically total control of Palestinian life by this radical organization and its leader Yassir Arafat had to be brought to an end. While prevailing thought in Arab capitals was that a military solution to the conflict with Israel was no longer possible, in Jerusalem the idea of a military solution to the conflict with the Palestinians emerged.

* 7 *

The greater freedom of movement and action the PLO had won in politically unstable Lebanon brought increasing disadvantages during the 1970s. What had once been considered a refuge from which the struggle for liberation against Israel could be waged had gradually become a place where all the political and military forces of the PLO were bound up in their own conflict. In the civil war of 1975–1976, when the Christian, Moslem, and Druse groups confronted one another, in large part because of the many refugees and the excesses of the Palestinian militias, the PLO fighting forces assumed a larger role within the Moslem alliance. In the south of the country, Israeli retaliations caused increasing friction with the Amal militias, who protected the Shi'a majority in this part of Lebanon. At the same time, the PLO now had to worry also about developments across the border of Lebanon—the extremely cautious but tangible relaxation in relations between Israel and its Arab neighbors, which, with the help of intensive American shuttle diplomacy through the disengagement agreements in the mid-1970s, led to Sadat's peace initiative in September 1977. Faced with the danger that the issue of Palestine might be pushed off the stage of the Middle East conflict and the refugees forgotten in their camps, the PLO reacted by becoming even more radical. It joined Iraq, Libya, and Algeria in a rejection front and prepared new, bigger terrorist acts from its Lebanese exile.

The latitude offered by Lebanon led to an extraordinary growth of the PLO. A large number of aid organizations operated in the camps; women's groups, labor unions, and student federations sprung up, creating national cohesion; over a hundred PLO offices abroad solicited political support. Nevertheless, the dominance of the military in the "struggle for the liberation of Palestine" kept growing. The struggle for cultural survival, democracy, equality and social justice had originally been considered equally important. Now it fell victim to both the propaganda war and the "armed struggle," driven by unfavorable circumstances and the lack of an independent public sphere that could have formed a counterweight to the vapid militancy of the leadership. The changing goals of the "armed struggle"—demoralizing the opponent, sustaining the conflict, consolidating national identity—could neither produce the liberation of Palestine nor improve the life of the refugees. For that, help from neighboring countries was needed along with a reversal in the West's position concerning

Israel. Without these two elements, a free Palestine was inconceivable. Thus, after Sadat's peace initiative, the PLO still hoped that spectacular attacks on Israel would make the militant government coalition under Menachem Begin react harshly, and provoke the resistance of Israel's friends and the Arab countries.

The strategy to improve or at least change the situation through a temporary worsening also aimed at the sympathy Israel enjoyed in the Western world as a place of refuge for the persecuted, and as the supposedly weaker side in the Middle East conflict. As the Palestinians saw it, the West's traditional solidarity with Israel, a product of guilt toward the Jews, colonial hubris, and the imperatives of the Cold War, ignored the real causes and motives of the conflict. The underdogs, the victims, were really the Palestinians. What could correct this error better than the image of militarily superior Israel hounding wretched and defenseless Palestinian refugees with excessive violence? It must have been a consolation to the PLO that even in the overwhelmingly pro-Israeli media of Europe and North America, a harsh Israeli attack quickly drove out the headlines of the Palestinian attack that had provoked the strike. Thus, the bloody competition for the status of victim and legitimate recipient of Western sympathy took off.

On Saturday, March 11, 1978, eleven members of Fatah landed in rubber boats on the coast south of Haifa. Their arrival in the late afternoon, on the rocky shore among fish-breeding ponds and white-crusted salt basins, went unnoticed. It wasn't until they were on their way to the nearby coastal highway that they were discovered by a hiker. The young woman, an American photographer who had come here to observe rare migratory birds, was shot. On the road, the group stopped two tour buses, packed all the passengers into one of the buses (according to police reports, there were seventy-one passengers altogether, including thirty children) and, shooting wildly out the windows at oncoming traffic, began a long bloody trip south. Near the Tel Aviv city limit, the bus encountered a roadblock hastily set up by the police and the army. In the ensuing exchange of shots, the bus caught fire, and more than half the passengers were killed along with nine of the eleven terrorists. Because the police assumed that members of the terrorist group had escaped under cover of dark into the dunes along the road, the broader surroundings, several wealthy Tel Aviv suburbs, were closed off, a curfew was imposed, and the area was combed all night by security forces. The sight of heavily armed troops marching through the quiet streets, helicopters circling over the houses, burning wrecks on the road, brought the battlefield right to the doors of the city.

The attack sent the Israeli population into profound shock. There had been previous infiltrations, but the assaults had been confined to border zones. Even the attack on a hotel on the Tel Aviv boardwalk, in which eleven civilians died, had taken place only a few meters from the landing place on the Israeli coast. This time a commando had succeeded in penetrating sixty kilometers into the heart of Israel through the main traffic artery of the country, causing unprecedented disaster and chaos. The reaction of the Israeli government was not long in coming. Barely forty-eight hours after the bloody end of the hostage-taking, an Israeli invasion army of some twenty-thousand soldiers moved into Lebanon. The Israeli air force and navy attacked Palestinian positions from air and sea. The stated goal was the "uprooting" of terrorist bases in the border area and the hinterland, from where terrorist missions had been launched into Israel. In the first days, Israeli ground troops occupied a strip of some ten kilometers north of the border.

In addition, air force and navy artillery attacked Palestinian positions in the coastal towns of Tyre and Sidon and in a suburb of Beirut, and bombed the city of Damur, less than twenty kilometers south of the capital. Damur was exposed to especially heavy attacks, clearly as punishment for the fact that the commando raid had started for the coastal road from here. Lebanese losses were high—some two thousand people lost their life, six villages were in rubble and ashes, and another eighty-two were badly hit. Over two hundred thousand people, a third of the residents of the south, fled north.

Judging by the extent of the military campaign, the Israeli government must have counted on a broad understanding of the allies for a large-scale counterattack. But the shock effect of the terrorist attack among Israelis was not reflected in the reactions of friendly governments. The U.S., struck by the heavy civilian losses on the Lebanese side, condemned the attack and demanded a withdrawal of Israeli troops. In a decision of the U.N. Security Council on March 19, 1978, a U.N. peace-keeping force was created at the request of the Lebanese government, to supervise the withdrawal and fill the power vacuum created in the south.

On the night after the acceptance of the U.N. resolution, Israeli tanks pushed deeper into Lebanon and occupied twice as much territory, as far as the Litani River. The goal was clearly to expand the zone of U.N. troop operations as far north as possible. At the same time, Israel took the opportunity to deal a final blow to the Palestinian guerrillas, who had sought safety a few days before on the other side of the Christian zone. Not until March 21 did Israel agree to the demanded ceasefire.

* 8 *

The Palestinian attack of March 1978 and the Israeli response in the form of "Operation Litani" showed once again the failure of a typical behavior pattern—the attempt of both sides to achieve political goals with military means and to avoid as long as possible the political process that could lead to a peaceful solution. In decades of conflict, both sides had looked to negotiations only for short-term advantages, while long-term goals and hopes seemed unattainable by diplomatic means. Both sides relied on a strategy of endurance and intransigence in which regional power constellations and the political priorities of the power blocks favored the Israeli side from the start. In 1948, the Arab states had been ready for a military intervention, but the rights of the Palestinians had not been the central issue. In 1973, when military intervention failed again, the impoverished Arab states, released from colonial domination only a few decades earlier, had to consider other means. Aside from Arab and Moslem countries, the Palestinian demand for a revision of the situation of 1948—return of the refugees, dissolution of Israel, and the establishment of an Arab state without privileges for Jewish immigrants—was supported only by the Soviet bloc. With the reforms under Gorbachev, the retreat of the Soviet Union from the Middle East and the renunciation of violence of the bordering states, the PLO had reached the point at which "endurance" was no longer enough. After all other hopes were thwarted, in 1988 the PLO recognized Israel in the borders of June 1967. For the first time, this opened the opportunity for negotiating on the basis of the Western model of solution. Only now, forty years after the establishment of Israel, did the PLO begin to play the negotiation card.

Nor did Israel—in the position of military and political strength—have much interest initially in a negotiated solution. A majority of nations, including the Soviet Union and its allies, had recognized Israel in 1948 and thus accepted the failure of a state solution for the Palestinians. For Israel, negotiations could only mean endangering what was obtained. But even in 1949, with the refusal to allow even a symbolic number of Palestinian refugees to return to their home, Israel violated international law and the wishes of the U.S. and other allies who had helped the Jews achieve a state in 1947. After 1967, with the settlement of the West Bank, the gap widened between Israel's military position and its political and legal situation. Since a diplomatic process inevitably had to be based on international norms, negotiations in the 1960s, as today, meant that Israel would have to give up territory and repatriate or compensate refugees. Therefore, the Likud government participated only reluctantly and pro forma after 1988 in the first indirect negotiations opened by the U.S. and the Soviet Union. Not until 1993, with the victory of the Labor party led by Rabin and Peres, did Israel seriously enter into negotiations with the Palestinians.

For more than forty years the dominance of the military approach had not brought the participants what they wanted, but often enough, the opposite. For Israel, "Operation Litani," the most comprehensive intervention into Lebanon to date, had brought unexpected and unwelcome consequences. PLO campaigns intensified and forced Israeli governments to take increasingly harsher countermeasures, which led to the invasion of 1982 and an occupation lasting almost twenty years. As for the PLO, they were forced to change their previous military strategy because of increasing impediments in the border area, and to start building a regular army, a development that led almost inevitably to the complete destruction of their military potential and the expulsion of the PLO from Lebanon. On the other hand, by weakening the PLO, those Israeli forces that would no longer tolerate Yassir Arafat and the PLO several hundred kilometers away in Beirut contributed to restraining their demands and redirecting them to the path of negotiations. The current result is that the sphere of influence of a PLO-led Palestinian administration now reaches to the city limits of Jerusalem.

* 9 *

The demonstration of Israeli power in "Operation Litani" had another unexpected result—Israel's involvement in the Lebanese civil war. The advance of Israeli troops and the air raids near Beirut impressed the Christian groups who, since the end of the last phase of the civil war in 1976, had seen a new threat in Syria's increasing role. Syrian troops had initially taken care of stabilizing the situation as part of the Arab deterrent force; but, after the withdrawal of all other Arab contingents, they turned out to be an occupier and protector of the Moslem groups, especially the Palestinians. In the fall of 1978, after a successful conclusion of the Israeli-Egyptian negotiations at Camp David, Syria had also become the main ally of the PLO within the Arab rejection front. For the Christians, the "Lebanese system" of dividing power between Christians and Moslems was at an end. Meanwhile, even two years after the fighting ended, Syrian troops made no arrangements to leave the Christian zone of Lebanon and directly endangered the economic and political autonomy that had emerged during the civil war, consisting mainly of the Christian bourgeoisie filling their pockets in a thoroughly unregulated and untaxed commerce.

While other Marronite groups within the "Lebanese Front" tried to get along with the Syrian presence, the two militias trained and equipped by Israel were in the middle of an armed conflict with the troops of the "protector," when Israel embarked on "Operation Litani." The Falangists led by the Gemayel family and the "Tigers" of the Chamoun family saw Israel as the only power that could still prevent Syria from turning Lebanon into a Moslem country. When the massive advance against the PLO provided proof of Israel's willingness to be more strongly engaged in Lebanon, these Christian groups looked to an expanded Israeli involvement to serve their own objectives.

Israel's ensuing involvement in Lebanese power politics, which led to the invasion of 1982, has since become the subject of several studies attempting to explain the incorrect estimates within the Israeli government machinery on which the far-reaching expectations of the 1982 offensive were based. The Israeli government under Begin and Sharon hoped that military intervention and cooperation with the Christian militias would destroy the PLO's military potential, banish the political leadership, and expel a large number of Palestinian refugees. Further results were to be the establishment of a purely Christian government, a peace treaty, the creation of a regional alliance, the neutralization of Syria, and the restructuring of the Middle East aimed at forcing the remaining Palestinians in the occupied territories into Jordan, and creating an ethnically cleansed Greater Israel.

The enlistment of Israel on the side of the Christians began with an adroit maneuver of the Falange. In the summer of 1978, after a few months of street fights and shelling between the Christian residential areas of Beirut and Syrian positions outside the city involving heavy losses, in which the Christian militias were threatened with total defeat, the Israeli government issued a warning to Syria that Israel would not tolerate a destruction of the Christian forces in Lebanon. As soon as this guarantee was given, Bashir Gemayel minted it into political coin. With hardly more than a thousand fighters, he began a counterattack against the three divisions of Syrian besiegers hoping to provoke Israel's direct intervention. The Israeli government reacted with a threat. It increased its troops on the Golan Heights and flew warplanes over the Syrian positions around Beirut. The threat was enough to make Syrian troops retreat.

Israeli government statements in those days conveyed the impression that the Christians in Lebanon were in a situation as precarious as that of the Jews in the 1930s. Israeli ministers and Prime Minister Begin constantly indicated that, in their view, the Lebanese Christians were facing "genocide." Analogies to the Holocaust were part of the basic propaganda arsenal of Menachem Begin and his Likud Party. On an almost weekly basis, the horror of the Nazi murder of the Jews was conjured up whenever the actions of the PLO and the inaction of the world in the face of the threatened annihilation of the Jews of Israel were to be denounced. But comparing the fate of the Jews during the Holocaust with that of the Christians in Lebanon was so patently absurd that even the Israelis, usually eager for such comparisons, seemed hardly convinced. The Israeli newspapers presented a completely different picture. An American journalist stationed in Beirut published a report in the Israeli press describing the leaders of the Christian militias as brutal and corrupt Mafia dons with a penchant for gold chains, cheap cologne, and armored Mercedes limousines, who were less concerned with defending their fellow Christians than with their income from illegal trade through illegal ports on the Mediterranean. From the beginning, the Israeli commitment to the Christians was not popular, nor was the Israeli leadership's belief in the alliance with the militias.

The leader of the Falange, Bashir Gemayel, had used the ceasefire in the struggle against the Syrians to eliminate his rivals brutally and to combine the Christian militias into a unified army, the "Lebanese Armed Forces," under his leadership. In the autumn of 1980, after a series of secret meetings with Menachem Begin, he managed to get a secret guarantee from the Israeli government. Israel pledged to protect Christian territories and armed forces against Syrian air raids. In less than six months, the Lebanese Armed Forces provided a suitable occasion for that. To undermine the "National Reconciliation Program" the Syrians had planned for Lebanon, Bashir Gemayel escalated the conflicts between his militias and the Syrian army in the provincial capital of Zahle. This town, at the edge of the Biqa Valley with a Greek Orthodox population of 150,000, controlled the most important connecting road and supply line between Beirut and Damascus and had been besieged for a few months by the Syrian army. When Syrian helicopters attacked the Christian hinterland, where the militias operated, Gemayel called on his ally.

On April 28, 1981, the Israeli cabinet met to discuss a limited air strike. The representative of military intelligence, as he stated later, immediately assumed a diversionary maneuver of the Lebanese armed forces aimed at involving Israel in the battles. Begin, the chief of staff, and the representative of the civilian secret service, the Mossad, who handled contacts with Gemayel and the Christian militias, were convinced, on the other hand, that the Christians were in a desperate situation and Israel was morally obliged to rush to their aid. The government decided to intervene. On the same day, Israeli fighter planes shot down two Syrian helicopters over Zahle, which were transporting troops to the Christian hinterland. Syria, which had respected Israel's "red line" so far, allowed Israeli intelligence flights, and had not taken any air defense measures in this part of Lebanon, installed modern ground-to-air SAM-6 missiles in the Biqa Valley the next day.

The siege of Zahle was ended two months later by negotiations. The Falangist troops, whose advance had triggered the crisis, withdrew, and Syria took back control over the valley. Only Israel came out worse. Stationing the SAM-6 batteries threatened Israeli air patrols and, as the government argued, constituted an obstacle to defense against PLO attacks. Despite Israeli threats and U.S. intervention, the missiles remained in the Biqa Valley. Thus, Israel's military interference ended with a setback and only created a new reason for the next intervention.

The constellation in the cabinet that led to the attack on Syrian troops in Zahle, the inefficacy of military intelligence warnings, the prime minister's firm ideological conviction that, as a Jew after the Holocaust, he was obliged to assist the Christians in Lebanon threatened with annihilation, the belief in the integrity and reliability of the Lebanese allies—all this was to find its parallel in the spring of 1982. Moreover, after the Israeli elections of June 1981, the political spectrum of the government shifted further to the right and Ariel Sharon, known for his unscrupulous methods, replaced the moderate Ezer Weizmann as defense minister.

* 10 *

The PLO saw itself in an increasingly complex situation in Lebanon. The Israeli retaliatory strikes increased the pressure of Syria and the Amal movement on the Palestinian leadership to stop launching attacks on Israel directly from Lebanese soil. In any case, stationing U.N. troops along the Israeli-Lebanese border in the spring of 1978 and the presence of Major Haddad's militia had made it harder to continue the infiltrations. At the same time, in view of the rapprochement between Israel and Egypt, the PLO was dependent more than ever on big spectacular military feats to sustain the interest of the world and the resistance to Israel. For a while, this could be achieved by attacks carried out from the sea or the occupied territories. Meanwhile, the PLO invested in longer-range artillery and missile batteries to be able to hit Israeli targets over the heads of the peace-keeping troops. In the spring of 1979, after the signing of the Israeli-Egyptian peace treaty, the PLO expanded their attacks. The almost daily shelling over the border provoked Israeli counterattacks that cost the lives of some two hundred Lebanese civilians in a few months. From the invasion in March 1978 to the end of 1980, Israeli ground troops carried out some twenty big advances into Lebanon. At the same time, there were a similar number of Palestinian missile and artillery attacks or infiltrations.

The result of the new strategic requirements, the tactical obstacles in the south and the aggressive reactions of the new Israeli government, was that the Palestinian militias increasingly turned into a regular army. While small guerrilla units remained advantageous in the occupied territories, the introduction of new weapons in Lebanon demanded an expansion of the logistical infrastructure. PLO armed forces in the south were combined into three brigade-sized units. Along with heavy artillery, radar-guided anti-aircraft weapons, and Katyusha rocket batteries, the troops received light tanks, armored personnel carriers, and a number of World War II-era Soviet T-34 battle tanks. At the same time, the Palestinian leadership began recruiting. The military transformation culminated in recruiting a Palestinian reserve army. Preparations for registering, mobilizing, and training all Palestinian men between the ages of 16 and 49 who were living in Lebanon were in full swing in June 1982, when the Israeli invasion brought military armament to an end.

The war of attrition reached its climax in the spring and summer of 1981. In April, the Israeli government launched the heaviest air and ground attacks since Operation Litani. The coastal cities of Damur and Tyre and Palestinian positions in Beaufort and Nabatiya in the south were fired on. The Palestinians responded with a two-day shelling of Israeli targets. In the following weeks, the whole thing was repeated with Israeli air raids on Sidon and Nabatiya and Palestinian retaliatory strikes in northern Israel.

After an Israeli air raid on July 10, 1981, the PLO fired missiles at the border town of Kiryat Shmona and the seaside resort of Nahariya. That triggered a new round of strike and counterstrike, which ended in a massive Israeli air raid on the Beirut headquarters of Al-Fatah and the Popular Front for the Liberation of Palestine, on July 17. The attack on Beirut resulted mainly in civilian casualties —more than three hundred dead and some five hundred wounded —and earned Israel a condemnation by the U.N. Security Council. Israel's massive attack on an Arab capital and the high civilian losses provoked unusually sharp protests among both allies and Israelis. The conservative U.S. government under Ronald Reagan postponed the supply of certain fighter jets for Israel indefinitely.

As shots were still being exchanged, U.N. authorities and a U.S. envoy began diplomatic efforts for a ceasefire. The PLO declared their willingness to agree to a truce, but expected that Israel would not engage in negotiations—even indirect ones—with the Palestinians. Meanwhile, a brand new element entered into Israeli politics—the population of the north was in a panic. Almost half the residents of Kiryat Shmona and Nahariya, cities with more than fifty thousand inhabitants, had packed their bags and moved in temporarily with friends and relatives. For nine nights, the remaining inhabitants of the north slept in bunkers, work in factories and fields came to a halt, and on television every single evening all Israelis saw pictures of columns of packed cars making their way south.

In ten days, 33 Israeli towns had come under fire 88 times and some 1200 missiles and grenades were lobbed into Israel. Six people died and 59 were wounded. Damage, especially to agriculture, was great. Compared to the losses on the Lebanese and Palestinian side, where hundreds of people fell victim to Israeli bombs and grenades during the same time, that was not much. But the Israeli population had never experienced such a thing. Moreover, there was the shock that, despite years of massive countermeasures by the Israeli army, the Palestinian armed forces could achieve such a military stroke.

On the tenth day, Israel agreed to a ceasefire, surprising all observers, not least the Palestinian leadership. Despite the efforts of the Israeli government to play down its consent to the treaty negotiated by the U.S., it was generally considered a political defeat. The government's behavior had led to a crisis in relations with the U.S. and to a cut-off in weapons supply. For the first time, the PLO appeared as an equal partner in negotiations. But certainly the harshest rebuff was seeing that Israel's military might had not been adequate to protect its own population or stop the Palestinian attacks.

For the PLO, all those were good reasons to maintain the ceasefire agreement. The attempt of dissidents to resume the struggle against Israel was nipped in the bud. Moreover, the agreement let the Palestinian side repair the damages it had suffered. New, better, more modern weapons came from the Soviet Union through North Korea, Syria, and Libya to the Palestinian armed forces, which now increasingly looked more like a regular army with a centralized command structure and effective battle units.

The U.S., worried about the growing influence of the Soviet Union in the region, began to regret their compliant attitude toward Israel's unbridled aggression. The pendulum of Washington's policy in the Middle East swung back toward Saudi Arabia and the Gulf states. But for the Israeli government, the ignominious outcome of the war of attrition provided more reasons for a new, even bigger military strike. Along with the Syrian anti-aircraft system in the Biqa Valley and the military potential of the PLO, there was now a third goal—preventing further political gains of the Palestinians. Defense Minister Sharon, along with Bashir Gemayel, now prepared plans for "Operation Peace for the Galilee," the campaign that began in June 1982 and led to my mobilization.

3

* EDUCATION OF AN ISRAELI *

The Zionism of Everyday Life

* 1 *

In the first year after my return to Israel in 1976, I was treated as a new immigrant. The new immigrant represents a special type in Israeli society, a blend of the admired Pioneer so important in Israeli mythology; the *shlemiel* or jerk from the Diaspora cast of characters, a naïve, even romantic person who does everything wrong and never has any luck; and finally the parasite, the *luftmensch*, who is lazy but shrewd and relies on the charity of the community. This figure of the "Oleh," the new immigrant, expresses the ambivalence of the old-timers toward the newcomer. The personal sacrifice the immigrant is willing to make by voluntarily accepting the experiment of the Jewish state earns admiration and respect. At the same time, he seems naïve and a little dumb, for he chose a path many Israelis would prefer to tread in the opposite direction. Everybody grasps the need to help the newcomer and support him. But the generosity with which the Jewish immigrants are treated—priority in housing, favorable mortgage conditions, tax exemptions—also provokes envy and resentment.

As a state, too, Israel relates ambiguously toward certain ethnic and social groups of immigrants. The country was intended as a melting pot of Jews, but Zionism had its roots in the Eastern European Jewish petite bourgeoisie, who were considered the real settlers of the new homeland. The expansion of the Zionist melting pot to other groups kept forcing the old-timers to defend their privileged position and their secular Eastern-European Jewish culture against the increasing stream of newcomers. Different levels of education and technology, standards of living, the position of women, different degrees of political freedom in the original society, all that has always made for tensions.

The waves of immigration from the beginning of Zionist colonization in the late-nineteenth century up through the 1930s are surrounded by myths and have always been idealized, while later immigrant movements have enjoyed less esteem. The process of "Aliyah," "ascent," the Hebrew word for immigration to Israel, is based on a hierarchy of respect. Those attracted by ideology are most admired. On the other end of the scale are those groups whose decision to emigrate was motivated by rejection, that is, anti-Semitism, or political or economic crises in their homeland. All this seems to contradict the reason for the emergence of Zionism, which was to aid the oppressed Jews of Eastern Europe.

The First Aliyah began with a few hundred young people from Russia, who were seen as the real Pioneers. It was triggered by the pogroms of 1881 in Russia, and the agricultural settlements they founded were financed by a benevolent aristocrat and run with the help of Arab farm workers, but they were considered motivated by love of Zion; they found an impassible, inhospitable terrain of swamps and unpaved roads. Little is known about most of them. That made them even more suitable to be cast into the role of the volunteers or vanguard so important to all national movements, whose model is to inspire future generations.

The Second Aliyah, a few thousand Russian Jews who wanted to realize their socialist ideals outside of Russia after the failure of the Revolution of 1905, occupied an ambivalent position in later estimates. This wave of immigration produced the first political leaders of the country, the socialist institutions, and led to the dominance of the Labor party and the East European Jews in the first three decades of statehood. Only the subsequent two Ascents were numbered. While the number of immigrants increased rapidly, in the eyes of the preceding generations their quality and popularity gradually decreased. The refugees of the 1930s no longer came out of "Zionism," but only "out of Germany"; those who sought refuge after World War II were second-rate. Given the desperate situation of the Holocaust survivors, the principle of "selection," of giving priority to that human material suited to rebuilding the country, had to be abandoned. This did not take place without grumbling and complaining about the uselessness of this "human dust." The mass immigration of Jews from Arab countries in reaction to the Israeli-Arab War of 1948 completely changed the perception of the Israelis. Where previous Zionist heroes arrived on the shores of the Promised Land and risked their life in the struggle against malaria and vile Arabs, the unwashed masses from the wretched quarters of North African cities now washed ashore. But it was more than class difference.

In the idealized expectations of Zionism, a renaissance of Judaism was to take place in Israel. But what emerged was a secular, Western civilization surrounded by a religious fringe culture that, partly by being marginalized and partly by being made dependent on the secular establishment, was incorporated into the new structure. Hebrew prevailed as a common medium, Jewish holidays were celebrated officially, and the State draped itself in symbols from biblical history, but that was the full extent of the connection to Judaism and the Jewish culture of the Diaspora. In their new society, the Jews who had previously been far from a state and close to God placed an idol in the center of their life—state, army, and nationalist ideology.

The groups that came from the Maghreb and the Arab countries of the Middle East after 1948, on the other hand, represented an older Judaism bound to the extended family and community and guided by religion, custom, and a traditional rabbinic leadership. The traditionalism of Arab Jews was thus on a collision course with the secular Jewish culture of Israel, with its class nature and a lifestyle determined by military service and devotion to national and Zionist goals. Moreover, these groups of immigrants shaped by Arab culture kindled a fear of "Levantinization" among European Jews. "Levantinization" stood not only for the fear of muddling the ethnic boundaries with the Arabs of Palestine, but also for the fear of losing the "qualitative advantage" vis-à-vis the neighboring countries, on which the European immigrants prided themselves.

The drawing of internal boundaries vis-à-vis the Jews of Arab origin was incisive and had far-reaching consequences. Within a few years, the core of the settler society—at the time of the establishment of the State some six hundred thousand mainly nonreligious Jews from Eastern Europe—faced double that number of newcomers, who were mostly poor and "underdeveloped" in the eyes of the old-timers. The Arab culture of these groups clashed with the emerging identity of the "Israeli," which began to be defined in contrast to the "Gentile," the non-Jew, but also in contrast to the "Arab," the hated opponent in the territorial conflict. The suppression of Arab-Jewish culture that now followed was done in the name of progress and "in the best interest" of the immigrants themselves. The European Jews could claim to be defending not only Zionism, but also modern achievements like women's emancipation. Since the core of settlers was identified with the Labor Party Mapai and the smaller leftist parties linked to it, voters from Arab countries were driven into the open arms of the rightist opposition, Herut and its successor, the right-liberal Likud coalition.

* 2 *

Taking care of a new immigrant is considered a patriotic duty and one many Israelis gladly accepted at the time of my immigration. The unexpected, almost total victory over the armies of the neighboring Arab states in June 1967 had triggered a euphoric mood in Israel. Helped by the myth of Israel in the West, a new kind of immigration was set in motion, bringing young, well-educated Jews from Western countries into Israel for the first time; they were at the start of their professional career and seeking the realization of their Jewish identity in Israel. The immigration of this group, who were not motivated by distress, seemed finally to fulfill the Zionist dream of the ingathering of the exiles and was a daily justification for the old-timers of the dangers and privations every Israeli accepted. Concern for the practical needs of the immigrant, his schooling in Zionist mythology and civics, transcended the often difficult daily life and fulfilled the modest spiritual needs of the mainly non-religious population.

I was also adopted like that. Two mentors appeared immediately to initiate me into my new life, two teachers and guides, whose care inadvertently but in an amazingly complementary way revolved around two supposed defects of my Diaspora persona. One of them was an older historian, the chairman of my department; the other was a friend whose devotion to the Zionist ideal had been somewhat responsible for my return in 1976.

In the 1930s, as a young man, the department chairman had immigrated from Hungary and could serve as an example of the "old settler." The myth of the founding generation who cleared the fields of stones and the country of Arabs had not yet been debunked and its influence in politics and society was still undiminished. In addition, he had his own personal style, a dramatic intellectuality that reminded me of prewar Hollywood films that portrayed Central European scholars or intellectuals as lovable eccentrics, impractical in life and love, but awkwardly committed to a high, unworldly ideal of learning that made them outsiders in a world driven by competition and conflict. My mentor had clearly been moved to emulate this cliché with its allusions to anti-Semitic stereotypes and the Jewish nationalist counter-ideal of the naïve Talmud scholar inept in matters of finance.

After a few conversations with me, he understood that I lacked "Yiddishkeit." He recommended several books with mainly spiritual subjects to rectify that defect. At that moment, I myself didn't know what he meant by "Yiddishkeit." Clearly, I lacked a certain cultural stamp that could help me to a higher form of Jewish identity or sensibility. The opposite of Yiddishkeit could only be Goyishkeit, the qualities of non-Jews, of Goyim, despised by Zionism and Jewish nationalism. In the bipolar world of Jewish nationalism, all non-Jews form a group surrounding Jews everywhere in Diaspora, who produce not only hatred of Jews and anti-Semitism but also the temptations of assimilation, a concept among Jewish nationalists synonymous with self-surrender and ethnic self-annihilation. The self-image and identity of Jewish nationalism emerged in contrast to this fictional "Goy."

A lack of Yiddishkeit was not a flattering diagnosis. It annoyed me. Had I not returned of my own free will to the land of the forefathers, as it is called in many nostalgic prayers, to the land of a future Jewish society I wanted to help build? Hadn't I thus shaken off my Goyishkeit and proved my Yiddishkeit? I understood that I must neither deny my supposed defect nor admit my anger, and agreed to follow his curriculum. Moreover, as a newcomer, I did not yet know the cultural code of Israel and was willing to learn new things.

My Yiddishkeit did not seem open to question. I had been born into a Jewish community where I was brought up as a Jew. My Jewishness consisted of this socialization. I didn't come from a religious family, was not pious and, as for Jewish ideology, had gotten a good dose of Jewish nationalism and Zionism on the way, but also a longing for acceptance and merging into the majority society. That hardly distinguished me from others of my postwar generation. Collective prejudice against non-Jews had been inculcated into me early on, but it had dropped off in my youth. "Goyim" or "Goyish" were terms I rejected, along with the nationalistic thinking and behavior they adhered to.

My mentor clearly doubted the intensity of my cultural and religious bonds to Judaism as well as the soundness of my ethnic awareness. Perhaps he distrusted my Zionist motivation and wanted to purge my harmful Diaspora influences. Or did he think that, as a German Jew, I lacked the imprint of East European Jewish popular culture, a proletarian Yiddishkeit, mythologized in Israel and in the U.S.? As a German Jew, was I already too assimilated, my Judaism too diluted to be saved by Zionism? Maybe he was right. At any rate, I was a new kind of immigrant who sought "self-realization" in Israel, an extremely individualistic goal that could not easily fit the categories of nationalism. After his first efforts to subject me to a Zionist metamorphosis, he abandoned all hope and dropped his educational program a few weeks later.

My second mentor was completely different. Born in Israel shortly after the establishment of the State, he was the prototypical "Sabra," a term taken from the name of a cactus fruit and applied to the native-born Israelis to describe the national character —prickly outside but tender inside. For him, the Diaspora, Jewish religion, history, and culture were important only because they all led to the establishment of the State of Israel and thus to their own demise. This attitude was shared by most Israelis. He taught at the university in the social sciences, which he also practiced in those days as a professional army officer. So he had two jobs and that, too, was a typical Sabra feature: a self-sufficient, competent, effective person, who never complained about the long work day, the small income, the lack of personal freedom, and the compensatory laziness. We were the same age, but otherwise we had almost nothing in common. He had married early, had children immediately, and with the same sobriety and resolve he had quickly arrived at all the other stages in his young life, studies and dissertation, a condominium, a career. Maybe that was why we liked each other. My life, guided much more by emotions than reason, seemed freer and less conventional to him and thus desirable. For me, it was the other way around. I admired and envied him precisely for his clear, sober attitude. What attracted us to each other also separated us, a tension that was later to become increasingly sharp in our political arguments.

Like many Israelis of his generation, my friend met his future wife in the army. For both of them, it was the first love, the first sexual relation, ending almost inevitably in marriage a few months after they were demobilized. The two of them sometimes alluded in conversation to this brief erotic period of their relationship in which they bonded for life. They told of evenings they had spent alone in lonely places on the sea, of a joint they shared, and the thrill of the erotic role reversals produced by their different ranks in the army. She had made lieutenant and he was a master sergeant.

Afterward, the two of them began to relate to one another as co-workers, who had to cope with a hard task together. Like many young couples of this generation, they lived at first with their parents, then obtained by marriage the right to a flat and, once established in their small apartment in a newly built neighborhood, they had to devote a large part of their income to pay off the flat and furniture. In this case, too, the husband had to work at two jobs to replace the wife's salary, while she took care of the babies, and as in so many other families, he disappeared into the army reserves for a month every year. They hardly had time for one another, for during the short Israeli weekends, from Friday afternoon to Saturday night, you visited family. All this looked to me like a militarization of life after graduation from high school. Between military duty and childbearing, there hardly seemed any room for what I then called "life."

The difference from my generation that had grown up in Western Europe could hardly have been greater. While I grew up with the leitmotif of liberation from tradition and of self-realization, my Israeli friends were introduced to the burdens and obligations of membership in a settler society that was permanently under arms and demanded a complete subordination of their own wishes to the needs of the collective. The emancipatory elements also present in their education seemed to be neutralized, at least temporarily, by these collective missions. One of the most important obligations consisted of reproduction, the "demographic strengthening" of Israel, which had to be borne by the women, whose national mission as mothers is embodied in various Israeli laws. Even if the "demographic strengthening" is sometimes motivated by the great losses of the Holocaust, the major motive is so obvious it no longer has to be mentioned—the struggle between Arabs and Jews in Israel and Palestine to oust one another.

My friend must have perceived immediately that I lacked his generation's strong emotional identification with the fate of Israel and its extreme sense of duty. So it was not surprising that, in outings and walks in the city, he often spoke of the heroism and self-sacrifice of the "Pioneers" when we climbed up to places that had played a role in building the land or in the struggle against the Arabs. Thus he tacitly created a hierarchy of willingness to sacrifice. At the top was the achievement of the elders, so enormous that his generation couldn't touch them. Along with admiration, I also thought I heard envy and regret at not being there himself, but also a certain annoyance that must have come from feelings of gratitude and guilt vis-à-vis these unattainable models. Then came his generation. Libertarian assimilated Jews like me brought up the rear; our primary goal was to get something from Israel, self-realization, and we were only secondarily willing to give something. His life was drenched in the myth of the pioneer generation.

Basically, both of us were romantic idealists. His ideals related to the nation, the people, and the state of the Jews, while mine related to the individual and society. For him, idealism meant not so much fidelity to the ideological premises of Zionism, but devotion to the country and willingness to act in practical matters. He spoke of Zionist ideology only indirectly, not as a goal but as a break with the past and everything foreign. Our conversations were often tinged with his rejection of the supposed materialism of Diaspora life and the decadence of the Western lifestyle, surprisingly simplistic ideas in a man of his education. They clearly were not based on his own experience but served as a contrast to the Israeli lifestyle so strongly idealized by him. This dichotomy concealed a jumble of nationalistic, anti-bourgeois, and socialist ideas indicating the broad substratum of Zionist thought stretching from communism to fascism.

His curriculum for me consisted of an extensive geography program, which wasn't titled "Know the Land" but "Love the Land." He gave me a list of places linked to the operations of the pre-state underground militias, the Israeli-Arab wars, and the economic and cultural achievements of the past fifty years. As a concession to convention, he had added a few ancient ruins and digs, but only those related to Jewish or biblical history. I assumed that I was to wander in the traces of his class trips. In his youth, class trips had been the proven means of exploring and acquiring an unknown land foreign to the parents' generation, and they still were. "Love of the Land" created in this way excluded everything that didn't relate to periods of Jewish settlement in antiquity and in the most recent past, in short, almost two thousand years of history. All references to Islam and the Arab population were absent, as well as the nearly four hundred years of Ottoman rule and culture. The guides and historical sources for this perspective were the Bible, the memoirs of a few Zionist leaders, a popular illustrated account of the Israeli-Arab wars and the oral tradition of the older generation, who had taken part in settling and conquering the Land.

Each in his own way, both my guides wanted to steer me out of the darkness and confusion of the Diaspora. The chairman of the history department wanted to transform me from an assimilated, diluted European Jew to a "real" Jew, while my Haifa friend wanted to make me into a "real" Israeli, which I wasn't in his eyes despite the fact that I was born in Tel Aviv. Thus, they unwittingly represented the two most important elements of Zionism, two ideas that contradicted each other and were pretty intangible, but which had excited millions of Jews and had moved hundreds of thousands to migrate to Palestine and later Israel. One was the desire for the survival of the Jews as a separate ethnic group and Judaism as a secular culture in an environment where Jews were neither oppressed nor assimilated. The other was the idea of "normalization," aiming at the future and negating the past and Diaspora. This meant that, once settled in their own state, the Jews were to cast off their "anomalous" features that had emerged through the distortion of minority life in the Diaspora, and to produce a "new Jew," the Israeli. One idea was to preserve a national identity created in the Diaspora, which we call "Jewish," the other was to assimilate the Diaspora Jew into the "Israeli."

What I still had left to learn was practical Zionism. That is, the attitudes and practical behaviors in political, but also in ostensibly non-political matters that are considered desirable or necessary in everyday Israeli life and that a newcomer must acquire to be able to live and flourish in this society. How, for example, should I behave with the Arabs of Haifa? In the very first weeks after I arrived, I confronted this question, when I wanted to transport my household goods from the port to my new flat. The attitude toward the Arabs of Israel was an extremely delicate subject, rarely discussed at that time, and then only in a remote, abstract way so that a newcomer had to orient himself primarily to tacit attitudes. In other areas, too, I learned practical Zionism through observation, trial and error, on such different occasions as an army physical and the purchase of an Israeli cheese.

* 3 *

My rented flat in Haifa was in a neighborhood dating from the time of the mass immigration in the early 1950s. This period is not designated by this revolutionary event that changed the face of Israeli society, but rather by the economic consequences. It is called the period of austerity, "Tsenna," the time of restrictions, shortage, and in terms of building, a strictly observed ugliness. The neighborhood comprised rental houses, had been erected by a government construction cooperative, and had a general store, a small gray-plastered structure isolated at the edge near the bus stop, the only possibility for shopping in the whole area. This establishment was known as a "Tsarkhaniya," a cooperative supermarket, which had served in the past more for the distribution of short supplies than for the joy of consumption. Here, I made all my purchases and came to know Israel from one of its most important aspects.

In those days, buying and eating habits of the Ashkenazi Jews from Europe were not yet oriented to the U.S., but rather to

Europe. In many respects, Israel was felt to be a Jewish outpost of the old continent, which had simply been transferred to the other end of the Mediterranean because of chronic disputes. England was considered a model of democracy and justice, Germany the epitome of industriousness and efficiency, and France a stronghold of beauty and pleasure. A sense of deficiency inevitably developed between the mother continent and its offspring, which was not easy to bear and thus the country found itself in a collective monologue jealously and competitively comparing local and foreign products. Officially, consumers were reminded of their Zionist duty to "Buy Blue-White," and Israelis who vacationed abroad were called "snobs," an epithet of considerable ambivalence. Beyond that, there was a complete if tacit agreement that anything imported was better. But, because of the protectionist economic system and the high tariffs, European goods were either not to be had or not to be paid for, and thus, many well-known European consumer goods were produced in Israel, hardly concealed as imitation, to satisfy the longing for everything foreign. In the neighborhood shop, there was a selection of two cheeses, which in appearance and name, but not in taste, were reminiscent of the European model. One was called "Emek" and, because of its red plastic rind, clearly meant as "Edam"; the other was called "Tal" and was obviously considered "Emmentaler Swiss" because of its holes. Along with "Kashkaval," which satisfied an East European nostalgia, these were the only hard cheeses that could be bought anywhere in Israel at that time.

In the shop was a fresh-foods counter, a metal giant that, shaking lightly because of the cooling unit, hummed reassuringly. The counter, with its eternally misty and dirty panes that considerately veiled the stacked goods, was staffed by two women who had assisted my investigation of the perishables a few times. Because of the religious dietary laws, which were strictly maintained here, too, despite the state socialist setting, one sliced meat and sausage, the other cheese. One day, one of the women pointed out a new Israeli cheese, which had apparently won first prize in a cheese competition in France. So was that the best cheese in the world, or not? she asked as she offered me a slice to taste. Since I didn't agree with the judgment immediately, she sought the support of her neighbor. "Who would have thought ten years ago," interjected the latter, "that Israel would produce the best cheese in the world today." Then she added that she had read that in the newspaper. It had been on the radio, too.

Obviously, as a recent immigrant from Europe, I was to confirm this statement. The cheese had no particular taste, which represented great progress as far as I was concerned. I couldn't say any more about it. But the subject had changed. The conversation revolved, as so often, around the tacit question: How much does government propaganda correspond with reality? The superiority of the cheese was not part of the credo an Israeli had to subscribe to. Nevertheless, I had to wriggle out of it somehow. I murmured finally that it wasn't so important if Israel produced the best cheese in the world or not. This evasive maneuver didn't have the desired effect. "Seriously," said one of them, "what do you think of it?" She gave me a second slice. I was now forced to admit that the cheese wasn't really as bad as I had thought at first. That was the open sesame. Both of them laughed and let me go.

The rule I had obviously maintained went like this: do not publicly contradict an obviously untrue claim that expresses a national conviction, but do let your doubt shine through. That will satisfy both ideology and reality. Both elements—agreement and doubt—were equally important. As I went off, I heard one woman whisper to the other, "One of ours?" That is, was I a Jew? "Why not?" answered the other. "There are some like that, too."

Naturally, everyday Zionism can also be found in areas demanding less sacrifice than patriotic eating habits. There are several paramilitary organizations that can be considered the heart of the settler society along with the army, which transmit the pioneer spirit and idealism of the founding generation to the Israel of consumerism. One of them is "Gadna" ("Youth Battalions") which provide Israeli schoolchildren with a paramilitary training and preparation for their army service. This organization emerged in 1948 from two pre-state paramilitary youth movements, and is run jointly by the Education Ministry and the army and has its own command. Even though Ben Gurion gave it the slogan "Not for war, but for peace" at its founding, it is meant to nurture and promote fighting spirit among Israeli youth. Along with shooting practice, marching, sport and scout camps, "Love of the Land" is also cultivated here through field trips. As in most youth movements of a military character, "Gadna" promotes devotion to the State, the romantization of military life, and trivialization of war. Years later when I visited "Gadna" camps during my service in the educational corps of the army I discovered how much the educational canon of "Gadna" overlapped with the Zionist youth movement in Germany that I had belonged to in my youth.

Another paramilitary organization is the Civil Guard. This civilian troop organized by the police consists of volunteers who patrol the neighborhoods of cities and villages at night to prevent or impede attacks on the civilian population. As insignificant as it might have been for the defense and safety of the "Home Front," it allowed a citizen to leave everyday life for a few hours and join the ranks of pioneers and volunteers of previous generations and make his contribution to the survival of Zionist society. At the advice of my mentor, I immediately enrolled in the first month. By immersion in this typical Israeli entity, I hoped to learn something more about the attitude called "Tsionut" ("Zionism"), by which the locals mean the "small" everyday Zionism. I joined the Civil Guard along with a fellow immigrant and flatmate, who missed the military component in his new Israeli life and was glad to be able to carry a weapon once again.

* 4 *

I had met my future flatmate on the ship from Italy to Haifa. On board, there were a few immigrants, who started talking together during the rainy crossing. That's where I heard the story of his life. He came from an English seaside resort, had traveled around the world a lot as a consulting engineer for textile firms, and had decided to change his life again before he turned fifty. He had always been a Zionist, and finally wanted to realize his dream of a life in Israel, to settle with his wife and two grown children in Haifa. A well-known textile factory had offered him a good position and now he had landed in Haifa as the family's vanguard in order to look for an apartment. While still on board ship, we decided to rent a furnished apartment together for the transition and share the joy and suffering of immigrant life for the first months. That now included the Civil Guard.

As a seventeen-year-old at the end of World War II, my shipmate had been conscripted into the British army and served in the British zone of Vienna. Thirty years later, he spoke of his disappointment at not taking part himself in the fighting. Shortly after he arrived in Haifa, he had asked the Israeli army about possible use. But at forty-nine, he was too old. He could at most accept the less bellicose and even less flattering assignment as a reservist in the military civil defense, "Haga," whose members examined briefcases and shopping bags for explosives at public buildings, supermarkets, and movie theaters. They do wear uniforms, but examining the contents of ladies' handbags neutralizes the masculine effect. Thus, he seized the opportunity to carry weapons once again by serving in the Civil Guard.

Our training began with an exercise on the firing range of Haifa. The weapons we were issued came from the American arsenal of the Korean War. The trainer explained to us that these were very safe weapons that were relatively accurate and not dangerous for the shooters. As a counterexample, he cited the small Israeli-made submachine gun, the "Uzi," at that time a successful export and very popular among police departments in the West. But in fact, it was much too dangerous to be used in peacetime. When one of the participants wanted to know more about it, the answer was that it scatters too much, was hard to aim. Moreover, at the slightest jolt, it goes off by itself. In contact with the enemy, that wasn't so bad, he added with a laugh.

Shooting practice was followed by a brief lecture. We heard that the night patrols were considered a deterrent. The probability of encountering an enemy attack was very small, but the prospect of catching a cat burglar in the act was somewhat greater. With the admonition that breaking and entering was not punishable by death, and the joking warning not to aim at cat burglars directly, we were dismissed. The whole thing took less than an hour and left me speechless. Carrying a weapon and its possible use were completely taken for granted. Nobody doubted that we were fit to walk around with weapons, and would shoot people if necessary.

Our first assignment followed a few weeks later. On a cool spring night, my flatmate and I patrolled the deserted streets of Haifa for a few hours and talked about life as immigrants. He told me of his vain struggle to bring to Israel the wine cellar he had built up over decades, a collection of several hundred bottles of mainly French wine he didn't want to leave behind. He had conducted a long correspondence about it with various ministries. Because of the large quantity, he had to obtain a commercial import license, he was told by the Ministry of Immigrant Absorption. The Trade Ministry, which was responsible for that, then explained to him why that wasn't possible. Even if he did get permission, the restrictions imposed to protect Israeli wines and to honor religious observance were many. That was beyond him. Weren't the bottles just as private as a stamp collection? And what did the rabbinate or the Ministry of Trade and Industry have to do with what he drank at home?

He was very bitter. Wines produced in Israel weren't potable; they couldn't even be used to clean the house. If you were used to decent French wines, or a good English Stilton cheese. . . . I contributed my own story of the cheese, and we spent the rest of the night in a conversation familiar to many immigrants from the West—how bad everything was in Israel and how much better it was over there. So here were the limits of practical Zionism. In the end, my flatmate admitted to me that he had left behind not only his wine, but also his beloved dog.

My first assignment in the civilian guard was also my last. My curiosity was satisfied and my entrance into the army ruined the pleasure of these adventures forever. My flatmate continued his service. When I moved from Haifa to Jerusalem and we parted ways, we stayed in touch. Years of disappointment ensued for him. He experienced setbacks and conflicts that weren't atypical for an immigrant. His marriage collapsed, his family went back to England without him, and he lost his position as department head in the factory. His conflicts at work could serve as an example of the experience of many immigrants. At first, he had felt useful and welcome in the factory as a Western expert and his work was seen as a Zionist contribution to building the country. His employer used his contacts with foreign firms to promote export and gave him a free hand. After a few years, the relationship began to go bad. Previously productive as an outsider and innovator, he now represented a foreign body. While he continued to consider himself superior as a foreign expert, his colleagues treated him with increasingly less respect. He kept denouncing mismanagement and mistakes, but his colleagues and superiors were no longer listening. The advantages he could bring to the factory as a newcomer had been exhausted. Now he was only a burden.

He became increasingly bitter, but that only seemed to enhance his Zionist spirit. Thus, he was one of the few whom I no longer dared see after I renounced Zionism and decided to leave the country. His loneliness and isolation increased. Like most immigrants, he was unfamiliar with the environment and did not feel "at home." His bond to the new homeland seemed to consist mainly of ideological abstractions. The Zionist promise that he would feel less foreign and more welcome in a purely Jewish environment clashed with the realities of being an immigrant.

* 5 *

More than a month after I arrived, the shipping container with my household goods finally came from Germany. Somebody recommended a small mover who had a truck and was willing to pick up the freight from the port and take it to my house, for a modest fee. At customs, where we had agreed to meet, the mover appeared alone. He was short, well-fed and approaching retirement age, and did not look like he could single-handedly drag the contents of my old flat up the stairs of the new one. As a new immigrant, I wasn't familiar with usages and was secretly worried that I'd have to undertake this work myself. The mover finally put an end to my concerns. "Don't worry," he said, "we'll take an Arab."

We went to Paris Square, the center of the old city of Haifa. Before 1948, the square had been called Sahit al-Hamra ("Red Square"), and had been the center of Arab Haifa and of trade and traffic. The droshkies and cabs had once stood here and buses had later gone all over the country from here. Now a ghostly scenery of past and future appeared, a collection of details that didn't add up. The observer was struck mainly by the abysmal sight of the former Arab business quarter now deserted and collapsed, by the traces of flight and destruction that looked fresh even thirty years later. Then the many churches and the few mosques of the mainly Christian Arabs of Haifa entered the field of vision, and they were partly destroyed too. From the square, you could still see the public buildings of the Mandate period, the main post office, the telegraph office, and the Jewish Agency, whose facades held out bravely in their own slower tempo of dilapidation. The city of Paris, which had given its name to the square during the most recent era of Jewish settlement, seemed not to be represented by anything, except the Metro station, the end of an underground cable car built by a French company, that began on top of Mount Carmel and ended down here in an ugly tunnel exit. And there was still the place the residents of Haifa called the "slave market."

Here groups of Arab laborers stood around smoking and waited for work. Whenever a potential employer approached, there was a rowdy jostling that must have appeared undignified even to an advocate of an unregulated labor market. Such places, where human labor is brought to market in such a basic fashion, can be found in many non-industrialized countries. But here, history gave another dimension to the relationship between employer and employee. Here, victor and vanquished, European colonist and Arab fellah, confronted one another. In its own view, Israel wanted neither to be a colonial state nor to maintain a system of Apartheid, but the bifurcation of society I saw here reminded me of both.

Haifa's fifty thousand Arabs had been the majority in the city until the 1930s. Their number had sunk to some three thousand after the expulsion and flight of 1948, and by the time of my arrival had risen again to about seven thousand people. As one of the few urban centers of Arab Palestine before the war, Haifa had accommodated the educated, politically active citizenry of a society consisting overwhelmingly of rural residents dispersed over Palestine's innumerable small villages. Those who remained were now employed in the industrial area of Haifa Bay, around the port, and as staff in the snack shops and restaurants of the city. The

Jewish citizens of Haifa prided themselves on an especially good relationship with their Arab compatriots. An Arab-Jewish meeting center for youth had been created, a common theater project, and the municipal administration dominated by Jewish leftist parties attempted to shrink the gap between the groups in other areas, too. For the Galilee, the most important settlement area of the Arabs who stayed in Israel, Haifa forms the urban point of reference. For the population of the occupied territories, as long as the Green Line could still be crossed, Haifa also offered employment as the most industrialized city in the country. So it is not surprising that, despite the troubled relations between Jews and Arabs, even in recent times, the Arab population has grown. In 2002, thirty-five thousand Arabs again lived in the city, under working and living conditions that are less segregated than in other Israeli cities and the territories.

After my mover learned the scale of the load at the port, he decided that we needed only one Arab porter. He engaged in negotiations while I waited in the cabin of the truck with the motor running. A few minutes later, he appeared with a middle-aged man who squeezed between us on the seat. As we set off, I was introduced to the economic principles of the system. The mover functioned as a contractor. He calculated a lump sum for the customer and from that, he covered his costs and that of additional laborers, and drew his profit. He bore the responsibility and assumed the entrepreneurial risk of a trip going wrong or taking a longer time. No, he wasn't guaranteed or insured. The customer himself had to assume the risk of damage, since otherwise the costs would be too high.

The Arab porter was a subcontractor. From his Jewish employer, he got a lump sum for his work, based on weight and parts of the load and on the number of floors. He shouldered the risk for his part of the job of unpredictable obstacles and complications that could make the assignment hard or delay it. His expenses consisted mainly of travel costs. He came, it turned out, from the occupied territories, from Jenin, not far from the Green Line. He made the trip along with other day-laborers in a cheap Arab jitney cab. When I asked him if he made the trip every day, he didn't answer. Instead, the mover answered as if we suddenly could no longer understand Hebrew and he had to interpret.

"No, they don't go home every day," he explained. "They sleep here somewhere." As he said "here somewhere," he waved his arm dismissively out the window. "When they have work late at night, they stay here." That wasn't allowed, but all the authorities closed their eyes to the illegal overnight stays of the inhabitants of the occupied territories. Both sides, employer and employee, profited from this uncontrolled and unregulated labor market, although in unequal measure. For inhabitants of the occupied territories, the income of a freelance worker in the heartland enabled a family with several children to survive on a subsistence level. The occasional savings of travel costs meant a considerable increase of income, particularly since staying overnight, organized by the employer or simply on the street, usually didn't cost much. For the State of Israel and the economy of the Jews, the commuting freelance workers brought great advantages. The employer did not have to pay for social benefits, the state invested nothing in the customary infrastructure of the labor market, and nobody stuck to any term of dismissal or any other obligations. The disadvantages of this system were also clear. Instead of building a partnership that would be mutually profitable and would bring peace for both sides through economic relations, the tendency to exploit and disregard the native population inherent in the Zionist enterprise was further reinforced. On the Arab side, this system meant the stagnation of the economy and society.

The occupied territories were not considered a foreign country, but the Arab inhabitants were considered foreigners. Israel regarded the territories as "terra nullius," a strip of land that belonged to nobody, a concept from the era of colonialism that opened the gates to arbitrariness. While the introduction of "guest workers" from other countries involves obligations and the maintenance of international rules, the labor force in the occupied remnant of Palestine was outside the law. Only someone legally employed in the heartland enjoyed the protection of Israeli labor law. After the outbreak of the first Intifada in the 1980s and during the second Intifada, the territories were regularly closed off for long periods, and the number of Arab commuters employed in Israel was drastically reduced for security reasons. To replace them, Israel imported workers from Eastern Europe and the Far East, who were allowed into Israel under extremely restrictive conditions on the basis of temporary contracts, since Israel as a Zionist state rejects the immigration of non-Jews for ideological reasons.

Our conversation in the truck took place in Hebrew. Later, when our Arab porter carried my cases and furniture up the stairs piece by piece, I heard my mover say a few words in Arabic for the first time. "Slowly, slowly," he called when a case threatened to bang against the wall. "Slowly, slowly!" was the shout with which he guided our porter around the bends of the stairs, case for case, floor for floor. "Slowly, slowly!" stayed in my ears for weeks. Upstairs in the flat, when we settled up and the porter was drinking a glass of water out of earshot, the mover took me into his confidence. "Sometimes they want to work, sometimes not. They work two days, take the money and run. I've worked with them a long time. They're not bad people. But you can't trust them."

* 6 *

The relationship with the Arabs forms the hardest chapter of everyday Israeli life that a new immigrant has to learn. The attitudes and opinions of the Jews about the Arabs, as historical opponent, fellow citizen in the State of Israel, and as a population living under Israeli occupation, have become the main subject of Zionism, after all other ideological fronts have subsided. The attitude to this group forms the adhesive of Jewish society in Israel. No other subject evokes so many emotions, no other question can separate the supporters of Zionism and Jewish nationalism so clearly from the dissidents and opponents of Zionism. In a discussion among Jews, anyone who goes on about "the" Arabs with prejudice, contempt, or aggression will usually get unquestioning agreement or, in the worst case, will appear as an overzealous patriot. Anyone who argues for the rights of Arab citizens or is worried about the situation in the occupied territories is considered a traitor or someone afflicted with the disease of "Jewish self-hatred," widespread among opponents of Jewish nationalism and Zionism.

Daily intercourse and the need to live together have created a pragmatic mode, in which the Jewish majority and the Arab minority in Israel can temporarily avoid the feelings fanned by inequality and ethnic conflict. This process of adaptation and denial, equally necessary for both the minority and the majority, reminded me of Germany. I had grown up as the scion of a formerly persecuted group in a society that had produced the persecution, and I had developed a feel for this difficult situation. The contrast with Germany could not have been greater. In Israel, a system of denial and repression of guilt and responsibility had emerged that enabled the Jews to maintain the idealized self-image of a group that behaved morally and sensitively and according to especially high ethical standards because of its own suffering. The Arab minority, with its tormenting feeling of humiliation and resentment vis-à-vis the majority always lurking beneath the surface, reminded me of the situation of the German-Jewish population after the war. Rage stood in a unique tension with the yearning for recognition as victim. The desire for confirmation of your own suffering and for acknowledgment of guilt is to be found among all victims of violence and injustice. For the Jews, this desire was largely fulfilled by Germany's public admission of guilt and the compensatory measures. Because of the constant attitude of denial of the Israeli Jews, this need is completely unsatisfied among the Arabs of Israel and the occupied territories.

The relation of the Israeli Jews to their Arab "fellow" citizens, the Arabs who remained in the Jewish State after 1948, is extremely complicated. On the one hand, they are members of an ethnic minority whose rights and freedoms have to serve for Israelis as a proof of the free and democratic nature of the State. On the other hand, they represent the opponent with whom the territory was disputed ever since the beginning of Zionist settlement, and the "ticking time bomb" of the high birth rate that threatens the "Jewish character" of the State in the eyes of the majority. But above all, the Arabs of Israel stand for a population that was humiliated, robbed, and displaced by the Jews, who will not take responsibility for it.

The great majority of Israelis blame the Arabs for losing their homeland. This strange construction, a reversal of guilt, of cause and effect, of the status of perpetrator and victim, is expressed in the official version of Israeli history as taught in the schools and presented daily in the media. It is so fundamental for the self-image of the State that every jolt to this ideological principle encounters implacable resistance. According to the quasi-official version of history, the Arabs of Palestine put themselves in the wrong with their incessant resistance to Jewish colonization and the creation of a Jewish State. In this view, the Jews only exercised their right of self-defense, hesitantly and unwillingly, and in doing so unexpectedly inflicted total defeat on the aggressor. Also the exodus of the Arab population from the future Jewish State is blamed on the Arab leadership. This led to the strange phenomenon that many Israelis pity the apparently unfortunate, politically immature Arabs of Palestine, who were incited to resistance by their own corrupt and despotic leadership and then ruined without a clue by these nationalistic charlatans. No causal connection is made between the destruction of the Arab society of Palestine and the colonization of the country by Jews from Europe, the gradual economic marginalization of the Arab population and their violent displacement during the war years of 1947 to 1949.

The tension between myth and reality is especially palpable in the question of the "historical" claims to the country. The idea of the superiority of the Jewish claim, and the corollary of the inferiority of Arab rights, is based on the romantic nationalist myth of the "return of the exiles" and the "restoration" of a Jewish state. This blend of religious messianism and modern nationalistic ideas is enriched by the idea of historical reparation. This much more purposeful myth alleges a guilt of Christian countries, arising from the historical discrimination and persecution of Jews that is to be removed by preferential treatment of Jewish claims over Arab ones. The decision of Great Britain, the future colonial power, in 1917 to reward the efforts of the then still small and insignificant Zionist movement with the promise of a Jewish homeland in Palestine is seen by many Jews in this mythic context to this day. The Arabs of Palestine, who from the beginning contested the pro-Zionist mandate granted Great Britain in 1920, also viewed this colonialist arrogation as the atonement of the Christian people toward the Jews—at their expense.

The notion of legitimate Jewish claims to Palestine and the view of forced self-defense were shared by public opinion in the Western world for decades. The attitudes of the governments of Great Britain, the U.S., West Germany, and other countries, who were responsible for the settlement of the Jews, the creation of Israel, and the consolidation of the status quo after 1948, promoted the continued denial and reinterpretation of events and thus constantly reduced the chances of an understanding with the Arabs. The consequences are tangible not only in Jewish-Arab relations in Israel, but also in the tension between Arabs and Moslems and the states of Europe and North America.

This many-layered process of denial among the Jews of Israel has resulted in political formulae and abstractions that more or less openly justify and defend the massive discrimination against the Arab population. For the first twenty years, the Arabs remaining in Israel were kept under military administration as a hostile population. After that, the reference to constant "security needs" prevented an open discussion about the living conditions of this group. Even today Israeli Arabs do not enjoy equal rights and remain subject to more or less subtle exclusion clauses in the laws of the state. But what hides behind all political and private discussions of the situation of this population is the "demographic" threat to a state created for Jews that has no place planned for other ethnic groups. The "Jewish character" of Israel is the all-embracing formula determining the relationship of Jews to the Arabs of Israel and the occupied territories. It is the consensus of the political parties, that the "Jewishness" of Israel translates to a demographic ratio of no less than 80 percent Jews to 20 percent non-Jews.

Every year on Independence Day, Israel's Central Bureau of Statistics publishes the latest numbers in this ethnic competition. In May 2002, on the fifty-fourth anniversary of Israel's independence, the ratio was 81 percent Jews to 19 percent non-Jews. According to the research of a demographer at the University of Haifa, nicknamed "the Arab counter," the portion of citizens considered Jews by religious criteria is only 72 percent of the total population. The rest of the population consists of 18 percent Arab citizens, 4 percent non-Jewish immigrants who exercised the right of return as spouses or close relatives of Jewish immigrants, 2 percent Arabs from the occupied territories living illegally in Israel, and 4 percent foreign workers. By this count, whose publication triggered a heated discussion of countermeasures, the

Jewish majority has fallen below the quantity that is indispensable for the "Jewish character" of the state. A mass immigration of Diaspora Jews could guarantee a Jewish majority. Should they stay away, the Jews of Israel still have the hope of a decreasing fertility among Arab women. Otherwise, without violence, the ethnic dominance of the Jews cannot be maintained.

* 7 *

Shortly after I arrived, I bought a postcard at a kiosk in Haifa. I had noticed the card—an old black-and-white photo—because it was sold in many places in the city and was pleasantly different from all other tasteless colored picture postcards. In the photo were the sea, a narrow beach, and a caravan of camels. On the back was the caption "Haifa Bay, circa 1900." It must have been the site of the port, the power station, and the refinery, built a few decades later, which replaced the once serene panorama with the mess of industrial plants.

What attracted me to the card was not only the charm of the photo. Old landscapes and cityscapes invite the viewer to compare "then" and "now." That's how I explained the obvious popularity of the camel card among the residents of Haifa. For locals, the card had an additional meaning not directly discerned by outsiders and newcomers. The sight of camels quickly evokes a smile among the residents of the industrial world. In Israel they often appear as a symbol for the lovably primitive past of the country and the medieval circumstances of the life and work of the Arabs. The subject of the postcard was the wonderful changes in the bay—progress from the backward to the modern. It implied that, until the Jews came, the area was stuck in the state of an empty wasteland, and only then did the period of industrialization and modernization begin in the country. It referred to a motif also known as "making the desert bloom" that still plays a big role in the internal and external propaganda of the State.

I took the card as an occasion to learn more about the history of Haifa. Until the 1920s, Jews had played hardly any role in the city. The first industries and modern agricultural methods were introduced in the nineteenth century by the German Templars, a pietistic sect, whose Haifa "German Colony" is now one of the most beautiful areas of the city. In 1905, the Turks linked Haifa to the Hedjaz Railway, leading from the Mediterranean to Damascus and the Arabian Peninsula. In the early 1930s, the British administration built the port and created a petroleum terminal for the pipeline from Iraq. The refinery was built in 1939 by a British firm, as was the power station, which was expanded in the 1950s with pumps and turbines supplied by Germany as part of the "reparations."

The idea that Palestine flourished because of the arrival of the Jews has a long history in Zionism. It began even before the flow of people, technology, and capital from Europe accelerated the modernization of the country begun by the Turks and the British. From the start, it was based on the idea that the Jewish settlers possessed a civilization superior to that of the "natives," who clearly had not been able to develop the land properly. It formed one of the justifications for taking over the country. The subject was well known by me and other immigrants, most of whom had been schooled in Zionist thought before their arrival, for in the myth that the people without a land would help the land without a people to flourish again, Haifa had an important place from the start.

In *Old-New Land*, the Palestine novel of 1900 by Theodor Herzl, one of the founders of the Zionist movement, Haifa was promoted as the international metropolis of a future Jewish Palestine. At that time, Tel Aviv, the current metropolis of Israel, did not yet exist. In Herzl's novel, the Jerusalem ophthalmologist

Eichenstamm describes the Zionist settlement to a visiting non-Jew: "Our old ground once again bears fruit." Herzl drew on his own trip to Palestine in 1898 for the novel. He went there to obtain an audience with Kaiser Wilhelm II, who was traveling through the Turkish province. The audience took place in November 1898, when the kaiser was staying in a tent city at the gate of Jerusalem. Herzl delivered a short address on the desired colonization of the "land of our fathers." "It cries out for people to build it up." Many Jews suffered from poverty, he added. "These people cry out for a land to cultivate." Thus, the Zionist enterprise was helpful for both.

The kaiser, who did not want to support the plan explicitly, answered with a deep insight: "The land needs water and shade most of all." Then he indicated the great heat, even in November.

In the novel, the non-Jewish visitor returns to the Middle East twenty years later and finds a Jewish state that had emerged as one of the most modern countries in the world. Everything is electrified, there is only large-scale agriculture, "open factories" where all work is done by the Jews themselves, no longer by the Arabs. Haifa has advanced to one of the most important ports of the world, a metropolis, reminiscent of Hamburg. The ophthalmologist Eichenstamm has become president and announces the maxim of tolerance on which Zion, the Jewish state, is oriented: "The stranger is to feel good here." Stranger meant the Arabs who lived in the country.

While Theodor Herzl formulated his conservative ideas on the colonization of the country, Marxist thinkers developed an argumentation within the Zionist movement that ultimately justified the displacement of the Arabs just as much as the idea of the superiority of civilization. According to the analysis of the Marxist "Labor Zionists," only those who cultivated and worked the land themselves could be considered legitimate owners. This argument was directed against the big Arab landowners of Palestine, whose estates were worked by Fellahin, the poor Palestinian farm workers. The Zionist left took the fate of these exploited masses to heart, as long as it could divert the claim to the young Jewish Pioneers from Eastern Europe, who wanted to liberate the land from the unfair property relations. But the solidarity of the dispossessed remained on paper. In the end, the land was to be "liberated" from big Arab landowners by the purchases of land by Zionist organizations. In most cases, the change of ownership meant the dismissal of the Fellahin, whose work was taken over by Jewish settlers.

The "liberation by labor" of the Zionist left had a double meaning. Along with the liberation of Palestine from Arab effendis, it also meant liberating Jews from their position as servants of capital. This idea, a reaction to common anti-Semitic stereotypes of the nineteenth century, had been carried to an extreme by Marx himself in his essay on the Jewish question. The social liberation of the Jews could be achieved only by liberating society from Judaism, he wrote polemically, equating Judaism with the capitalistic money economy. The Zionists, who often observed Jewish life in the Diaspora through the same filter as the anti-Semites, adopted this point of view and castigated the ostensibly "unproductive" life of the Jews in Europe, who were stuck in commerce and "parasitical" positions. Along with the return to agriculture, the Zionist demand for "productivization" was to cure the Jews of Diaspora life and let them convalesce as "New Jews" on their own soil.

The kibbutz also pursued the goal of this "proletarianization" and liberation by farming. But the idea of equality and the communal ownership of the means of production propagated by the kibbutz did not extend to their Arab neighbors, who felt only the disadvantages. The low prices of agricultural products in Palestine, bound to the poverty of Arab farm workers, made it hard for the Jews to compete with their products in the market. Production in Jewish enterprises had to be made cheaper. This was possible only by lowering the costs of living and this function could best be undertaken by the kibbutz and other cooperative forms of settlement. Thus, "proletarianization" brought the Jews into a much better competitive position. At the same time, the leaders of the Zionist labor movement could represent and justify taking the land as a progressive project and as a Jewish share in the "victory procession of history." Here, too, the effect was the gradual displacement of Arab farm workers.

A joke I picked up in my first year in Haifa summarizes these Zionist myths and the relation to the original Arab population: A grandfather stands on Mount Carmel with his grandson and looks down at the bay. "Look at that, my child," he says proudly. "We built all that with our own hands." The boy looks at his grandfather in amazement: "Grandpa, did you used to be an Arab?"

* 8 *

As a new immigrant, I existed between two worlds, the old life in Europe and the new one in Israel, where I was still an outsider. I soon noticed that it was easier for me to get along with newcomers than with the old-timers. That was understandable. As immigrants we were in the same situation, at least temporarily, despite all differences of origin and motivation. In other respects, too, we had more in common with each other than with the Sabras, those native-born Israelis. Despite the warnings of the old-timers not to get stuck in a "ghetto" of Europeans and Americans, that's precisely what happened. In my private life I hung around almost exclusively with new immigrants, in my work almost exclusively with Sabras, who were disdainfully called "the Israelis" by many new immigrants, even though most of them had citizenship and so were also Israelis. At work Hebrew was spoken, among friends

English, the Lingua Franca of all immigrants. I soon knew as much about life in Leningrad, Toronto, or Helsinki as about life in Israel, maybe even more. If the marriages in my circle of friends in Haifa and Jerusalem can be considered a gauge of integration, the experiment of the "melting pot" failed completely. Not a single marriage was made with an "Israeli." The immigrants stayed among themselves.

Less than a year later, I began to shift my life from Haifa to Jerusalem. A few months after I arrived, I had been offered several positions, all of them in Jerusalem. One of them, at Yad Vashem, the official Memorial for Heroes and Martyrs, could be limited to a few days a week, so I decided for the time being to spend the weekend and the ensuing work days in Jerusalem and the rest of the week in Haifa. My sudden popularity had a reason —I had been discovered by scholars from Germany and by the German-Jewish institutions in Israel. A former German Jew, a member of the institute I was later to direct, named the phenomenon: I was "roped in." That immediately revealed his origin. He had belonged to a Jewish-Zionist student organization in Germany that maintained an informal "old boys" network in Israel. Quite unexpectedly, contact with this group of prewar immigrants gave me what I had sought in vain in Germany, a cultural point of contact that could link my German and my Jewish identities. Instead of developing my Israeli identity, I devoted myself with great pleasure to the insular world of the "Yekkes," the Jews from Germany.

During my Jerusalem weekends, I also met my future wife, a biologist from Amsterdam who had just completed a doctorate at the Hebrew University. Her circle of friends also consisted of immigrants. In terms of religion, most of her friends were traditional, celebrated the holidays, observed some of the dietary rules but not others, and complied with other religious commandments in that eclectic way that can be considered typical of this big group of "traditional" Jews. They were neither non-religious nor Orthodox, but at the same time they had too little interest in belief to join one of the non-Orthodox currents that took religion "seriously." That was not the only reason that made me an outsider as a completely non-religious person in this group. All immigrants I met were politically conservative and shared the current Zionist view of the emergence of Israel and the conflict with the Palestinians. Political discussions in my new circle of friends usually ended in the same confrontations, and I had to keep answering the not unwarranted question of why, given my position, I had come back to Israel at all. People like me seemed sensibly to steer clear of Israel.

Unlike professional integration, social integration was arduous. Even in the Jewish state, immigrant Jews are primarily foreigners and are assimilated first into groups of previous immigrants from the same country. So, my experience with the Yekkes was not atypical. As for Sabra society, it referred to the immigrants as "Orientals," "Russians," or "Americans." This reinforced old national or cultural identities, which the new immigrants were supposed to shed. In my circle of friends, people began to feel like Swedes or French, often more intensely than they had in their countries of origin where they had been considered Jews. Even the Jewish identity that was to unite all Jews in Israel quickly turned out to be a separating element: quite unexpectedly, the difference between the Jewish identity that had grown up in the Diaspora and the new identity of "Israeli" assumed great significance.

In the years after the founding of the State, the identity of the "Israeli" had crystallized primarily out of two opposites—the Diaspora Jew and the "Arab." Both types served as melting pots for negative qualities, against which "Israeliness" was defined in positive contrast. The prejudices about "ghetto Jews" among Israelis, which I encountered for example in history lectures for officer candidates in the army, could have made even the most confirmed anti-Semite blush with shame. This initially very sharp separation from the Diaspora, however, was subjected to countervailing forces. The constant coming and going of immigrants and emigrants, the financial and political support of Jewish organizations so necessary for Israel, as well as the recourse to European roots needed for the confrontation with the "Levant," alleviated the initially strong anti-Diaspora thinking of the Israelis. However, the stigma of "ghetto mentality" stuck longer to the alleged centers of Diaspora "decadence," Western Europe and the U.S. The taint of decadence in particular, the idea of some anemic, sickly lingering of Jewish life in the Diaspora, was a commonplace notion among Israeli intellectuals, a prejudice that, adorned with scholarly arguments, even made its way into serious journals. More important was the misunderstanding in the opposite direction. The Jewish identity of the immigrants, intensified and reinforced in "Aliyah," the ascent to Zion, made it very hard to connect with the new "Israeli" culture.

The consequence was visible in my circle of friends. Many of my fellow immigrants from Europe or North America found friendships and spouses among the "Jewish" types who had not given up their original Diaspora identity, and even felt closer to the traditionalism of the Oriental Jews than to the nationalist, secular Israelis. The alienation felt in Israel by immigrants with a strong Jewish or other cultural stamp seemed hardly reconcilable even at the time I came to the country. The "Yekkes" were an example of that. Even after forty years, many of them still spoke no Hebrew, suffered from the "boorishness" of the Israelis, and waited impatiently for the summer vacation every year when they set off en masse to Switzerland to recover from the "Levant."

Meanwhile, "Israeliness," as the dominant culture of the country, has diminished. The increasing dimension of the Ashkenazi Orthodox communities, the emergence of independent parties among the Oriental Jews, and the immigration of Jews from Russia have changed Israel completely. A new political avant-garde, the rightist Zionist Pioneer movement of the national-religious camp, and its success in settling the occupied territories, have finally challenged the hegemony of secular nationalism and thus of "Israeliness."

How to deal with the Holocaust in Israel was another chapter the newcomer had to learn. Most of my fellow immigrants from Europe were children of survivors and had experienced the consequences of the Holocaust in their own families and communities. Persecution of the Jews formed the central element of their Jewish identity. The great majority of the Israelis, on the other hand, had not been directly affected by the Holocaust, even regarded Nazi persecution of the Jews as a national humiliation and shame. In Israel, the Holocaust ethos, maxims referring politically and morally to the Holocaust, was first expressed in political discourse. Here, it was the "lesson" of the Holocaust that was the focus, not the victims or the survivors. The Zionization and utilization of the Holocaust created a sense of alienation among many immigrants, both of the older and the younger generation.

Even though the pre-state community in Palestine hardly identified with the fate of the Jews of Europe, its leaders had used Nazi persecution of the Jews as an argument for a faster development of statehood even before 1945. In the crucial diplomatic negotiations of 1947, the Holocaust became the central argument. After that, it formed the basis for the Israeli demand for the political and economic support of the West and for the solidarity of Jewish groups abroad. The first center-right government of Menachem Begin, which came to power in 1977, extended the Holocaust ethos to relations with the Arabs. The religious, ultra-nationalist settler movement, "Gush Emunim," that arose just as I returned to Israel also used the Holocaust to legitimate driving the Arabs out of the occupied territories and for their own radical anti-Gentile positions. The "Gush" developed a strange political vocabulary that fed on the language of the Nazis and reversed the relationship of occupier and occupied for all intents and purposes. When the representatives of the Arab population protested the settlement of Jews in the West Bank, it was implied that they wanted to make the West Bank "Judenrein." Respect for human rights and laws were "democratic excesses." Sympathy and scruples for the Arabs was condemned as a "ghetto mentality." The tendency to use the Holocaust to justify political or military measures was strengthened during the Lebanese war. Nowadays, Israel presents itself as an entity that has received its legitimacy and its mission from the Holocaust, assigning a subordinate role to European Jewry and its organizations.

* 9 *

What had to strike every newcomer directly was the incredible energy and restlessness of the Israelis. Israel was obviously not a normal state. Many myths have sprouted around this special nature of the country, this exception among the nations, where the laws of history seemed to be null and void. Already nineteenth-century Jewish nationalism had portrayed the Jews as a special case in human history and now a Jewish State was created under what seemed like exceptional, almost miraculous circumstances. The victories of the Israeli army, the rapid building of cities, roads, and factories, the reclamation of the desert, the absorption of enormous masses of immigrants from all countries, the revival of the language, the flourishing of the sciences—all that appeared to many as extraordinary and unique and was also gladly presented like that in public. These myths tempted, inspired, and enchanted people, but at the same time they also had to blind and confuse. Many old-timers were used to this dramatic façade, no longer noticed many things, or had drawn their own conclusions, which gave them a little sleep at night amid all the sparkle and splendor.

But it was the omnipresence and intensity of the myths that made it hard for a newcomer to orient himself in the new homeland. I often felt that a large part of the historical and political reality was completely beyond normal perception. Leading political figures and their acts seemed superhuman, political decisions referred to a time and space that was far away from here and now, and the language of everyday politics sounded more biblical than the Bible. I regularly asked: What kind of country is Israel really? What is the precise meaning of a "state of the Jews"? Who really is a "Jew," and who isn't? And what are the consequences for society and the political system? Is Israel a modern nation state? A democracy according to Western standards? Or a system of Apartheid, an "ethnic democracy," where only Jews have full civil rights?

The character of Israel as a "Jewish State in the Land of Israel," as it is called in the Declaration of Independence, or as a state of the Jews, as many would prefer, is established in a series of basic laws. In the basic law of the parliament, the Knesset, Israel is defined as "the state of the Jewish people." In another basic law, the Law of Return, every Jew is granted the right to immigrate to Israel. This right extends to the first level of non-Jewish relatives of an immigrant, whose right to citizenship can also be transferred to non-Jewish parents, spouses, and children. Initially, it was enough for a person to register in the local office of the interior ministry and guarantee that he was a Jew. The special status of immigrant and its benefits were automatically recognized, and the person could be issued a passport or a personal ID. Nationality was linked to the Jewish religion. In 1960, a definition of "Jewish" was added. Now a person had to be born of a Jewish mother and not belong to any other religion, or to be converted to Judaism according to religious, that is, Orthodox Jewish law. After a test case against the monopoly of the Orthodox interpretation, the clause referring to religious law was deleted in 1970. In the ensuing decades, the ambiguity of the Judaism clause allowed the State to accept a large number of immigrants from Russia and Ethiopia, whose Judaism was controversial in terms of religious law. Behind this practice stood the desire to increase the percentage of the Jewish population vis-à-vis the Arabs. The court decision also settled the conflict surrounding a basic question: Was nationality now mainly dependent on the profession of the Jewish religion or on origin? From now on, the ethnic element enjoyed priority over religion in Israeli nationality. In other words, the State of Israel had to act primarily as the guardian of the ethnic group.

The Jewish nature of the State is also reflected in the laws on education, which prescribe a Jewish curriculum for all Jewish students, in the dietary provisions of the army, in the prohibition of pig-breeding, in the introduction of Saturday as a general day of rest, in the state symbols and in the jurisdiction of Orthodox rabbinic courts for marriages, divorces, and other matters of family law pertaining to Jews. For adherents of other religions, courts were established under other religious jurisdictions. This autonomy in religious matters originated in the need to bring extremely diverse groups with different traditions and various degrees of secularization under a common roof. But in the process, the establishment of generally valid norms and values was circumvented, perhaps even deliberately avoided. In practical terms, to this day the norms of Jewish Orthodoxy apply to most citizens.

Is it because of this legal fixation of the state's ethnic nature that Israel is now a nation state like those that emerged in Europe in the nineteenth and twentieth centuries? This parallel has often been drawn in the history of Zionism. According to this argument, when the European peoples formed their nation states, the Jews went off empty-handed. Even worse, they were the victim of this development. The nationalism of European peoples excluded the Jews, argued Herzl, and forced them to develop their own nationalism and the desire for a national state. This idea of the inevitable course of history, in which the Jews were caught up unwillingly and innocently, made it much easier to accept the radical idea of the colonization of a remote territory inhabited by others as a normal, inevitable step toward nationhood on the European model. Critics also went along with this idea. Thus, the historian Hans Rothfels described the establishment of Israel as the anachronistic renaissance of a nation state, which could not be explained without "Adolf Hitler's turning back the clock."

The historicity of the Jewish nation that was to re-emerge in Palestine was mainly a figment of the imagination. This applies in various degrees to all "nations," which call on extremely dubious historical origins and continuities. While in European nation states already existing countries and populations combined or reinterpreted themselves as a "nation," the idea of the Jewish nation and its return to statehood after two thousand years lacked all constituent elements: cultural and linguistic cohesion, territory, and last but not least, the people. The historical kingdoms of Israel and Judah, with their feudal priestly caste and central temple service, were the scene of the emergence of Jewish monotheism, but the Judaism we know today emerged in the centers of Exile, as well as in the community of Palestine, and developed into a decentralized, non-hierarchical religion of extreme adaptive force and diversity. The people also adapted to their far-flung and different surroundings and, even if they often lived on the periphery of society, became bearers of heterogeneous, multicultural traditions comprising both Jewish and non-Jewish elements. The idea that emerged in the nineteenth century of the "Jewish people," as a group united in essential aspects, and that of the "Jews" as bearers of national character traits, were conceptions of nationalist ideology, both Jewish and anti-Jewish, and stood in glaring contrast to the variety and diversity of Jewish groups in the world.

The overwhelming majority of the population intended for the nation was never consulted and lived far away in other countries.

Of the thirteen million Jews in the world at the time of the establishment of the state, some six hundred thousand, barely 5 percent, were in Israel itself. Even fifty years later, two-thirds of the Jews in the world are still outside the state created for the Jews. The increase of the Israeli share in the Jewish world population is to be ascribed only partly to immigration and partly to the higher birth rate among Israeli Jews. Nevertheless, Israel claims to be the state of all Jews and to act in their name and their interests.

Since there is as yet no constitution, the Declaration of Independence of May 1948 continues to serve as a source of general ethical principles and state goals. In the same clause declaring Jewish immigration and the "ingathering of the exiles" an official mission, the State promises to increase the welfare of all inhabitants and to protect their rights and freedoms on the basis of full equality. These two missions—the promotion of Jewish interests in Israel and elsewhere, and the protection of the interests of all inhabitants of the country regardless of race, religion, and gender —are clearly contradictory. This contradiction is expressed in the inequality of Jewish and non-Jewish parts of the population, but there is more.

An amendment adopted in 1994, Section 13 of the criminal code, illustrates this problem. The amendment gives Israeli criminal law jurisdiction over crimes abroad, not only for offenses against the body, health, and property of an Israeli, but also for crimes against Jews and Jewish property. During the passage of the law, the justice minister at the time emphasized that it applied to crimes aimed against Jews as Jews, and does not extend to crimes against Jews for other reasons. This law was to reaffirm the nature of the State of Israel as a state of the Jewish people. This is a unique and extremely bizarre construction that creates a one-sided link between the welfare of the state and that of Jews and Jewish institutions abroad that cannot be influenced by those it protects.

The character of the state as a protector of the Jewish ethnic group limits the rights of all citizens of the state, not only Moslems and Christians. In no other democratic secular country, for example, is a Jew prevented from marrying a non-Jew. In Israel, this can only be done through the detour of a marriage abroad and the retroactive recognition of the marriage in the country. In no other democratic country is a Jewish child obliged to attend a school with a Jewish curriculum. In other words, in no other country is a Jew forced to maintain his own group and culture by law.

Israel is not the state of its citizens, nor does it want to be—Israel sees itself as the instrument of the Jewish people. Nor is Israel a country of immigration in the conventional sense, since neither for the immigrant nor for the absorbing society are economic reasons paramount. Old people are accepted along with the young, the educated along with the uneducated. To this day, the State has neither controlled nor limited immigration. One exception is the management of the mass immigration of the 1950s, when the Jews coming mainly from Islamic countries were sent to the dry and barren territory in the south, to the parts of the Galilee that were "cleansed" of Arabs, and to the Negev which had long been uninhabited by Jews, to "Judaize" those areas. This banishment to the Negev, Israel's Siberia, had such undesirable social and political consequences that steering migration streams had not been tried again since. As long as an unbridled immigration remains necessary for the demographic competition with the Arab minority, Israeli society will have to continue to make its resources available to integrate the returning members of the nation. The differences between a civil state and a settler state are clearest at this point. In countries like Switzerland, it is up to the civic community, the smallest political unit, to decide whether to give a newcomer the right of citizenship or not. The possibilities of the state to regulate immigration are thus radically limited.

Israel has no firm borders, hardly a definable territory that can be designated as Israeli or Jewish. On the one hand, that is because of the lack of historical continuity. With the often cited exception of a single village, there is no place in the historical area of settlement where Jews have lived continuously. The Jewish groups who stayed here throughout the centuries were subject to the same fluctuations, the same migratory factors as other Diaspora communities. The Jews' link to their original homeland, which Zionism relies on, had long ago assumed a spiritual character and the historical "Land of Israel" was less a concrete than a mythic place. Moreover, the borders of the biblical empires, as far as they are known, were far from the modern Zionist settlements along the Mediterranean coast, which were ruled in biblical times by the Philistines, the Palestinians.

At the beginning of the Zionist migration, the historical area of settlement was barely inhabited by Jews. Thus, building the nation was primarily an act of colonization and subjugation of the land. That happened gradually. Beginning in the early twentieth century, the Zionist movement purchased land wherever there was an Arab seller, and so a constantly growing number of agricultural settlements were created. The goal was to settle Jews who would create the economic, political, and territorial conditions to settle even more Jews. From the mid-1930s, when the partition of the country became a possibility, settlement took on an additional function—the conquest of land by disrupting the contiguity of Arab settlements. The targeted purchase of land, and the establishment of scattered settlements in areas densely populated by Arabs, would later justify claims to include the entire area in the Jewish state. The U.N. partition committee appointed in 1947 tried for months to solve the problem of the disrupted space and to draw a border around the non-contiguous Jewish settlement clusters. Despite the many remarkable solutions that were found, the Jewish territory contained a large number of Arab inhabitants and hence the motive for their later displacement and expulsion. After 1967, this unscrupulous and short-sighted policy of breaking up Arab population centers by settlement was continued in the occupied territories. Thus, conquest by settlement remains at the core of the Jewish-Arab tragedy.

The peculiar dynamic of the settler state keeps Israel and its neighbors constantly on their toes. In little more than thirty years, the idea of the Jewish nation developed from the concept of agricultural colonies for poverty-stricken refugees through the idea of a homeland with an international charter and a Jewish-Arab federation to that of a sovereign state in 1948. Today, Israel is a binational state ruled by Jews, with an ethnic democracy at its core and a colonial rule at its periphery. Essentially, the State of Israel remains the constantly changing shell for a still developing national idea, a cover that has slowly filled with people and reality and thus is continually shifting the internal and external borders. This dynamic produces the great energy many people admire about Israel, but also the great unrest and unpredictability.

* 10 *

In my first years in the country, I learned a lot about the Israel of the people and started appreciating it in unexpected ways. I began to reject the other Israel, the Zionist utopia of a state for Jews, which assigned non-Jews lesser rights, and the ever more militant nationalism required by the whole enterprise. The confrontation with political reality triggered in me a process of rethinking whose details were almost imperceptible. Often, it was only in retrospect that I noticed how far I had distanced myself in one or another question from conventional points of view. I seemed to want to hide from myself that I had become an outsider in a society that valued reliability and ethnic solidarity.

In late 1977, I had moved completely from Haifa to Jerusalem. I had given up the position at Haifa University and was now working part of the week on a research project for Yad Vashem and part on a book project for the Leo Baeck Institute. My girlfriend and I married in the summer of 1978 and moved into a flat near the Hebrew University. From the door of our house, a path led through the thicket of bushes over a dry riverbed up to the imposing building of the National Library, where I spent most of my days. Studying German-Jewish history was like a healing balm on my painful identity gaps. Like other young Jewish historians from Europe I, too, encountered a welcome side effect of my profession. Questions of identity could be resolved in scholarly pursuit of Judaism and could be "objectified." At any rate, the problem of mutually exclusive cultural identities I had faced in the special situation of postwar Germany and that had brought me to Israel, diminished. With age, group identities became less important and I no longer had to seek a reinforcement of my "Israeliness."

Shortly before I left Haifa, I had met two young Americans who worked in the Peace Corps in an Arab village near Haifa. I was eager to hear more about their experiences there and invited them to visit my wife and me in Jerusalem as soon as they could. A few months later, the two showed up at our house. At dinner they told of the horribly poor conditions in the village and the paltry sums the Jewish State provided the Arab minority for schools, health care and other public needs. One of the two described the situation like this: "The village is hardly more than a labor camp where Arab workers spend whatever time they have off from working in the Haifa industries." The term "labor camp" fell like a bomb on the table. My wife was annoyed that the speaker, a non-Jew, made an analogy to the Nazis' treatment of the Jews. I considered the term exaggerated, but didn't find it completely unjustified. After all, Arabs lived in this country in a subordinate position and appeared in Jewish society almost only as a cheap labor force.

Now the cat was out of the bag. In the ensuing weeks, my wife and I argued repeatedly about the incident. She maintained that, wittingly or not, our guest's expression concealed an anti-Semitic thrust, which I still excused and defended, in a "Jewish house." I accused her of avoiding the criticism with her anger over the choice of words. By charging our guest with anti-Semitism, she could reject his observations out-of-hand as prejudiced and wrong, without having to deal with the issue itself. My wife insisted on judging things from a Jewish perspective and from a Jewish sensibility, which was nourished by the experience of the Holocaust and anti-Semitism. I refused to judge such questions from a "Jewish" point of view. For me, the universal political maxims of human solidarity were paramount and not ethnic or national ones. This event, banal as it was in itself, pointed to a conflict that was to involve me more deeply.

That year, for the first time, I experienced "Yom Yerushalayim," "Jerusalem Day," celebrating the "liberation and reunification" of the city in June 1967. The date of the anniversary followed the Jewish-religious calendar and fell on a different day of the Christian calendar every year. The Jerusalem municipality organized celebrations, the political parties had their own parades, and even the Chief Rabbinate located in Jerusalem held thanksgiving services. Everywhere, the so-called "liberation" was seen as a miracle and the fulfillment of a dream of two thousand years. The resurrected state of the Jews had its old capital city back. The site of the former Temple and the western retaining wall of the Temple Mount, the so-called Wailing Wall, were once again under Jewish control, and Jews returned to the Jewish Quarter of the Old City, which was evacuated in 1948. National and religious zeal coincided in the idea of a liberated and reunited Jerusalem as in no other issue. The streets were decorated with flags and patriotic posters, shops and public enterprises gave their employees a day off, and even those who weren't so nationalistic could take advantage of the many cultural performances planned for this day.

Not all parts of the city celebrated. The holiday was controversial, for one, because the "reunification," as the annexation of the eastern part and the surrounding Arab villages was officially called, was not recognized internationally; and secondly, because the Arabs, now formally under Israeli rule, had nothing to celebrate. The Arabs of Jerusalem, some hundred thousand people, had their own memorial day, the anniversary of the defeat and the beginning of the occupation. The date for this day was set by the Christian calendar and fell on June 5. On this day, the inhabitants of the eastern part marched in a memorial procession to the four monuments the Jewish city government had approved as sites to commemorate the killed Arab soldiers and civilians. During the memorial rally, as on other such days, the East Jerusalem shopkeepers closed their stores, a gesture defined and fought by the Israeli government as a "commercial strike."

In June 1978, for the first time, the two memorial days fell in the same week. The Jewish holiday took place on June 2, the Arab commemoration three days later. The parades were held in the same area, even in the same street, which separated the new part of the city from the walled Old City and had formed the border between Israel and Jordan until 1967. The Jewish march began on the square in front of city hall, site of one of the notorious walls, which between 1948 and 1967 served to protect the Jewish side from snipers. To mobilize the sympathies of the Western world and emphasize the commonality of interests, Israeli governments of the time compared this wall to the Berlin Wall, as if Communism had carried out its atrocities here too. The square in front of city hall, named in the 1920s for the British General Allenby, whose troops had conquered Palestine in World War I, has since been dubbed "Zahal Square," "Square of the Israel Defense Forces." The broad street leading down from here along the Old City wall to Damascus

Gate and from there to the northern suburbs of Jerusalem, had been named by the British for Suleiman the Magnificent, the Ottoman sultan who had built the splendid city wall in the sixteenth century. Now it was called "Street of the Paratroopers." Beyond Damascus Gate, the street is once again called "Suleiman the Magnificent." Before 1967, the Jordanian municipal government had named this part "King Hussein Street," after the Jordanian ruler at that time. The Jewish municipal government, which originally wanted to rename the whole road "Street of the Paratroopers" in memory of the conquerors of Jerusalem, out of consideration for the new Arab fellow citizens, had made do with substituting Hussein not with the famous Israeli elite brigade, but only with the politically less awkward sultan.

On the Jewish holiday, I joined my wife and a few friends, and now stood embarrassed and lost on Zahal Square, waiting for the march to begin. Meanwhile, among friends and colleagues, I was accused of a nagging "negativity" about everything concerning Israel, a charge I stubbornly denied. But as soon as I got to the meeting point, I regretted coming. The spectacle reminded me of mass marches of Communist and Fascist regimes and immediately dashed my hopes of not being conspicuous for "negative" comments on this day.

I no longer know what triggered the fight, nor can I remember the details precisely either. What I do remember only too well is the sharp, painful insight that I had wound up on the other side. The discussion was extremely pedantic and all unpleasant. I stated, half in jest, that "liberation" refers to people, but here only stones had been liberated. My friends had a different opinion. Free access to the holy places and the guarantee of the free exercise of religion, which wasn't protected under the Jordanian regime, represented liberation. Moreover, the division of the city had been an unbearable situation. I insisted that, for one part of the Jerusalemites, the conquest of 1967 represented a great catastrophe and decent people couldn't celebrate that. Israel's independence was also celebrated, answered my friends, even if Israel's victory in 1948 meant the defeat of the Arabs. I myself, a West European Jew who had come to Israel for Zionist motives, had used this victory. They were right. I was no longer the same person who had decided to return to Israel two years earlier. I had not consciously made these changes, which now moved me to the other side of the divide. I didn't really like them, and I would have liked nothing better than to consider them a passing bad mood or my "negative" character. My happiness, my future in Israel, the whole plan of my future life was thus put in doubt.

* PART 2 *

4

* TO EACH HIS OWN *

A Jewish Youth in Postwar Germany

* 1 *

My dissatisfaction with life in Israel raised a simple question: Why had I come in the first place? What was I seeking in this country? I kept posing this question with rising panic and an increasing awareness of having made a wrong decision. What alarmed me were not only the consequences but also the cause of my confusion. I could no longer find a clear answer to the question of why I had returned to Israel. This problem became the central theme of an internal dialogue I conducted in subsequent years, and still do, albeit from different starting points. Only at this place in my life, when my attempt to achieve an unambiguous identity as a Jew or an Israeli had floundered, did I set out on a sustained process of self-examination about my Judaism, my Jewish childhood in postwar Germany, and the shaping forces I experienced within the Jewish group and the non-Jewish surroundings. Collective processes aren't the only source of an individual's development and attitudes, but they do determine the ground on which we shape our individuality. In my case, and in that of my postwar Jewish generation, the experience of the collective—persecution and displacement—impregnated all fibers of the individual to an extent observed only in extraordinary times. Resistance to the claims of the collective resulting from these events was still undesired and burdened with guilt. The time and place of our youth created a complexity that neither our parents nor we could cope with. Given the catastrophe of the Holocaust, the swelling tide of Zionism encountered little opposition in the Diaspora. Anyone who was not deeply committed to the Jewish religion or to socialist or liberal humanism was swept up in the surge of nationalism.

The prospects for the flourishing of a new Jewish life in Germany were not favorable in any event. In the political self-image and the public debate of the young West German republic, the return of Jews, and the so-called "reparations" and reconciliation, did attain a central significance; but on the other hand, nationalist thinking and distinctions still existed and were even reinforced. Back in the nineteenth century, the contrast to the "Jew" was important in the emergence of the "German," the modern national identity of "Germans." Was identity- and continuity-generating contrast to be felt less sharply after twelve years of the Nazi hate campaign, and in view of the constant crises of the postwar era? If you were a "Jew," you could not be a "German," and vice-versa. In this respect, the new beginning in 1945 only drove these attitudes and feelings underground. Officially, a politically correct wishful thinking prevailed. Politicians now spoke of a "Jewish person" and hoped to overcome the negative connotation of "Jew" and the nationalist traditions associated with it. The old distinction between "German" and "Jew" was morally re-evaluated with the additional new meaning of "perpetrator" and "victim." But this was mainly a politically correct form that covered the old content. That made it even harder to overcome those distinctions.

Among the Jews in Germany corresponding views emerged. In the social isolation of the postwar communities, nationalist attitudes grew out of the stock of traditional coping strategies that used the Holocaust to validate a new Jewish separatism and radical Zionism. The non-Jewish environment of postwar Germany was considered dangerous and "bad," while the Jewish community was considered the embodiment of good. The absence of persecution seemed like an ephemeral, atypical phase of the attitude toward Jews, while the anti-Semitism of German society—indeed every "Goyish" society—was considered chronic. No wonder that a new Jewish identity in Germany hardly developed. Even though tens of thousands of Jews settled or resettled in Germany, only a few could take this existential step with the necessary openness and willingness to adapt to the environment.

I grew up between these sharply demarcated group identities of German and Jew, perpetrator and victim, whose significance only increased as the Holocaust grew more distant. The desire for assimilation to the majority culture, present especially among children of immigrants, and the need for belonging and protection in the minority group, were mutually exclusive. These conflicting loyalties and the internal split they produced made normal development practically impossible.

* 2 *

The political and biographical experiences my parents brought to this situation were extremely contradictory. They had to integrate their experience of persecution by the Nazis and their collaborators into the new life, along with their repeated loss of a homeland as well as their stigmatization as "Jews" and as "capitalists" under the new regimes of Eastern Europe. Above all, their hope for a better life had to be maintained against their distrust of

Germany. When I was born in 1951 in Tel Aviv, my parents had come to Israel only shortly before. Repeatedly uprooted and displaced—first by the political restructuring of the Austrian Empire after 1918, then by the Holocaust, and finally by the split of Europe after 1945—they had not had any rest since their school days in Czernowitz and Prague. They now confronted a fourth round of departure and search for a new home, because of Israel's precarious economic situation in the early 1950s as well as my father's political sensibilities that were repelled by Israel's nationalism and militarism.

In the spring of 1951, my parents had found a temporary residence in North Tel Aviv in a building with a flower shop on the ground floor. Fresh flowers were considered a luxury at that time and were seldom available. The shop apparently subsisted mainly by selling the many small and large houseplants that occupied almost all the space, leaving only a narrow aisle from the entrance to the counter. During the week, the customers were mostly women, and on the weekend mostly men. Rush hour was Friday noon, when the neighborhood men fulfilled their traditional obligation to thank their wives for doing the housework all week by bringing flowers for the Sabbath. My father also followed this custom. Along with other habits, it formed a canon of marital rules, which he maintained strictly during his life and which seemed to link the many different episodes of his life together more reliably than other adhesives.

My parents shared the flat with several other families. Every family had its own room; the kitchen and toilet were shared. There was no bath. To avoid the annoyance of a common kitchen, my mother had concocted a cooking place in our room. The trunk with which my parents had come to Israel formed the base and a gas burner was the stove. With this kitchen appliance I was bathed. A bucket from the flower shop served as a tub. It was filled with water in the kitchen, dragged cursing to our room by my father, and put on the burner. As soon as the right temperature was reached, the gas was turned off. My mother put me in the bucket and started washing me, constantly warning me not to wriggle around in the bucket under any circumstances. Nevertheless, the construction couldn't always be kept from tipping over. Then the bath water spilled on the stone floor, while I, fished out in time by my mother, floated happily over the site of the misfortune.

The house was at a corner of Rehov Ben Yehudah, a popular street of shops in the northern part of Tel Aviv. The area had grown because of an increase in the flow of capital and people from Germany, who had also found refuge in Palestine in the 1930s. The streets were named after the heroes of the Zionist movement. Eliezar Ben-Yehudah had revived Hebrew as a modern language and was considered the author of several linguistic creations. Our cross street was named for Aaron David Gordon, a romantic-religious socialist influenced by Tolstoy, whose glorification of agricultural work had made a profound impression on the Zionist labor movement. In the area around Rehov Ben Yehudah, there were still a great many German-speaking immigrants, who cultivated their mother tongue among themselves and considered learning the language of Israel an unnecessary labor. Everybody had to know that the Hebrew word "rehov" meant "strasse" in German, but many persisted in calling Rehov Ben Yehudah Rehov-Ben-Yehudah Strasse. That was done in an affected smugness indicating that the speaker was thoroughly aware of the error, but didn't want to condescend to take the language of the locals seriously. This arrogance often concealed a lack of linguistic talent or simply the difficulties for adults of learning a new language. In the best case, this blasé attitude could be considered the cultural self-assertion of an immigrant group that saw itself as the representative of a high culture and a significant western civilization exiled in the province of the new Hebrew, where nationalistic kitsch still prevailed. With "Rehov Ben Yehudah Strasse,"

German nationalism spoke through the mouth of a German immigrant to the Polish Jew, the bourgeois assimilated Jew of Western Europe to the proletarian Jewish immigrant from Eastern Europe.

My parents also shared the view that, given the difficult situation, knowing Hebrew was not one of the highest priorities. The immigrant generation of 1951, mainly refugees, first had to feed itself and find its place in a rapidly expanding society. In the four years since the establishment of the State in 1948, 700,000 immigrants had come to Israel. They were absorbed by a Jewish population that had numbered only 680,000 people in May 1948. The years 1948 and 1949 brought the highest rates of immigration ever known in Israel. For every thousand old-timers, there were over two hundred immigrants, most of them destitute, who required housing, work, and material support. The record year of 1935, when some 66,000 Jews had fled to Palestine from Nazi domination, had triggered an Arab uprising against the British colonial government and its protégé. This time, the wave of immigration entailed the spectacle of big tent cities, the *Ma'abarot*, erected by the government as emergency accommodations on the outskirts of the cities.

My parents held onto their mother tongue for other reasons, too. All friends and relatives spoke German and all shopping could be done in German. The language and affinity to German culture unexpectedly became significant in Israel, forming one of the few continuities with their previous life lost forever back beyond the years of persecution and immigration. My mother had grown up in a German-speaking milieu in her hometown of Prague and had attended the German school. My father came from another island of German language and German-Austrian culture in East Europe, Czernowitz, the capital of the Bukovina. There he had attended the German Gymnasium, and then the college for world trade in Vienna. In 1922, he had moved to Berlin. In the current poor circumstances, my parents' German education meant a kingdom not to be taken from them by persecution and war, a hallmark of their bourgeois origin, which also seemed to include the guarantee of a better future.

My father had found work in a wholesale building supply. His job was to get the orders out of the warehouse, carry them to the yard, and then help the buyers load their trucks. Later, when he told me about his time in Israel, he always referred to his work with the same description of details, thus clearly avoiding naming his function in the firm. My father was then a warehouse worker, an activity he regarded as disgraceful, unsuited to his education, abilities, and experience, and that represented a demotion for him. Moreover, he was already fifty years old and suffered from the physical effort of loading heavy iron parts outside in the heat.

My parents longed for a place where they could finally build a new life in peace after the years of persecution and migration. They vacillated about staying in Israel. The country had not been their real destination, but was considered a way-station and a gate to the West. After the Liberation and the end of the war in Europe, my parents had each independently wound up in Bucharest, where they met and married in 1947. Their temporary stay in Romania was an exigency that threatened to become permanent when the "Iron Curtain" came down. Israel was one of the few countries for which the Romanian authorities granted an exit visa in the late 1940s, and thus my parents boarded a ship in the Black Sea bound for Haifa, without knowing their final destination. Once they arrived, they began weighing the possibilities of life in Israel. My father's sister and her family, who had come to Palestine before the war, and my grandparents were then living in Tel Aviv. But the presence of family did not make conditions easier. The country was at the end of a war that had expanded its territory, along with the hostility of the neighboring states. The political future of the country was completely unclear, and the economic situation offered middle-class immigrants hardly any prospects for a new beginning in their former professional or social position.

But where were they to go? My mother came from a big family, was the youngest of five brothers and two sisters. The oldest had died in a concentration camp. The others had scattered all over the world. One of my mother's brothers, a pharmacist, lived in New York. He had followed the family profession and had once been chosen to take over my grandfather's pharmacy. He wanted to help my parents and had already signed the affidavit enabling us to immigrate to the U.S. But it took four years to get a visa. Anyway, my father worried about the prospect of life in the U.S. At his age, he felt that he wasn't up to the hard competition of the American labor market and while he knew Greek and Latin, he didn't know English. Two of my mother's other brothers had landed in Brazil and had opened a shop for radios and household appliances in Sao Paulo. But didn't they speak Portuguese there? The rest of my mother's family had been living in France since the 1920s. In 1933, after graduation, my mother had also settled in Paris, and after the Wehrmacht invaded, she had followed her brothers to the free zone in the south of France, where they survived the war in hiding. But my father's ignorance of French also made France out of the question as a destination. My father's family was much smaller. Aside from those who lived in Tel Aviv—his parents who were over ninety and his sister—he had a brother who worked for the British military administration in a small German town, Mühlheim on the Ruhr. He lived in the guarded and fenced area for members of the British military government in Düsseldorf, capital of the British zone of occupation.

* 3 *

Moving to West Germany in the early 1950s seemed less problematic than later. Many political refugees, including Jews, wanted to contribute to the creation and success of a democratic state and didn't even wait for the official new beginning in 1949 to return to their homeland. Even among those who had to choose between staying in exile and returning on the basis of living standards, cultural affinity, and other more general factors, the idea of a "break with the past" had to be paramount. The Nazis were defeated, the major perpetrators of the war and the persecution of the Jews were dead or in prison, and the new constitutions of the federation and the states were the most progressive Germany had ever had. Among Jews, the attitude was hardly unequivocal. In the early 1950s, two points of view concerning Germany began to take shape, and still form the poles of the opinion spectrum—a differentiated political view oriented to political realities in West Germany, and a nationalist approach that believed that under the surface of democratic and pluralistic structures, the eternally authoritarian and racist Germany was still present. One attitude was expressed in the decision of the most important Jewish organizations and the Israeli government in 1952 to cooperate with the German government to compensate Jewish victims of Nazism, in the so-called "reparations" project that lasted for decades. The other attitude crystallized around the protest against this very same compensation agreement. In his speech against entering negotiations with Germany, the leader of the parliamentary opposition in Israel, Menachem Begin, shouted to a crowd in Jerusalem in January 1952: "Every German is a Nazi, every German is a murderer, Adenauer is a murderer!" Henceforth, a basically anti-German attitude and the evocation of the Holocaust could be considered a characteristic of Jewish postwar nationalism. This attitude, which has become more strongly encoded, has always counted as the most important weapon in the arsenal of nationalistically oriented Jewish organizations, which appear as fighters against anti-Semitism and "forgetting."

In any case, the return of Jews to Germany was considered out of the question. In 1948, the most important Jewish organization in the world declared that Jews should never again settle on the "blood-soaked German ground." Anyone who did was ostracized. The motives imputed to them were reminiscent of the Zionist nationalist distancing from the "ghetto Jews": anyone who settles now in Germany is motivated by greed. Until the mid-1950s, international Jewish organizations boycotted the newly emerging Jewish community organizations in Germany along with their umbrella federation. In negotiations over heirless and community property of the German Jews, the new community organizations were not considered the successors of the prewar ones. Instead, two "successor organizations," created by the most important world Jewish federations, negotiated with the occupation authorities and the German local authorities. The new communities had to apply to them for funds to finance social services and the rebuilding effort. In the first decades after the war, a pragmatic position with regard to West Germany and a thorough antagonism against everything German seemed to have led a peaceful coexistence within the Jewish organizations that created the "Conference on Material Claims Against Germany."

With their decision to emigrate to Germany, my parents found themselves not only at the crossroads of two opinions about their destination, but also at the junction of two Jewish streams of migration: one led to Germany and the other, much bigger, out of Germany. After 1945, over two hundred thousand survivors of the camps and refugees from East Europe had made their way to the Allied occupied zones, mainly the U.S. zones in southern Germany and Austria, and waited in Displaced Persons (DP) camps for the possibility to leave. This came only with the establishment of the State of Israel, which about half the DPs made their new home. As the emigration pressure subsided, other popular destinations, the U.S. and Canada, also opened their gates. By 1953, more than 90 percent of these refugees had left Germany. Until the closing of the last DP camps in 1956, the rest of them spread out over the newly emerging Jewish communities. At the same time, the number of Jewish returnees from exile increased and the immigration of Jews from East Europe began, but to a much smaller extent—both probably attracted by the passing of the various components of "reparations" by the Bundestag and the Bundesrat in the spring and summer of 1953.

Even before, the German states had offered support to the survivors and refugees, but with another objective. The Jewish DPs were a thorn in the side of the local authorities; they were involved in brawls with the German population and participated in the black market. Unlike the eleven million non-Jewish slave laborers and deportees, who had found themselves on German soil after 1945, they were considered non-repatriable. Thus the "reparations" began with small payments that tried to compensate for the time in concentration camps and other prisons, but were aimed mainly at motivating the survivors to leave Germany. It was a bounty that set a standard for later benefits. For every day in a concentration camp, former inmates received a compensation of one U.S. dollar.

In comparison, the obligations accepted by West Germany in the Luxemburg Treaties of 1952 were much more comprehensive and spectacular. But they were not aimed at attracting the Jews to stay, return, or resettle, either. The German-Israeli agreement providing goods and funds worth 3.5 million Deutschmarks was to compensate the State of Israel for the costs of absorbing five hundred thousand refugees in the period 1933–1950 at $3000 per capita. The West German Indemnification Law, offering compensation for personal losses, went far beyond that sum. This law, the core of "Reparations," constituted a gigantic undertaking, which treated the Holocaust as an enormous insurance case and promised to examine and repay all possible damages.

Between March and July 1953, both measures were adopted by the Bundestag and the Bundesrat, under the scrutiny of the international press. The effect abroad was considerable. When

Chancellor Adenauer visited the U.S. for the first time in April 1953, he was greeted warmly by the government, the population, and representatives of Jewish organizations. The effect the German government hoped to achieve with Reparations seemed to occur—a rehabilitation of Germany among their former enemies and the influencing of American-Jewish "financial circles," regarded by German conservatives as vital to ease access to credit and markets for the German economy.

Most Jews who settled in Germany at the same time as my parents shared this view of a chastened Germany aware of its obligation, which was willing to make great sacrifices in the middle of reconstruction in order to reconcile with the Jews. Their hopes originated in an expectation they shared with all emigrants—that prospects for a life in the country of destination were better than in the country of origin or in exile. Understandable as their optimism was, influenced by the publicity campaign of the West German government, the opposite attitude was just as reasonable and much more widespread. Of the almost three hundred thousand German Jews who had left Germany in time, 95 percent decided not to return there. In the early 1950s, most exiles had already spent fifteen years in another country where they had created a new life. It was only the Jews who had chosen Israel who found the prospects offered in Germany relatively more favorable. Ten percent of the former German-Jewish refugees returned to Germany from Israel, a rate of return twice as high as the whole group. It was this group of emigrants that my parents joined. We were part of those 48,000 Israelis who sought their salvation outside Israel between 1948 and 1953, during the biggest wave of immigration to the country, because they could not find suitable work, could not find their way around the language, could not bear the politics or the climate. We traveled with Israeli passports that had a special note: "Valid for all countries except Germany." On the last page of my parents' passports, which I still have, the note of the Israeli Ministry of Finance is still attached, indicating that my parents had acquired 151 Pounds Sterling and 20 U.S. dollars in foreign currency to pay for their travel and their new life.

My parents could hardly imagine what was really in store for us in Germany. A former resident of Düsseldorf, who had fled to Palestine in 1939 with his family and now returned with my parents, had stayed in the city briefly a few times since 1948 as an attorney. He knew the situation much better and had left his wife and two sons in Israel. He warned my parents. Not only was the country devastated, the people were deeply traumatized. In truth, hardly anybody valued the return of Jews.

* 4 *

My earliest memory of Germany is a cat. She sat very close on a branch in front of my window and looked at me. I remember the tree and the village where we lived. There was a village lime tree, a village well, and a village green, surrounded by decorative, white-washed little houses with their red roofs. It was a very special village we lived in, friendly and picturesque. Established in 1937 as a model Nazi settlement, it was in North Düsseldorf on the former site of the Nazi fairgrounds, "A Toiling Nation," and had originally been named Wilhelm Gustloff after the Nazi Gauleiter of Switzerland, who had been promoted to martyrdom in February 1936 by a bullet from the Croatian Jewish student David Frankfurter in snow-covered Davos. In 1945, the twenty little houses had been rechristened "North Park Settlement," and were taken over by the British Army of the Rhine, which set up its headquarters in the Nazi fairgrounds. Even if the little houses were a propaganda facade, the living was good here.

We rented house number three. In a series of photos my mother began making of our new life with her AGFA box camera, it forms the background of scenes of an idyllic childhood—the boy with his father, the boy with children from the settlement, the boy with a goat. It seemed a radiant beginning and my mother must have sent these photos all over the world, capitalizing on the fake scenery in her own way. Years later, I came upon another series of photos in which the house appears as background. I found them in the journal of the German Settler Federation of November 11, 1937. One bore the caption "The Settlers of Wilhelm-Gustloff-Settlement Await the Führer" and shows a crowd of children and a group of adults who "waited for their Führer in a festive mood." Further on, it says: "Their radiant eyes may have rendered some of their thanks to the Führer, owed by German homesteaders to their Führer and Chancellor." Other photos show the Führer visiting our house and two children who tossed seeds to a flock of chickens in the front yard. The caption here reads: "Feeding chickens, a favorite job of the settlement children." I also remember the chickens.

The Jewish community organization in Düsseldorf had re-emerged in the summer of 1945. The first members were mainly residents of Düsseldorf, who had lived through those years in hiding or as spouses of non-Jews or who had survived the camps. They included the future wife of my uncle, my father's brother, who worked for a "successor organization," the "Jewish Trust Corporation," created by the British Military Administration, and who was responsible for our presence in the city. As a girl, my aunt had been snatched by the Germans from Poland, saw the end of the war and the liberation as a slave laborer in a big Düsseldorf munitions factory, and had remained. This small group, which had come together by chance, was joined by other returnees and soon by people from the refugee camps. Religious services were held in rented halls, for where the Düsseldorf synagogue had stood until 1938 an ugly bunker now jutted up to the sky. In 1948, a private house was turned over to the community organization for religious services and administration.

The house was in an elegant residential neighborhood north of the "Horgarten," the palace gardens, and dated back to the turn of the century, Germany's Gilded Age. The ground floor had painted windows and the facade was decorated with garlands and other Jugendstil motifs. This décor was rare in a city whose center had been largely destroyed by air raids and where many rococo, Empire, and Jugendstil facades were repaired by crudely knocking off the stucco ornamentation. It must have been the house of an attorney or a physician, the office downstairs where the sanctuary with the Torah scrolls now was. Upstairs, where the community organization offices were, the family had once lived. For us children the most important room was the small hallway at the foot of the stairs, where we played during religious services or meetings, completely ignorant of what was going on around us and what had happened here only a few years earlier.

Our small community was so colorfully mixed that it was only in the eyes of the outside world that we seemed to form a unified group, as "the Jews" or as it was then still called in embarrassed circumlocution, as "Jewish people." There were the few who had survived in Düsseldorf or the surrounding villages. Then, there was a handful of political emigrants who mostly for political reasons had come back soon after 1945. There were the camp survivors, captured and deported somewhere in occupied Europe by the SS or the Wehrmacht, and who had sought safety in the British Zone after the liberation and were now too sick or too tired to move on. There were the few returnees from exile in England or Israel, who wanted to reoccupy their old shops, factories, or homes. There were the attorneys who specialized in compensation and restitution law and wanted to settle in the state capital to be near the state court of appeals and the state compensation office. And there were people like my parents, who decided to live in Germany because of their language and upbringing, their "affinity with the German culture," as it was called officially.

The original community numbering some two hundred people kept expanding and contracting until it reached around nine hundred members in the late 1950s. The change in growth came in 1956, when the West German government announced the payment of "immediate aid" for returning former citizens and thus seemed to have prompted the return of hesitant Jews from Israel and Latin America. With the political development in East Europe, Stalin's show trials against prominent Jewish Communists, the "anti-Zionist" campaigns, and the 1956 revolt in Hungary, many Jewish Poles, Hungarians, Romanians, Czechs, and Slovaks fled to Germany, including those who wanted to join the community organizations. The handful of Jewish immigrants from Prague and the Bukovina who had come to Düsseldorf in the early 1950s attracted other fellow countrymen. Thus, Düsseldorf also became an important international center of exile of both these groups, and the Prague and Bukovina "associations," to which my parents and I belonged, began to influence the community as a whole. With the growth of these German-speaking, East European groups that were educated with a special passion for German culture, not only did the ethnic and social composition of our community change, but the traditionally tense relationship between "Eastern" and "Western" Jews also took a special turn.

Until the eighteenth century, Jews in Eastern and Western Europe had not seen each other as strangers. Only with the gradual disappearance of legal and social barriers and the unequal processes of emancipation and acculturation of Jewish groups in individual countries did the differences and the sense of disparity increase. In Germany, the unfortunate situation of the Jews was recognized and denounced by the champions of enlightenment early, but the discriminating special status remained until the end of the nineteenth century. Thus, unlike their fellow Jews in other Western European countries, legal equality came not at the beginning of the cultural and social process of integration, but at the end. During this long period of uncertainty, the German-Jewish minority was exposed to increasing demands for stronger assimilation. This pressure created a pronounced sensitivity among German Jews with regard to the unassimilated Jews of Eastern Europe. When the Russian pogroms of 1882 triggered a powerful migration of Jews toward Western Europe and the U.S., this need for distinction turned into a defensive position. Jews had to be assimilated and emancipated in their countries of residence and if necessary fight for their rights there. The constant moving must stop, according to the argument. In the eyes of many German Jews, the "Eastern Jews" asking for absorption disturbed and endangered the process of Germanization. They seemed to confirm the thesis of "Jewish rootlessness" and threatened the whole group with a relapse to marginality and lower class status. The results of this episode in relations between the two groups were still to be felt in the 1950s. Despite persecution and exile, the returning and surviving German Jews still considered themselves "German" and distinguished clearly between themselves and the "Eastern Jews." Even now, the collective achievement of past generations that had produced a cultural synthesis between Judaism and Germanism was to be upheld and defended against intruders. What threatened to upset the synthesis was not only the idea of the incompatibility of "German" and "Jewish" in Nazi and nationalist thinking, but also the allegedly unpolished "Only-Judaism" of the Eastern Europeans that once again seemed to endanger the willingness of non-Jewish society to accept them.

The "Eastern Jews" who settled in Düsseldorf, on the other hand, formed a unified group only in the eyes of the German Jews. In reality, here too, historical circumstances threw together people from many Eastern and Southern European countries, who had been more or less assimilated in their homelands and could relate to one another only through the unfamiliar Esperanto of their common Jewishness. There were a few scattered Jews from Hungary,

Czechoslovakia, Yugoslavia, Romania, and mainly from Poland. They included former DPs, who had been in Germany since 1945, and people who had fled in the years afterward from the Eastern Bloc countries. In social terms, the image of the "Eastern Jews" did not fit the cliché either. This group included physicians, pharmacists, and engineers as well as unskilled laborers and people whose professional development had been interrupted by ten years of persecution and flight. More or less in the middle between the "Eastern Jews" and the "German Jews" stood the group that comprised my parents, German-speaking East Europeans from Prague and the Bukovina. Socially, people from this group got along as easily with "German Jews" as with "Eastern Jews," got on better with the non-Jewish milieu and in many ways held this extremely heterogeneous community together, which, aside from their common identity as victims, had barely anything in common.

Social differences in the postwar communities seemed just as glaring as in the big German-Jewish community organizations fifty or a hundred years earlier. The German Jews had long ago turned into a middle-class minority, who could consolidate their status by admission to the universities and the professions or by the acquisition of land and industrial property. Despite persecution and exile, this status could usually be regained to some degree through restitution and compensation. The destitute Yiddish-speaking "Eastern Jews," released from the concentration and DP camps, and the emigrants from the Iron Curtain countries were in a quite different position. They had lost or given up everything. Even possessing an education counted for little, as the physicians and attorneys among them still had to gain the right to practice in Germany. Unlike the former German citizens, the newcomers had no legal claim to stay in Germany and first had to be acknowledged as refugees in order to get permission to remain. Many felt unwelcome by both non-Jews and Jews. Even among their children, the feeling of "being stranded" and the temporary nature of their life in Germany held on for a long time.

The West German Indemnification Law also treated the three groups composing our community unequally. Victims of persecution who had lived in Germany before the outbreak of the war or by the deadline of December 31, 1952, could claim all damages by persecution, including the loss of property and wealth and the impairment of professional or economic advancement. The loss of property, wealth, and profession, however, had to have occurred within the country. Thus, for all intents and purposes, the DPs and refugees who did belong to the group that had full rights because of the deadline were excluded by this regulation. All those who had never previously lived in Germany and had settled there only after 1952 were compensated only for the period of imprisonment, wearing the "star," and damage to their health caused by "racial or political persecution." West Germany was not obligated to pay general reparations, so did not have to pay for the results of "normal" acts of war or the occupation. Thus, the burden of proof was imposed on the persecuted, who had to show that the damage to their health had occurred because of factors that deserved compensation. Even a concession of the authorities of certain states, including Nordrhein-Westphalia, who were entrusted with implementation, demanding only that these groups make an "acceptable" causal connection, didn't help much. The rate of rejection of applications for "health damages" was 50 percent. Proving that back troubles or a lung disease had arisen precisely in the ghetto or concentration camp was harder fifteen years later than documenting the destruction of household goods, the loss of a dwelling, or dismissal from a job. What concentration camp inmate could present the certificate of an SS physician or had bothered about evidence of health right after the liberation?

Whichever group you belonged to, without an expert attorney the individual could achieve nothing in view of the hopelessly complicated material; and even with the help of an attorney, you often got little enough. Between 1953 and 1965, the eleven West German compensation offices received over three million applications from about a million people. About half of the applications were rejected out of hand by the authorities, three hundred thousand were handled by the courts, and eight hundred thousand were finally denied altogether. In Düsseldorf, the site of one of these offices, dozens of attorneys were concerned exclusively with compensation cases. The complication of the law, a result of the complexity of the fate of the persecuted and the variety of the persecuted groups, produced a new type of "reparation attorney." In the Jewish community organization of Düsseldorf, Jewish reparation lawyers claimed and maintained the leading role from the start. Financially, they formed the upper class in the community, were the mediators and spokesmen to the outside world and the authorities, and provided many with income and papers.

The existence of such a group of spokesmen and providers, the large number of immigrants and refugees many of whom were politically inarticulate, the big differences in income and social position, mistrust and distance vis-à-vis the non-Jewish surroundings—all that gave the community an anachronistic character associated with the social and cultural isolation of a nineteenth-century East European "stetl." Many Jews spoke of a "ghetto situation." Attitudes prevailing in the non-Jewish environment also contributed to this feeling. There was no longer any systematic exclusion, but the line of cultural distinctions was drawn even clearer. After twelve years of anti-Semitic propaganda and persecution, no one could expect that German society had freed itself of the traditional nationalistic differentiation between "German" and "Jew." Moreover, the war, the defeat, and the complete destitution of the immediate postwar period led to a degree of solidarity among the German population that the Nazis had only dreamed of. "German" as an identity was probably more monolithic in the postwar period than in 1939.

* 5 *

For us children, education about the Holocaust began early. When I was nine years old, my parents pressed a few brochures in my hand, three brownish pamphlets of the Government Information Service, with the strange titles, "A Woman's Story," "Of Life, Struggle and Death in the Warsaw Ghetto," and "The Struggle against the Final Solution of the Jewish Question." That I still remember clearly the mood and the moment of the presentation can only mean that it was both significant and painful. I saw this embarrassed speechlessness of my parents only once again a few years later when they were suddenly confronted with the need to enlighten me sexually. The three brochures lay long unread on the table in my room, until one day I found them again on my bookshelf, lined up by a clearly worried mother between Enid Blyton, Karl May, and Erich Kästner. At some point, I picked up one of the brochures and started leafing through it. It was the report of Grete Salus of her imprisonment in Auschwitz, written in 1945. I read a few sentences, and leafed through it, scared and confused, went on until my eye stopped again on a few lines. Thus, I turned the pages, disturbed by the enigmatic, mysterious events, and drawn through this glance into a mysterious, forbidden world. I had already picked up words like "concentration camp" and felt their oppressive atmosphere. But now the connections weren't clear to me either and I didn't understand that it concerned my parents. Only the unique tension the subject evoked in them was conveyed to me. Thus, the other brochures remained unread.

What drove my parents to "enlighten" me in this way and so early? Like so many questions about their history during and after the persecution, I didn't ask this one during their lifetime. I maintained a tacit "hands off" about all these subjects. The whole thing could not really be kept silent. So all my parents had left was a linguistic and emotional control, a method other Jewish and non-Jewish parents also used to answer questions about war and persecution. My parents expressed themselves only in short, concise generalities about that time and their own fate, and thus clearly conveyed the feeling that any inquiry was undesirable. There was also a news blackout about what we were doing in Germany, another awkwardness that followed from the first. At the same time, they sought my sympathy for what they had "gone through," as they usually put it. This happened by way of extremely cautious revelations, covered with strict prohibitions that included the hint that they would have endured or done anything for my sake. So I felt guilty without knowing why.

What prompted this abrupt introduction into the secret world of the Holocaust can only be guessed. In 1960, when the scene in my room took place, a wave of anti-Semitic events went through the country. In Düsseldorf, the new synagogue that had been inaugurated only two years earlier was smeared with swastikas and the famous slogan of "Juden raus!" "Jews Get Out!" My parents reacted with fear to this incident. They packed me and their suitcases and left for a short "vacation," as they said, to Amsterdam, where they stayed in a hotel. The hasty presentation of the three brochures may also have been a prophylactic out of concern that outside events might soon introduce me to the subject even more roughly. In the same year, for the first time, serious doubts also arose about our future in Germany. My father, who had constructed for himself a more or less independent professional life, tried to find a foothold in France, and we spent the summer with relatives in Paris. As long as my parents were making headway in Germany, they had had a good reason not to expose me to the burdensome knowledge of the Holocaust. Perhaps they thought that the less he knows, the better he'll get around in his non-Jewish environment. Only when they themselves began to doubt the correctness of their decision of 1953 did they break the silence, even if in a strange way.

Most parents of the Jewish children I grew up with made do with abstract, summary remarks when their experiences during the persecution came up. The reason for this was the understandable argument that the young generation should be spared knowledge of the "horror" as long as possible. They relied on the non-Jewish milieu in this respect, for there, too, people wanted to keep the awareness of what had happened to the Jews as far away as possible; nor was it mentioned in school. Among Jews, there was really a whole series of personal reasons for remaining silent. All those who had been in the camps had to get over the traumatic memories that often intruded involuntarily and threatened their life in the present. The same was true to some extent for those who had survived the vestibule of hell in the ghettos and in hiding, surrounded by the constant threat and fear of death. "To let bygones be bygones," ignoring the past at least temporarily, was a widespread coping strategy. Other Jews, who had fled to exile in time, felt ashamed in view of the misery of those who suffered the worst, and were silent about their own experiences. Only very few spoke openly and with clear feelings about their fate. Similar rules clearly applied among our non-Jewish neighbors. Anyone who was directly responsible kept quiet about it. The others kept quiet out of solidarity. For other reasons, widows and orphaned families, or the victims of the horrible bombardments of German cities, did not discuss their fate. Thus, one set of reasons for the silence prevailed among the parents of my non-Jewish classmates and playmates, and another among the parents of my Jewish contemporaries.

A nuanced view of the Holocaust, including the motives of the perpetrators as well as the experiences of the victims, could not be pleasant for any modern society. Thus, to a certain extent, the survivors generally felt pressed to restraint or silence. In countries like Israel, Germany, or France, the memory of the war, the occupation, or the Holocaust also had important political functions. So it is not surprising that the memory of the survivors conformed to general formulas or had to conform, even when not always successfully. In Germany, for the Jewish immigrants and returnees, the memory of the Nazi period was still in the way of integration, even seemed to question a successful integration. Either the individual had to trivialize experiences contradictory to the environment, as observed among Germans or German-speaking Jews, or had to continue living in a non-conformity tolerated by the environment, a lifestyle practiced mainly by former DPs. Restraint, linguistic control, and conforming your own experience to group formulas corresponded to a general need shared by non-Jews and Jews alike. All German society looked "ahead." The collective had institutionalized regret, atonement, and reconciliation in the compensation measures and in contacts between official representatives, and thus made a personal position unnecessary. "One" talked about it without having to say anything oneself. Postwar society with its colorful blend of Jewish and non-Jewish persecuted, displaced, and bombed out, soldiers' widows and war-wounded, of Nazis, anti-Nazis, non-Nazis, of collaborators and apoliticals, in which every individual could have presented the collective with another bill, seemed to have agreed on a series of catchphrases that allowed it to talk about what had happened, and at the same time neutralized painful elements of memory antagonistic to a positive self-image or the national cohesion. In fact, everyone would have liked to portray himself as a victim, for most people felt they were. On both the Jewish and the non-Jewish side there were similar collective topoi, in which one's own group appeared as a victim of a powerful opponent and the sufferer of an historic injustice.

* 6 *

In the historical awareness of the Jews of Europe, persecution and suffering have always held a central position. Over the centuries, the history of horrors by non-Jews and the occasional eruptions of persecution has been handed down from generation to generation like holy relics representing a higher truth. The trail of a collective debate with persecution and the perplexing idea of "dispersion" can be found in the traditional treatises of religious scholars—that blend of exegesis, theological and historical speculation that represents the most important medium of Jewish culture in the pre-modern age. With the beginning of secularization and cultural adaptation, religious culture lost its binding force along with its role as consoler and interpreter of history. For most Jews it was replaced by secular, national ideas. But the idea of the biblical "nation of Israel" that had survived for two thousand years as a religious community at the margin of society united only through faith in God and Torah, could not be as easily recast into the modern concept of the nation based on the unity of language and territory and aimed at the homogeneity of living conditions. The "Jewish nation" was still dispersed, both territorially and linguistically. Given the enormous variety of Jewish life in the Diaspora, a few simple generic elements emerged that could serve as common characteristics of Jewish identity. The most important is identification as a persecuted or discriminated minority.

The motif of systematic persecution and discrimination by the Christian and Moslem milieus, of the "vale of tears," where Jews had been trudging since their exile, was developed by secular authors and historians in the nineteenth century and accepted eagerly by the Jews of Europe. This idea also explained the relative backwardness of the Jewish groups, pointed to the guilty, and left no doubt as to who had to improve the situation of the Jews. Being the object of permanent persecution and eternal hatred, even when totally unjustified, was hardly a flattering thought. Another generic element seemed to offer consolation for that—converting the negative anti-Jewish stereotypes into the idea of the Jews as morally superior people, who became the victims of atavistic counterforces because of their moral superiority. Here, too, traditional ideas from the religious culture came together to form a new national myth.

The Holocaust represented a frontal attack on all these ideas. While there was a widespread tendency to see Nazi rule and the Holocaust as exceptions and a "breakdown of civilization," Jewish thinkers within the religious or Jewish-nationalist traditions took pains to emphasize the continuity and explain the Holocaust on the background of Jewish experiences. The local state rabbi in Düsseldorf, Robert Geis (whose son was my classmate at an ultra-conservative Gymnasium on Düsseldorf's Königsallee, founded in the sixteenth century, where we were the only Jews among eight hundred non-Jewish students) expressed that idea when he unveiled a memorial for victims of the Nazis in the Jewish cemetery in the 1950s: "[Hitler] took us very seriously, truly bloody seriously, more seriously than we wanted to take ourselves. In his simplifying way, he saw through all our forms of life down to the deepest core of our essence. For him, the Jew was the person from whom the visions of the Prophets could emerge again at any moment . . . the person who would never be tired of believing in a world of justice and peace. The Jew was the person of social empathy." Geis then quoted from *Mein Kampf*: "The Jew is the creature of another God. . . . I compare the Aryan and the Jew and if I call the one man, I must call the other something else." And Geis concluded: "As creatures and followers of God, we were bound to be the most dangerous public enemy of the Third Reich and in all our suffering, we still say 'yes' to that." Stylizing the Jews as the predestined victims of a satanic power and elevating them to the counterimage of absolute evil, Rabbi Geis expressed a widespread view. The Social Democrat Ludwig Rosenberg, future chairman of the German Trade Union Congress, persecuted by the Nazis as a trade unionist and a Jew, wrote something similar in 1957: "It was the fate of the Jews, representatives of all humanity, to be the special target of the hatred of the non-humans. With the burning of synagogues, not only the prayer houses of a religious congregation were assaulted, but also the belief in eternal values."

This myth of the Jews as representatives of "eternal values" and as "public enemies" of evil emerged in all Jewish communities. It covered the increasing nationalism of a group that had been jolted by the nationalism of other groups. The myth assumed a special significance in Israel where animosities were not only in the past. In the daily confrontation with Arab opponents, the alleged verdict of history—that Jews are on the right side and their opponents on the wrong side—was a timely boon. The Arab opponents were stylized as the new Nazis, the Jews of Israel as the intended victims of an anti-Semitic policy of extermination. Equating Israel's experience of "victimhood" with that of the Diaspora created an unhealthy dynamic in which the alleged "persecution" of the Israelis radicalized the opinions of the Jews in Diaspora, and mobilized them in the struggle against the "persecutors" and critics of Israel, who were allegedly motivated by anti-Semitism. Thus, the myth contributed to prolonging the suffering in the Middle East and deepening the injustice that has been done to the Arabs of Palestine in the name of the Jewish nation.

* 7 *

Among us children, the members of our own group were simply considered better people, if not even the best, the surrounding society as suspect, but much more interesting. This didn't make us any different from other immigrant groups who distinguished between an intimate, secure internal world and an inhospitable, alien external world. While the school tried to prepare us for a successful life in German society, many of us learned in the privacy of our parents' home or the Jewish environment to despise non-Jewish society and to distrust non-Jews. In this respect, there were great differences in the Jewish community. German and German-speaking Jews had a much easier time with the non-Jewish surroundings, the barriers of social and professional integration were low for them, and behavior "inside" was hardly different from that in the outside world. For immigrants from Eastern Europe, on the other hand, who were still alien both culturally and linguistically, the incomprehensible environment easily seemed like a hostile, monolithic whole. This split between internal and external worlds was deepest and most lasting in a certain group of my Jewish contemporaries, the children of relatively younger concentration camp survivors from Eastern Europe.

In their youth, these parents had fallen into the maelstrom of persecution, which had spewed them out in 1945, most without parents or relatives. The younger ones were sent to Israel by aid organizations or were adopted by families in the European Jewish communities who had not suffered during the Holocaust, most in England or Scandinavia. The "adults," those who were about twenty when the war ended, came to DP camps as refugees and quickly—often too quickly—established families. Most had no professional training or academic education beyond a few grades in grammar school when the Holocaust interrupted their life. Many had learned the Hebrew of the prayers and the holy writing as children; many were illiterate in all languages. The communities they came from no longer existed, relatives lived overseas, seldom in Germany. These were the people who had children my age, and these were the children I associated with most often. Only later did I realize that these families were the hardest hit in our community.

The parents almost all worked in small businesses in wholesale or retail trade in the traditional branches of textiles, carpets, and jewelry, or they ran bars. Here the disadvantages of the lack of training and language and the weak social starting position could be made up for with the traditional methods of hard work, help from the family, and support from the community network. In the early days, hardly anybody earned much, but everybody had enough to live on. Another advantage, perhaps even the biggest one, was the limited, formal, well-controlled contact with the outside world of non-Jews. Here the need to avoid the surrounding world as much as possible could best be fulfilled, at least for the parents. The children, who were also required to keep the separate spheres of life, were in a different situation. They attended public schools, played in the street, and associated with the neighborhood children. They were immersed from the beginning of their school years in the non-Jewish environment and had to find their way there, indeed their future, with neither the encouragement nor the necessary equipment from their parents.

We all owed our parents gratitude, loyalty, and indulgence for what they had suffered. But these children were required to evince a solidarity with their parents' suffering and to share their hatred of everything "German," which was quite unbearable. This alliance against the environment hardened not only behavior toward the outside, family life itself also became atrophied. These children were also expected to accept their parents' unpredictable, irrational behavior with patience and understanding, to offer them the emotional support and existential stability they themselves needed as children. What immediate and long-term results all this had depended on the concrete behavior of the parents, who were not always consistent in their attitude, and on the children's wealth of imagination.

My Jewish friends quickly learned to evade these far-reaching limitations nimbly and to interpret the complicated, often hardly logical code of behavior to their advantage. Most of these parents had imposed a strict ban on bringing non-Jewish friends home. It was hard enough not to be able to invite their friends home, but how could they explain to them that they weren't welcome in their parents' home as non-Jews? The real reasons could not be cited and so new excuses were constantly concocted—my parents nap in the afternoon, my mother is sick, my father can't bear any noise. The parents' demands often went further. In accordance with their own practice to limit relations with non-Jews to formal, business transactions, they expected their offspring to follow a similarly limited, utilitarian relation to their non-Jewish friends and classmates. Thus, their children learned to justify association with non-Jews with motives of necessity—help in homework, or their classmate's math skills. Other friendships were simply kept secret.

Another of the parents' habits that was just as unfortunate for their children was to call non-Jewish Germans simply "Nazis." Everyone was honored with the shout of "Nazi!" who evoked the speaker's displeasure for some silly reason, as when a neighbor didn't greet them in the street. The custom of one father became a joke among us children: he used to curse other drivers by stopping the car, rolling down the window, and, without regard to age or sex, shouting at the person in question: "You old Nazi!"

Later, when we were older, this sharp separation between "Jewish" and "German" was also mixed with worry about the long-term maintenance of the tribe. Every sign of sexual maturity was greeted with the rhetorical question: "You won't get involved with a *shiksa*?" For us boys, "shiksa" was clearly the most dangerous special form of the genus "goy." However, in relations with the other sex, a few nuances were to be observed. Jewish girls were expected to be virgins when they got married—to a Jewish man. The same final goal also applied to us boys. As far as virginity was concerned, the parents apparently had less trust in the self-discipline of their offspring. When a sexually active young man had to be prevented from going to bed with girls of his own group, affairs with *shiksas* were permissible if they followed the general rule of being limited to a formal, utilitarian "acquiring experience." Naturally, danger was lurking behind this back door, and so the parents of two friends not illogically sent their boys to the whores when they reached a certain age, as a birthday present we all envied. To maintain the tribe, they paid the high price of having this as their sexual initiation.

My parents had settled on the other end of the behavioral spectrum of attitudes toward the non-Jewish environment. They gave me a differentiated image of German society and encouraged me to begin my life in Germany as light and free as possible. But they also drew boundaries in another way. They sought and found non-Jewish friends among the risk-free groups of political emigrants and anti-Nazis, and otherwise practiced great restraint and caution. By regularly attending the theater and concerts, they also cultivated a formal association with the environment and a typical social mode that had been practiced before the war by the German-Jewish bourgeoisie. "Going out" gave them a sense of social integration they had not really achieved. My father, who still cultivated the affability and manners of the imperial province of Bukovina, kept warning me to be especially polite and considerate toward non-Jews. He wanted his son to make a good impression "as a Jew." He himself greeted female employees, even bank tellers, with a kiss on the hand, regularly brought flowers and candy for business associates, and seldom appeared in public without gloves and a hat. How much his odd social manners resulted from the wish to appear especially "impeccable" because of his

Jewishness can no longer be determined. Born in 1902, he belonged to a generation of Austrian Jewish bourgeoisie that kept their group consciousness sharp in Jewish national student associations like "Emunah" ("For Judaism and Science!") or the "fighting" "Hebronia," which still practiced the fencing duel and which my father belonged to in Czernowitz and Vienna. Judaism was a matter of "honor," which sometimes had to be defended with a drop of blood against all-German associations like "Wotan."

It was not only our parents who avoided the difficult, central questions of our life. As far as the new Jewish life in Germany and the problems of youth were concerned, the Jewish public and the Jewish community organizations were almost mute, too. In 1958, a new community center was opened in Düsseldorf, comprising a big synagogue, an administration and office building, and a youth center. With this undertaking, the community organization demonstrated that a permanent resettlement of Jews in Germany had turned out to be possible and desirable, and by building their own youth center they indicated the only means to guarantee the community in the long run: to bind Jewish youth to Judaism and to Germany at the same time. In practice, however, what happened in the youth center had the opposite effect.

Most activities offered us were no different from those in Catholic or Protestant youth centers. We did handicrafts, photography, ping-pong, played music, and danced with the same goal: to keep "our own" young people off the street and bind them socially and culturally to the group. "Jewish" activities consisted of a weekly hour of religion that introduced us to Jewish holidays and prayers, and the broader Jewish youth work that, however, was not undertaken by the community itself. That was in the hands of the "Zionist Youth in Germany," an Israeli organization founded in 1959, which held weekly meetings in our community and organized camps for all Jewish youth in Germany three times a year. The goal was to make us immigrate to Israel right after finishing school or training. The Zionist youth movement spoke of its task in Germany as an "evacuation" of all Jewish youth to Israel. The allusions to the emergency situation of the Nazi period were no accident. Then, too, there had been an evacuation of Jewish youth to Palestine because a continuation of Jewish life in Germany seemed impossible.

The establishment of "Zionist Youth in Germany" went back to an appeal of the Jewish Agency that spoke of the "few tens of thousands of Jews who still remained in Germany," who "have neither a Jewish nor a Zionist nor a human justification to stay here." An urgent situation demands extraordinary measures. Thus, several Zionist parties, who were usually rivals in Israel and elsewhere, joined together into a single organization and established local groups in a dozen big communities. In almost all cities, the activities took place in the youth center or in rooms of the community. Here and there, the conflicting missions and perspectives of Zionists and community organizations led to friction—after all, the Zionists rejected the re-establishment of the communities and Diaspora existence—nevertheless, the ideologically important youth work remained in the hands of the Zionist Youth in Germany. With the exception of two community organizations, the Jewish organizations in Germany gave up their most important mission without a struggle.

Until the 1950s, Zionism had had a hard time almost everywhere in the Diaspora. The experience of the Holocaust and the establishment of the State of Israel began to ease the tensions and a mutually advantageous coexistence of community and Zionist organizations developed, with one side donating money and the other identity. But this model could not be transferred to West Germany where the community existence was too insecure and the goal of the Zionist organization was not support for Israel, but emigration. Why didn't the community organizations do more to defend the new Jewish life in Germany? Did those in charge secretly feel that returning to Germany was unreasonable and unhealthy for children? Some parents forbade their children to attend the Zionist youth groups and didn't let them go to the vacation camps. A few were explicitly anti-Zionist. But parental resistance wasn't directed primarily against Zionism or the idea of emigration, but rather the destination. They hoped that, after finishing school, their offspring would opt for the U.S., France, England, or Canada. All of them—parents, educators, community leaders—hardly showed support in favor of what they themselves had begun: a new Jewish life in Germany. Maybe it was too early for that. As immigrants, their concerns were mainly material. Maybe the feelings of shame or guilt that arose from life in Germany were too strong to deal rationally with this question. In any case, we children had to find our own way in this difficult situation.

In their general cultural agenda, the community organizations also refrained from promoting or influencing the process of integration. The difficult question of continuity with the prewar communities was lurking here. The new organizations preferred not to carry on the tradition of German Jewry before Hitler, and not to continue the centuries-old Jewish communities in their own towns destroyed only a few years earlier. There were many motives for this deliberate distancing. In Düsseldorf, the only remnant of the old community organization was a partially destroyed cemetery. Among the leading members of the new community established in 1945, there were initially a few old residents of Düsseldorf, but their number and importance quickly declined, while the portion of new members who didn't come from Germany grew steadily.

The German Jews among us and the groups from the islands of German culture in Eastern Europe sought continuity, albeit cautiously, almost defensively. The desire for continuation aimed at a distant, idealized past of German Jewry, at the heroes of the Enlightenment and successful assimilation. Hardly anybody seemed interested in the recent history of the Jews of Germany or Düsseldorf. In Düsseldorf, as in most other cities, erecting memorials and museums was left to the initiative of non-Jews, municipal governments, and churches. It was as if the concrete idea of what the Jews had gone through in their own city, their own street, just a few years earlier, could not yet be endured. The lack of interest in the fate of the local prewar communities, however it was justified, was the most direct expression of the repression of memory that accompanied the "new beginning."

In the late 1950s, my parents along with about twenty other Jewish families established a study group that met once a month in private homes and tried to cultivate German-Jewish culture. The members held lectures and readings, and discussed them over tea. They "educated" themselves, not with Schiller or Goethe, the heroes of a previous generation of German-Jewish bourgeoisie, but with Moses Mendelssohn, Heinrich Graetz, and Kurt Tucholsky. When the study group met in my parents' house, I sat with them, touched by the seriousness and the conspiratorial atmosphere, and took in the words of Glückel of Hamlin, Rachel Varnhagen, Heine, and Celan, like magic formulas. The whole thing lasted barely five years.

The leaders of the community organization regarded this activity as an elite separatism of "German" Jews that threatened the unity of the community. For years, they fought the study group and finally managed to put an end to it. A compromise was found. Members of the study group were to open their cultural aspiration to all members of the community. A "cultural committee" was established, similar to the already existing community committees for religion, youth, building, and finance. Representatives of the study group and representatives of the community board were now to provide "culture" to the community. My mother was a member and, as a student, I was also involved in it for a few years. The culture produced by the committee constituted a victory of majority interests, represented in the meetings by a member of the board, usually a reparations attorney. The committee decided on guest appearances of the quiz show host Hans Rosenthal, Israeli folk dance groups and singers, and orchestras or comedians, who appeared twice a year at the community organization balls. Jewish culture was an apparently endless round of harmless black-tie-optional entertainment.

Thus, my contemporaries and I grew up in a strange vacuum: Our parents' origins lay buried under the ashes of the Holocaust or had disappeared behind the Iron Curtain, history and memory of family and homeland fell under the silence shrouding "the past," and for many of us, German society was out of the question as a model or a goal of assimilation. This sketch could have come directly from the textbook of Zionism. An isolated Jewish minority lives unloved and alien in the surrounding society, unable to integrate culturally and socially, constantly aware of the danger of renewed discrimination and persecution by the majority. The only solution seemed to be emigration to Israel. Not only was my generation in Germany extremely receptive to these nationalist and Zionist ideas, they had virtually nothing to oppose to them. Parents and milieu presented no counterimage, no alternative diagnosis for our feeling of alienation and isolation, and no alternative therapy. Thus, the negative self-image, shared by Zionist and anti-Semitic ideologies, was tacitly continued: that traditional Jewish life in Diaspora is abnormal and must be changed by intervention of one sort or the other.

* 8 *

In 1956, we moved from the northern to the southern part of Düsseldorf, near the university clinic. After the rustic idyll of the former Wilhelm-Gutloff Settlement, we wound up in an environment of workshops and small factories, surrounded by allotment gardens, in a residential neighborhood with the small red-brick multifamily homes of the prewar era and their carefully pruned shrubs in the front yard. We rented the upper floor of a building on a little street that led only to the thicket of the allotments and to a bucolic scene that indicated the peculiar ambitions and special personality of our landlord. The move was arranged by an American-Jewish official, who had lived with his family in the attic flat since the end of the war and now went back to the U.S. Another Jewish family lived on the first floor, and the landlord lived in the middle.

The owners of the house were pious Catholics, belonged to the active core of their congregation, and had two daughters, both a few years older than I. On Sunday, four members of the family left the house, all dressed up, and after mass, five of them returned, accompanied by the priest, who always came to lunch on that day. In the garage next to the house, they took in laundry and ironing, and behind the house, they kept a big flock of geese that pecked around under the fruit trees and constituted the agricultural part of the family enterprise. The father, who also bred rhododendrons, had worked for the British military authority since the end of the war. He came from a family of Catholic anti-Nazis, and it was no accident that he had taken two Jewish families into his house.

Renting a flat was clearly one of the most difficult problems for a Jewish family. There was still a housing shortage, caused not only by the destruction of the war but also by the presence of a large number of refugees from the East. If you could find a flat, you had to count on a rejection as soon as it turned out that the future tenant was Jewish. Obviously, the landlord was not open about it and those involved could only speculate about which motives were behind a refusal. In any case, searching for a flat was easier for German Jews than for those who spoke only Yiddish. In general, relations with the neighbors were usually fraught with tensions and mutual distrust. Names and addresses of landlords "friendly to Jews" were passed around. Members of the Jewish community informed each other about which shops one could buy in and which officials were "friendly to Jews" and who was an "old Nazi." At that time, the words "friendly to Jews" and "Nazi" were components of almost every one of my parents' conversations.

A joke that made the rounds among my parents' Jewish friends caricatured the fear of discrimination and the consequent constant distrust of the non-Jewish environment: Two Jews applying for work as a radio announcer, are waiting to be interviewed for the job. The first one, a stutterer, is called in. A few minutes later he comes back, disappointed. The other applicant wants to know why he didn't get the job. "Th-th-they're a-a-all a-a-anti-S-s-semites!" replies the failed candidate.

The most important strategies to avoid degrading experiences in the non-Jewish environment were foresight and precaution. With the help of our new landlord, my parents created an imaginary map of the neighborhood marking the shops and firms to keep away from. As soon as I was old enough to be sent to the corner to "shop" with a few pennies in hand, I was also introduced to this map. Thus, the butcher where I had often picked up a piece of sausage was suddenly off-limits, and my mother now spoke of a "BDM type" who stood behind the counter. What "BDM," the Hitler Youth for school-age girls, was I didn't know, but from now on, I gave the woman a warning and fearful look through the display window on my way home from school, like Hansel and Gretel keeping the evil witch in check. I couldn't grasp the idea that people rejected or even hated me only because of the accident of my birth and my affiliation with a group through no fault of my own. At a later age, too, I reacted with surprise and what now seems amazing naïveté when a disparaging remark was made about Jews in my presence or when I myself was the object of anti-Semitic insults. To a large extent, that was self-protection. But even then,

I obviously assumed instinctively that anti-Semitic attitudes were more the exception than the rule, and that it was better to keep away from certain people and situations than to distrust the whole environment.

As my awareness of a group identity and the alleged differences between Jews and non-Jews increased, I noticed remarks and incidents more often. Some were not to be ignored, like the expressions of the boisterous sons of the owner of a corner pub with a penchant for violence, who called me "Jewish pig" on the way to school. But others I had to ignore, like the greeting of a classmate on the second day of school in the Gymnasium. On the first day, during the roll, religious affiliations were made public. Mine was declared to be "Mosaic," a euphemism for "Jewish" that was considered less offensive. My ten-year-old classmate must still have been unfamiliar with the word and its use and had probably asked at home. The next morning, when I entered the classroom, I came on him carving a swastika on my part of our shared desk. Until we graduated eight years later, neither of us talked about the incident and the postponed brawl came only at the beer-soaked stage of the graduation party.

The fact that we lived in the house of anti-Nazis was the most significant influence on my view of the German environment as a child. I felt at home in our neighbors' house and was treated like a member of the family. Our landlord told me of his youth in a way that suited my intellectual capacity. His parents had forbidden him to join the Hitler Youth, and so he had suffered from the teasing of his classmates and the comments of his teachers. I could understand these experiences and his situation only too well. He also told how he had managed to avoid military service by volunteering for the police force. Then, a moment came during training when he regretted his decision and cursed his parents' political orientation. At a Düsseldorf swimming pool, as a non-swimmer, he had been pushed off the diving board so that the swimmers among the recruits could practice life-saving. He served as my model for the political and moral scope open to the individual during the Nazi years. When the mood in my parents' home became more difficult because of external circumstances, I spontaneously adopted our neighbors as a substitute. These good people then gave me the emotional support that helped me later as an adult to master the problems stemming from my parents' years of persecution and uprooting. Because of them, I was spared the impression of a monolithic, hostile German society that afflicted many of my Jewish contemporaries.

My life increasingly began to run on two separate tracks. At the age of twelve, I joined the Zionist youth group in the youth center of the Jewish community. At the same time, as usual at that age, my friendships with my non-Jewish classmates in the Gymnasium became more intense. I became a member of two different circles of friends, one Jewish and one non-Jewish, indicating the two worlds I belonged to and wanted to belong to, but which could not be mingled. Many of my Jewish friends distrusted my obviously equal friendships with non-Jews, while my non-Jewish friends silently made the most varied conjectures about the closed world of my Jewish life. I kept the two groups of friends apart as much as possible, and for a few years it felt completely normal to live in two worlds.

Some of my non-Jewish classmates and their parents were interested and curious about my origin. Many passed over the fact in silence, but most of them responded to me with an embarrassment typical of that time. Almost everyone felt obliged to remark on my origin, mostly with well-meaning, laudatory comments about Jews or Judaism, which seem to repudiate negative stereotypes but actually acknowledged them. Other comments about my Jewishness, just as often and ostensibly just as unavoidable, were exonerating. "With their economic success and their undeniable superiority," went the rhetorical question, "didn't the Jews themselves contribute to the hatred and prejudices against them?" Gradually, I began to react just as sensitively to these ostensibly positive judgments as to the negative ones, as they both made me aware of the stigma I bore in the eyes of the environment. But what bothered me most was the emphasis on the differences between "us" and "them." I insisted on belonging to both worlds.

I discovered the ideological justification for these differences in the Jewish youth center. In the weekly meetings of the Zionist youth group, we were introduced to the history of the Jewish people, Zionism, and Israel, practiced Israeli folk dancing, sang Hebrew songs, and discussed the political questions of the day. I was especially impressed by the seriousness with which "real" things were discussed, Judaism, the political and military problems of Israel, the Holocaust, existential problems we faced in Diaspora, everything naturally from the perspective of Zionism. The ideological training, like all ideological training, was quite simple. We learned that life in Diaspora was dangerous for us Jews and prevented us from a free development; that only our own state could create a remedy. It was tacitly accepted that we Jews knew only one form of life—as a separate group or a separate people. The possibility of cultural mixing or "assimilation," the polemical opposite to Zionism, was considered an illusion.

We devoted most of the time to the history of the emergence of Israel and the Middle East conflict. This must have been the main difference from the indoctrination of Zionist youth in European Jewish communities twenty-five or fifty years earlier. The Holocaust had clearly verified the Zionist thesis, and the Jewish state had meanwhile become a reality. Now it was a matter of defending it. With constant repetition, all the well-known arguments were drummed into us: Israel was the only legitimate answer to the Holocaust; Arab resistance was unjustified, Jewish rights to the land superceded those of the Arabs. In the 1960s, as today, Israeli propagandists focused on Palestinian violence. I still remember the depressingly long lists compiled by the Foreign Ministry in Jerusalem and distributed by the embassy in Bonn, indicating places and times of attacks. Before 1967, it was landmines used by the "Fedahin" to drive out the enemy. At night on isolated roads along the border, several times a month, they took many victims among passing soldiers, but also among the civilian passengers of public buses.

About half of the eighty or so active young people between twelve and eighteen years old in the Jewish youth center were members of the Zionist youth, the same ratio as in other Jewish communities. We shared the need for seriousness and "authenticity" with our whole generation, which was reacting to the materialism of the environment and to the first postwar wave of consumerism from the U.S. But none of us caught onto the one-sided interpretations dispensed at the meetings, and most of us eagerly opened ourselves to the thought that a life in Israel would solve all our problems. I responded to the attraction of the political and social utopia as well as to the pathos of Israel's heroic struggle against an overpowering enemy, without getting into a conflict of loyalty with my non-Jewish world, at least not for the time being. Neither I nor my fellow Zionists saw participation in Zionist activities as a direct reason to immigrate to Israel for real. In fact, the effect of the indoctrination was more subtle. It undermined the basis of our life in Germany.

The Zionist youth vacation camps were held twice a year in neighboring countries. That was no accident. Across the border, we were supposed to feel free of our unfortunate existence, of the hypocrisy and adjustments forced on us by a life among "Germans." The main function of the camps was to get the members out of the normal context of their daily lives, bind them to one another socially and ideologically, and persuade them to immigrate to Israel. The effort to create a social link to Zionist-oriented youth in other cities soon showed results. During my six-year membership in the Zionist youth movement, during vacation camps and mutual visits I met hundreds of Jewish youth from all German Jewish communities, surely a third of the twelve hundred Jewish youth in Germany of school age who were members of a Jewish community at that time.

An Israeli flag waved over the tent camps or youth hostels rented by the Zionist youth in Denmark, the Netherlands, or Switzerland. On the kitchen doors, lounges, and bedrooms were signs in Hebrew, and we were encouraged to learn as many Hebrew expressions as possible. Every morning we gathered for roll call, were counted, stood at attention, sang the national anthem, raised the flag, and then did some Israeli army exercises. We learned Israeli songs and dances, attended courses every day on some Zionist subject, played scouting games, sang around campfires, performed skits. The human model conveyed to us was both simple and impressive: Diaspora Jews were materialistic and groveling; Israelis were generous, brave, and had a strong sense of community. Our Zionist ideals consisted of a special blend of nationalist and socialist elements, a potpourri of European culture: a little bit of German *Wandervfogel* romanticism, a little bit of the kibbutz, a little bit of the army. Those were the most exciting events of my youth.

All that had tempted generations of youth in the most varied political movements: contempt for a conventional bourgeois lifestyle, willingness to sacrifice, devotion to higher goals, and the paramilitary drill, which gave a touch of adventure to it all. This anti-bourgeois revolutionary attitude of bourgeois children went in tandem with a high degree of conformity. Political dissent, a deviant view on the Palestinian question, was inconceivable. There were only moderate and radical Zionists, the latter more socialistically oriented, the former more persuaded of the worldview of Menachem Begin's Herut party. Even among their opponents, the representatives of the Zionist right enjoyed the reputation of excessive but praiseworthy idealists, who were "ready for everything," "knew no forgiveness," could not be led astray by the sanctimoniousness of the non-Jews or the cunning of the Arabs. The Israeli "emissaries," who directed our vacation camps and the organizations, belonged to one of the ruling socialist Zionist parties in Israel; most were members of some kibbutz and were posted abroad for a few years. Many had nice-sounding Hebrew first and last names from the Bible reminiscent of the heroes of Hollywood films like "Exodus." They had dropped their old Yiddish, Slavic, or German names out of idealism, clearly along with their independent political views. Thus, the virtues of conformity necessary in kibbutz life also served as a model for training our own character.

Most moving were the Holocaust commemorations. The history of a resistance act was read out or told to us, six candles were lit, "one for every million," and songs were sung, mostly American Yiddish shmalz, "My Stetlach Belz," the "Partisan Hymn," and the Israeli national anthem. We all wept. The date of the commemoration ceremony complied with the "Memorial Day for the Holocaust and the Ghetto Uprising," a legal holiday in Israel since 1951. Since the date follows the Hebrew calendar, it falls on a different day each year in the Christian counting. The memorial day we knew from our own community organizations was November 9, the anniversary of Kristallnacht 1938. The commemoration took place at the memorial plaque before the Düsseldorf synagogue that was burned down in 1938, consisted of a brief speech and the Kaddish for the dead. The Warsaw Ghetto Uprising and the liberation of Auschwitz were also commemorated in Jewish communities. These celebrations held in most Diaspora Jewish communities had a traditional religious form and were designed to remember the victims. The Israeli Holocaust memorial day was far from every religious form and meaning and filled a political-national function.

The law of 1951 placed the Israeli Holocaust memorial day between the beginning of the Warsaw Ghetto Uprising (April 19) and Israeli Independence Day (May 15), in order to produce a link between the two events. The central Jerusalem celebration I participated in for the first time years later reminded me unpleasantly of the death cult of fascist and communist movements. Youth and young soldiers of both sexes marched together with survivors in a military formation to an outdoor theater, planted themselves between big torches and read brief biographies of victims, each youth representing one dead person. Thus, people who had been killed randomly and arbitrarily were treated as soldiers who had fallen for the fatherland. This was intended to give meaning to the "sacrifice" of these people, since their death had contributed to the rise of the state. Comparable celebrations of the Zionist youth spread such ideas also among us, with great effect. We learned that armed resistance against the Nazis and their collaborators was the only appropriate reaction, while a passive attitude of the persecuted was tantamount to collaboration. We were not aware that we were thus doing a great injustice to the large majority of Holocaust victims. Nor did we understand the social implications of the fact that the "State of the Jews" was really built on the principle of race. Our eyes were shut tight in that horribly naïve certainty that the world owed us something. To be against Zionism or Israel, we learned, was to be against the victims of the Holocaust.

* 9 *

My increasing acceptance of Zionist thinking and my consideration of possibly returning to Israel were painful for my father. But all he could do was to point me to his own hierarchy of civilization, in which, despite Hitler, German culture and "education" were on top and the Israeli lifestyle and manners were on the bottom. His attitude was shaped by his experiences. In all the years since our departure, he had visited Israel only once for a few days for his mother's funeral, and hadn't stayed a minute longer than necessary. In vain did he try to divert my obvious enthusiasm for the vacation camps and their scouting romanticism into other channels. He enrolled me in the "Falcons," the youth movement of the Social Democratic Party, which he considered his political homeland and presented as a model to me of the successful integration of opponents of the Nazis, victims of the Nazis, and Nazis. But his influence on me was limited, precisely in the question of a life in Israel. I had no doubt that it was his personal disappointment that determined his opinion about Israel. We never settled the issue. Even when we parted on the eve of my move to Haifa, he still presented his experiences to me as a deterrent example, an argument I could easily reject out of hand. Like every son, I was firmly convinced in that merciless way that I could do it better and would not repeat his mistakes.

That he based his criticism of Israel on personal experiences corresponded to the general tendency to express deviant opinions about Israel only with great restraint and caution. Among the Jewish bourgeoisie of Western Europe, who were traditionally skeptical about Zionism, Israel was considered "unrefined," and Israelis coarse and uncouth. This social and esthetic argument often concealed a basic criticism. Before Hitler and World War II, Zionism in Europe and America had been a minority movement rejected or combated by almost all community and religious organizations. Orthodox groups were upset about the secular messianism that didn't want to leave the Jews' return to Zion to divine Providence. Reform Judaism did not regard Jews as a nation and saw their messianic traditions aimed at all mankind. The anti-emancipatory tendency of Zionism worried almost all organizations who feared that Zionism would undermine the struggle for freedom of religion and equal rights by questioning the achievement and propagating an alternative to emancipation. Even among those who thought of Judaism primarily as a nation, a revival of a national life was considered unnecessary and a location in the Arabic province was not considered exactly tempting. A self-initiated national segregation under the leadership of a handful of boorish radicals from Polish or Russian stetls was hard to sell to a Jewish establishment striving for recognition and integration. After the Holocaust and the establishment of the State, these attitudes changed radically.

Now it was no longer possible to express basic criticism of Israel or Zionism in Jewish public life. The State in its double role as persecuted and savior could be assessed only from internal Zionist perspectives—from the standpoint of rightist Zionists, who criticized the willingness of the socialist governments to compromise with the Arabs and denounced the nepotism of the kibbutzim and trade union enterprises; and from the perspective of leftist Zionists, who regretted the hard course of action that had been necessary in 1948 against the Arab population, and worried about the humanity of Israeli society. The three religious currents in Judaism—Orthodox, Conservative, and Reform—also gave up their anti-Zionist position and began to orient their policy to the interests of their parties or organizations in Israel. Thus the boundaries of legitimate discussion about Israel were established in Jewish public life. The non-Jewish public began to follow the same rules. Opinions that basically rejected the Zionist arguments, widespread only yesterday, were now outside normal discourse.

In the Düsseldorf Jewish community, there were only very few members who could be considered anti-Zionist in a political sense, and only a handful of active Zionists who planned to immigrate to Israel. The great majority was somewhere in the middle, was pro-Israeli and pro-Zionist, but not active Zionists. That was an attitude typical for most Diaspora Jews, in which the individual identified with the fate of Israel and was willing to support the State morally, politically, and financially. At every opportunity, holidays, and worship services, money was collected for about a half-dozen Israeli purposes—for the two main Zionist funds that had been created before World War I to finance the acquisition of land and the building of the infrastructure, for social purposes in the military, for the handicapped, for the improvement of the position of women, for the universities. Beyond money, the community member could express solidarity with Israel in many other ways, from buying Israeli products to vacationing in the Land. Commitment to the State became the central component of community activities. Israel had captured the place that had once been taken by other philanthropic tasks—feeding the poor, caring for the sick, providing dowries for brides, washing the dead, and so on—those remnants of the largely autonomous Jewish life during the Middle Ages that had once been the heart of the community, but had become unnecessary in the modern state.

My father's fairly inconsistent attitude was also typical. In the privacy of his own home, he gave free reign to his dislike for Israel and its affairs, but in the community and the many Zionist philanthropic federations he belonged to or gave money to, his commitment to Israel was exemplary. This was an expression of the same ambivalence seen in religious observance. What was allowed in private was not acceptable in Jewish public life. Israel had become the content of Jewish life, in community work as in private identity, and provided a point of reference for a Judaism in which traditional belief had hardly any more meaning. In the 1967 war, this turning away from traditional content and the turn toward Israel reached a climax. Afterward, the attacks of "Black September" seem to have cemented the fate of the State inseparably with that of the Jews in the Diaspora. From then on, the buildings of the Jewish Community of Düsseldorf presented the image of a beleaguered fortress, defended by police with submachine guns, armed security guards, fences and other measures—ostensibly proving the Zionist hypothesis of the inevitability of Jewish persecution.

5

* TWO PHOTOS *

A Search for Identity between Germany and Israel

* 1 *

At the age of seventeen, I was drafted into the Israeli army. Even though I was a German citizen living in Düsseldorf, I received a mimeographed order to report from the Israeli embassy in Bonn, filled out by hand and provided with the logo of the Israel Defense Forces—an olive branch twined around a sword in a Star of David. I still remember the shock my parents and I felt after we had deciphered the writing. There was a moment of silence. My father was mute because he felt guilty, my mother because the idea that her son was to be a soldier left her speechless. Both of them clearly felt responsible for putting my life at this unpleasant pass because of their move to Israel. After all the years, the past had caught up with us, this brief, half-forgotten time when my parents were in Israel and I happened to be born. I was silent out of amazement. I was astonished and confused, unable to express or grasp my conflicting feelings.

My father tried to dismiss the letter as meaningless. He called the Israeli embassy in Bonn, but didn't seem relieved after the long conversation. The embassy had informed him that all Israelis, even those abroad, were subject to military duty between the ages of seventeen and fifty. Shirking this duty was considered desertion and treated as such on arrival in Israel. This was not an altogether exact description of my legal situation, as it turned out later. I was advised to take care of my military status if I wanted to get in and out of Israel unscathed. From the perspective of the State, the draft was plausible. Israel was in a state of war; unlike the Arab countries, it had a small population and urgently needed soldiers. Israeli citizens, wherever they lived, had to fulfill their civic duty.

Serving in an army, even the Israeli army, was out of the question for me. I identified with the ideals of socialism and humanism and not for a minute did I consider putting on any uniform. I didn't feel like an Israeli and my political opinions vacillated between the pacifist and anti-nationalist ideas of the postwar period and the Zionist and nationalist notions of my Jewish education. In this, I resembled many of my Jewish contemporaries, but hardly all. In certain circles, serving in the Israeli army was considered a welcome vehicle of consolidating Jewish identity and loyalty to the community. In many young Jews, the aura of the Israeli army was like a Jewish counterpart to the Foreign Legion. At the time, for me, the arrival of the draft notice meant only that I would have to accept the procedure mentioned by the embassy if I wanted to keep open the possibility of future trips to Israel. So, from now on, I regularly applied for a deferment of my military duty, sent the same short text every year to the military authorities in Tel Aviv, and every year I received the same positive decision. That's how the army entered my life.

Though born as a citizen of the State of Israel, I had not set foot in the country since 1953. The blue passports my parents and I had used until naturalization in Germany had lain unused in a drawer since the 1950s. The statement on the first page of the Israeli passport, that I was of "Israeli nationality," corresponded to reality as little as the sentence on the first page of the West German document that "The holder of this passport is a German." Aside from the formulation, I didn't feel at ease with either of the two statements, but for very different reasons. The strange construction of German citizenship hindered my identification as a "German." It was based on an ethnic German-ness and was closed to me if only because of the Nazi past. There was no neutral citizenship identity enabling minorities and immigrants to feel they were members of the community despite their origin. I felt even less an "Israeli." The differences from the real Israelis, the citizens who lived in the country or who had grown up there, were only too clear to me. What I felt for the country often corresponded only to the loose cultural and emotional bonds linking Diaspora Jewry with Israel. That didn't require citizenship. I would have liked to substitute the clarity of a "homeland," a place, a region, or a landscape, I could connect with, for the complexity of a "nationality." But I didn't have a homeland either. My roots were in the Austro-Hungarian multinational state, Stefan Zweig's "World of Yesterday" that had vanished back in 1918; the country where I was born, Israel, was foreign to me; and the country where I lived considered me foreign. I was really at home only in the language, the only thing that encompassed my various cultural and geographical identities, but at the same time, all contradictions and conflicts, too.

After a while, the arrival of the draft notice did have an effect. Clearly, it had unwittingly influenced the emotional balance between my conflicting identities, and had given new impetus to my longing for a homeland. Even if army service was out of the question for me, for the first time I did feel a concrete relation to the land of my birth. I was curious—about the country I came from and the possibility that a homeland could be found there for me after all. Yearning for an unequivocal identity and a way out of the conflict with my German environment formed a constant impetus. Initially, it had driven me into the arms of Zionism and now it pushed me toward Israel, even though I hadn't realized it yet. I decided to spend the summer vacation with relatives in Jerusalem, whom I knew only from photos and greeting cards.

It was 1968. That summer, two photos were taken of me that foretold the split of later years and the clash of political ideas and life plans. The first photo shows me running through a Düsseldorf commercial street arm-in-arm with two classmates during a demonstration against the Vietnam War. Behind us are a poster with Ho-Chi-Min's white-bearded face and many rows of other demonstrators. In the other photo, I'm standing next to an Israeli soldier on the roof of the former Jordanian police station in Jericho, which had then been under Israeli occupation for exactly one year. The photo was taken on a visit to my cousin, who had an important function in the administration of the occupied territories and was nicknamed "King of Jericho." I'm wearing a khaki-colored uniform shirt, very unmilitary shorts, and holding an Uzi machine gun pressed to my chest.

In many respects, 1968 was a watershed for me. I looked for a relationship to the country I lived in, independent of my parents' experiences, and tried to make my own judgments about politics and history. From this moment on, I began to leave my parents' home, even if it took me more than a year to leave my parents' flat. I began to distance myself from the Jewish community, the Zionist youth group, the world of the Bukovina and Prague associations, from my Jewish friends, even from my own Judaism. I was just seventeen years old, but the circumstances of my youth urged me to grow up fast and be independent. I started to steer a different course and before me, not yet visible, were the rapids of internal conflict.

* 2 *

My Zionist education, aimed at fundamentals and history, had hardly prepared me for the real Israel and especially not for the Arabic character of the country. Landscape and architecture, sounds and smells referred to the Orient and the Arabic culture of the majority population, of Jews from Arab countries and the Arabs of Israel. Only in Tel Aviv and in other smaller towns on the sea, shaped wholly by European Jews, did I recognize a familiar atmosphere. Nevertheless, the people were still foreign to me. It was during a few days on a kibbutz, among the Pioneers of Zionism, who then still served as a model for the society, that I felt the differences most keenly. These were people who radically rejected the cultural influence of the Diaspora and Europe. They wanted to be cut from only a single block, and strove to re-invent themselves as farmers bound to their own soil in only one generation. The culturally more complex Jews abroad, "my" Jews, on the other hand, lived in a much more interesting state of cultural and social androgyny that for me represented the true "Jewish" condition.

My stay in Israel was the first long trip I had made by myself. After a short tour, I spent a month in Jerusalem and the occupied West Bank with my cousin. He lived in a neighborhood of the Jewish new city dating from the 1930s, in a flat that really was too small for him, his wife, and their three children. Even according to the Spartan but very generous standards of Israeli hospitality, there was no room for me. My cousin put me up in a monastery on the border between the western and eastern parts of the city, across from the Old City wall, not far from Jaffa Gate. My small, sparsely furnished cell offered me a cheap lodging and a marvelous view of the Old City. The Christian environment and the Christian ritual, which were just as familiar to me as the Jewish ones, the situation in No-Man's-Land, all felt pleasant and familiar and surrounded me like a protective capsule in the Israeli milieu, where I unexpectedly had to cope with feelings of loneliness and alienation. My cousin took me to the movies and theater and tried to introduce me to Israeli culture, as he understood and appreciated it. Nothing he did could have made me realize more sharply that I did not belong in this country either, and made me more disappointed. But my exploration, fortunately, did not remain limited to questions of identity. The situation in the country, one year after the conquest of East Jerusalem and the other parts of Palestine that had remained in Arab hands since 1948, was very interesting, and my cousin's position in the administration of the occupied territories opened unexpected perspectives for me.

In the last twelve months, Jerusalem had undergone enormous change. In June 1967, after nearly twenty years of isolation, the part of the city belonging to Israel, an enclave in a Palestinian-Jordanian area, connected to the heartland of Israel along the coast only through a highway corridor, had become part of the Orient again, with the conquest of the Arab part of the city and the West Bank. Residents of West Jerusalem went on expeditions to the Old City, which had been off-limits to them for two decades, to the markets and the modern East Jerusalem commercial streets. Curious groups of Arab citizens were seen wandering through the downtown area of the Jewish part. In the flats of my parents' friends and relatives strange collections were to be admired, touristy knickknacks from the Arab market next to shell casings and shrapnel brought home from the war by the husband or son. The dark carved tables, cabinets, and chairs were also new, a special kind of war trophy, picked up cheaply in the villages and monasteries of the surrounding area in the rage for antiques after reunification with the Orient. These objects looked like souvenirs from a trip abroad. Nothing indicated that a war had taken place right before your door and the enemy still lived two streets away.

My cousin had fought in all Israeli-Arab wars, had made a career in the police and other services, and now had an important role in one of the most sensitive locations of the occupied territory, the only open border crossing between Israel and an Arab state. He directed the Israeli customs post on the Israeli-Jordanian border crossing at the Allenby Bridge near Jericho. To me, my cousin seemed like a high provincial functionary from a short story by Chekhov, aware of his power, generous, and above all rules. In his company, I had access everywhere, unconditional and unlimited, like a subordinate in the entourage of a powerful person. Every day in his jeep we sped down from Jerusalem to Jericho, barriers were lifted, the guard posts pushed aside the barbed-wire entanglements or wooden trestles, straying camels got out of our way. In Jericho, my cousin occupied an imposing structure built by the British as a police fortress in the 1930s to keep an eye on the local population after the first Arab uprising against the Zionist enterprise. From 1948 to 1967, the Jordanians had used it as a police headquarters. Now it had fallen into the hands of the Israelis and now Arab residents of Jericho went in and out as petitioners. On our first trip, my cousin's driver had told me the legends circulating about my cousin. The locals apparently called him the "King of Jericho" because of his great power over the only commercial crossing between Israel, the West Bank, and the Arab countries.

My cousin did his best to play his role as occupation officer as convincingly as possible. He had to impress the local Arab merchants, to intimidate smugglers, and stop Palestinian guerillas from smuggling weapons and explosives over the Allenby Bridge into the occupied territory. But where should a Jew from Czernowitz, who had come to Israel in 1948 as a kid of twenty, have gotten models for the proper attitude, behavior fitting a representative of the occupation force? My cousin seemed to rely on his instinct. His rules were simple—to demonstrate "strength" at all times, and even in the most difficult situations, to maintain an impeccable attitude worthy of a man in his position. For the worthy attitude, there was a Zionist model presented by the founder of the Revisionist movement, Ze'ev Jabotinsky, with the term "Hadar" ("Brilliance"). This meant the radiant, proud conduct of the New Jew, the contrast to the Zionist cliché of the weak ghetto dweller, oppressed by the yoke of the Diaspora. So my cousin was shining. Demonstrating strength was more difficult and could easily lead to an overdose.

One morning, when my cousin and I were still at breakfast after the ride from Jerusalem, a few Arab dignitaries of the city requested an interview. The group of dignified old gentlemen entered and my cousin asked them to sit down in chairs at his desk. He ordered coffee for them and then turned back to his breakfast and me, as if we were still alone. Breakfast consisted of several courses. We first had a small salad of tomatoes and cucumber, cut into tiny pieces in the style of the country and sprinkled with fresh mint that grew behind the house among the rubbish. Then came scrambled eggs. And, somewhat later, a plate of fried potatoes. A breakfast of toast and jam, a soft-boiled egg, might have provided a basis for easier tasks. My cousin took his job seriously.

A good breakfast puts the day on the right track and creates an agreeable disposition. Meanwhile, the visitors were satisfied to attend our breakfast in silence. Prayer beads clicked, the small cups of black coffee clinked, and only an occasional throat-clearing pointed to future conversation. The big ceiling fan, which usually circled slowly, was turned off, and from the desk, only the rattle of fork and knife answered the sounds of the waiting men. According to local custom, the chairs the gentlemen sat on were lined up along the wall. In front of them was a low table with the cups and a tray of untouched fruit. Coffee was offered and accepted, but the fruit was apparently beyond an invisible line that could not be crossed with dignity. Time passed, my cousin was still busy with breakfast. If the visitors felt humiliated by the wait, they concealed their displeasure. Defeat demanded steadfastness, while victory allowed compromise, and so after a good half hour, my cousin left his breakfast. I was sent out of the room, and the interview could begin.

It wasn't easy to hold court in this city of muddy streets, dilapidated houses, and stinking gutters. In the north, behind the tiny commercial quarter and the mounds of ruins of biblical Jericho stretched an enormous refugee camp. Countless small clay huts lined narrow alleys and formed a checkered pattern with the trickle of sewage. The camp was half deserted and collapsed after the refugees of 1948, who had been housed here under miserable conditions, had fled once again or had been driven out in 1967, this time to the East Bank of the Jordan. The regular artillery duels over the Jordan, still held by Israel and Jordan even a year after the war ended, were often heard there. Even if the explosions were manifest only as a muted, hardly perceptible tremor of air, the population registered them precisely. Their sensitivity to the various omens of war was amazing. Once I saw the passersby around me scatter from one moment to the next and disappear into the houses, even though I myself hadn't noticed a sign of danger. Only after a while did I discover a dust cloud on the horizon. Soon after, the rattle of tanks was heard and heavy Israeli Centurion tanks crashed through the town on their way to the border.

On the small square in front of the former police station, my cousin had put up big, whitewashed stones in the dust to mark the way to the entrance, surround the flagpole, and indicate his parking place. One of his staff repainted them whenever a tire or a shoe left a black mark on the white stone, picked up litter, and kept the entrance square clean and neat. Our driver, who often sat in the open door of the car listening to the radio, kept him company, along with a soldier in the guard house at the entrance, who had to check IDs but usually read the sports pages of the paper. Even under the conditions of this impoverished, pathetic dot on the edge of the desert, an Israeli official still had to represent the State and convince the locals of the superiority of Israeli civilization.

My cousin was not a squeamish type. In the rather frequent moments of danger when there was shooting in the town or at the border, he could react coolly. Once we were standing right on the bank of the Jordan and watching traffic over the Allenby Bridge, when shots suddenly came from the Jordanian side. We ducked behind the sandbags. Only my cousin remained upright. When an assistant tried to pull him under cover by his trouser leg, he refused, concerned only to show his own people his courage and the enemy his contempt. What I observed in him didn't fit my image of the peace-loving Jew, an impression reinforced later in his house when I came face to face with his war trophies. During the battles on the Golan Heights a year before, my cousin had shot a Syrian officer. While the battle was still going on, he had climbed out of his armored vehicle, stripped the corpse, and taken the uniform. Now it hung washed and ironed in the bedroom closet where he proudly showed visitors the bullet hole. His wife later told me how much she had had to overcome to wash the bloodstained uniform. This experience pushed me to a deeper layer of my cultural identity. My cousin's attitude somehow seemed "un-Jewish." I almost heard my father say: A Jew doesn't do that! On other occasions during my stay in Israel, I also realized that my vague notions of a peace-loving, tolerant Judaism were a myth that couldn't be reconciled with the facts.

My cousin quite obviously expected that sooner or later, I would come back to Israel as an immigrant, and he began making plans. Meanwhile, my feelings about the country and the prospect of a life here began to develop in another direction. I had to recognize that I had little in common with the people here. Being with young Israeli soldiers my own age serving in Jericho every day, made me see that I would always feel foreign in this group. The political gap seemed wider than ever. The humanistic values implanted in my youth made me react very sensitively to many aspects of life in Israel. The ethos of the leftist parties and institutions that had seemed attractive to me before, seemed much less credible after a year of occupation. The adjustments I would have to make to be a real Israeli now seemed unrealistic. The years of Zionist indoctrination in the Jewish youth center as preparation for immigration to Israel seemed to have had little effect. On the contrary, after my experiences with Israelis I felt unequivocally affiliated with Diaspora Judaism.

In the last weeks of my stay, the conversations, soliloquies, impressions, and insights of the trip intensified into a melancholy mood. I had parted from Jerusalem, my cousin and his family, and had gone to a children's home in the north of the country, where I was to live and work for a week as a volunteer. The home, in a suburb of Haifa, had been built in the 1930s for the "Youth Aliyah," a branch of the Zionist movement that had brought some five thousand children to Palestine from Germany, Austria, and other countries between 1933 and 1939. The buildings and grounds of the home called "Ahava" ("Love"), which now housed children from Oriental immigrant groups, were in a dreadful condition. Money and help for renovations were urgently needed, and both were provided by a Jew from Düsseldorf, who had come through this home as a refugee child. It was because of him that I worked there as a volunteer that summer. The home was in the broad, flat Haifa Bay, amid the cotton fields of the nearby textile factory. At night, to find a little peace after the children's shouting and to enjoy the cool sea breezes, I ran aimlessly along the fence through the fields. On the very first evening, I met the night watchman of "Ahava." The man spoke a precisely cultivated and educated German, called "Weimar German" in Israel, to distinguish it from the corrupt language of the Third Reich. He came from Czernowitz. As soon as I told him my name, he exclaimed: "The son of Willi Brecher?" It turned out that he had known my father as a child. Now he began to tell glowingly about the adventures of their common youth, as if they had happened just yesterday and not sixty years ago. His reminiscences referred to the Gymnasium before and during World War I, when Czernowitz was still the capital of Austrian Bukovina.

The former classmate seemed to recall most an especially memorable characteristic of my father—that he had been an assiduous charmer and had enjoyed a corresponding reputation. It also turned out that my father had kept me in the dark about his membership in a Zionist youth group. Then my father's friend told me about his own life. He had immigrated to Palestine in the 1930s and had worked until shortly before as an official in the city administration of his town. Now he was retired. Since a government pension in Israel wasn't much, and his two grown daughters still needed financial help, he supplemented his income, like so many retirees, by working as a night watchman.

Then I had to tell about my father. As I sketched our lives in Germany, the night watchman kept interrupting me with questions and amazed exclamations. He had also heard that many Bukovina Jews had settled in Düsseldorf. How do they make out there? How do the Germans behave? I caught myself painting an especially rosy picture of the situation, because the opinion seemed to hold in Israel that Diaspora Jewry shaken by crises would soon experience its defeat and appear repentant in Zion. The night watchman sighed. Quite clearly, he would also have preferred defeat. I couldn't help comparing his situation with my father's. How would our life, my life, have looked if we had stayed in Tel Aviv in 1953? I had always admired my parents' courage at settling in Germany at that time, but at the same time I accused them of not thinking of the results. I was the one, it seemed to me, who had to suffer the consequences. Naturally, I could understand my father's desire to avoid the fate of his night watchman classmate. He had decided to emigrate for economic reasons and proved to be right. But couldn't they have chosen another country and spared me this unbearable feeling of not belonging anywhere?

Without being aware of it at the time, I had drawn a lesson from those last weeks. I was dejected. As little as I felt "at home" in Germany, Israel was no alternative. So, for the time being, there was no way out of the situation that plagued me. The first trip to the land of my birth ended with this disappointment. As I later noted, many of my Jewish contemporaries in Germany had similar experiences. Almost all who spent any time in Israel in these years came back chastened. Strong as the centrifugal forces were, the experience of alienation and antagonism in the non-Jewish world, Israel offered no solution. The special circumstances in the postwar Jewish communities in Germany had obviously created an especially resistant strain of Jewish group identity, which could not easily be converted into the identity of the "Israeli." Moreover, because of the continuing state of war and the material conditions of life, Israel could hardly be a match for the prosperity and liberalism of the West. Among the Jewish left, Israel's political development after 1967, and the anti-Israel turn taken by the New Left in Europe and America, made for an additional distance. Thus, I wasn't the only one of my leftist-Zionist friends who turned away from Zionism at that moment.

As I helped clear the grounds of "Ahava" and supervised the children splashing in the big, dirty swimming pool of the home, my mind was elsewhere—with a girl in Düsseldorf I had just met. By chance, my girlfriend and her mother had planned an eastern Mediterranean cruise that summer and were to stop in Haifa. A whole day was planned to tour the Holy Land, and so, as I took care of the children in the home, I waited impatiently for my Düsseldorf girlfriend to enter the port of Haifa for her twelve-hour tour of the country.

* 3 *

The entrance of my non-Jewish girlfriend into my life complicated everything a great deal. The two of us belonged to that small group of "politicized" youth, as it was then called, who were committed even as students to various groups and committees. So it wasn't surprising that, right at the start, we had come to talk about the historical burdens that weighed on our love. My girlfriend told me that, as a young man, her father had been an enthusiastic supporter of Nazism and still was, according to her. During the war, he had been an officer on a submarine. From this circumstance, we concluded, in his favor and ours, that he couldn't have participated in the persecution of Jews. But we didn't know that precisely. My girlfriend also reported the reaction of her mother, who—unlike her father—had been told the secret. "Child," the mother said, "consider very carefully whether you want to get involved with this young man. These people don't have an easy life and you'll have to share their heavy fate." I also had to confess to her that my parents' not always tacit hopes aimed at my finding a Jewish spouse. That made everything much more thrilling.

The new friendship aggravated my conflict, which had been brewing for some time. It drew me away from my Jewish environment even more. For a few years, my two worlds had coexisted without great friction, but now a decision was clearly in the offing. My Jewish contemporaries were also at a crossroads. Some stayed within the Jewish community or Jewish society, others submerged themselves completely in their non-Jewish world. For most of them, graduation from high school meant a change of residence or environment, and the old methods of dealing with the split were no longer effective. Many of my Jewish friends who had suffered from especially strict reservations imposed by their parents against the non-Jewish world seemed to have been waiting only for this opportunity. As soon as they left their parents' home, they changed sides and, for all intents and purposes, were lost to Judaism and Jewish society forever. Among others, for whom the borders between the internal and external worlds hadn't been drawn so clearly, a long conflict emerged.

In the year after my trip to Israel, I started commuting between the two worlds. I'd spend a few months with my girlfriend and my non-Jewish friends, would then break up with her and my non-Jewish friends and join the Jews. One or two months later, I'd make a break and a turn in the opposite direction. That was repeated a few times until my environment was fed up with it and I suffered a crisis. I withdrew and, in the next months, I spent my free afternoons, evenings, and weekends alone in my room. I stared out the window, photographed the clouds, and tried to understand myself. At least in one respect, my feelings were unequivocal. I wanted to be with my girlfriend and among my non-Jewish friends. That was the group of people I had chosen myself, who shared my interests and political tendencies. I had almost nothing in common anymore with the Jewish contemporaries I had grown up and attended Jewish youth groups with. But strong bonds of ethnic solidarity tugged me whenever I tried to get away from the Jewish group, triggering doubt and guilt.

I tried to be as clear as possible about my contradictory feelings. First, even if I didn't want to admit it, I distrusted non-Jews just as much as my Jewish contemporaries did. Could I trust the non-Jews? Wouldn't I encounter prejudice in non-Jewish society sooner or later? Behind this distrust was the fear of injury and rejection. Then came the question I felt was at the core of the conflict. I myself didn't despise German society, but what did non-Jews think of me as a Jew? Could I appropriate a German identity, assimilate into a society that had prejudices against Jews? Generations of young Jews had posed these questions, but Nazism and the Holocaust had lent them a new edge. Finally, maintaining the tribe weighed on me. Was I betraying the victims of the Holocaust if I was absorbed completely into German society? My answer to this question was no. I was willing to defend Jewish life in Diaspora at any time against threats, but maintaining the group was not a goal for me. If I derived any mission or duty from the Holocaust, it led in the opposite direction—to eliminate ethnic boundaries and prejudices. If, because of general social and cultural processes, Judaism was to disappear completely someday, it would reduce the cultural variety in the world, but nothing more.

The search for acceptance in the non-Jewish society of West Germany was an emotional risk, an uncertain venture. No wonder I was now plagued with a yearning for a place where I belonged naturally and without question. I envied my non-Jewish friends because they didn't have this need. They had no special sense of affiliation, no national pride; but in this respect, they didn't lack anything either. In postwar German society, the issues I had to deal with as a young Jew in Germany—group identity, homeland, nation—were almost completely suppressed and so my non-Jewish friends believed they had long ago gone beyond these questions. For that reason, my laments about my homelessness often encountered misunderstanding and must have lent a nationalistic tinge to my search in their eyes that it didn't have in mine. It was German identity that was closed to me because of its ethnic dimension and that triggered my search. There was the idea of "constitutional patriotism," corresponding to the concept of civic patriotism in the U.S., which was propagated by the major parties to counterbalance German nationalist traditions. But, for the time being, the idea of Germans of Bavarian, Jewish, and Turkish origin sharing a common civic identity was still utopian.

This unadmitted or suppressed dimension of "Germanness" made the search for a place in German society even more difficult. It also led to counterreactions among my Jewish friends. Many of them seemed to follow the motto: "If you insist on your ethnic identity, so will we. Anyway, we Jews can do it much better." Here the myth of the Jewish community as a separate, reclusive group, which had been saved from antiquity to the present only by an absolute will to survive, played an important role. This notion of a powerful Jewish identity fascinated both Jews and non-Jews, formed the source of double-edged compliments, and gave my ostensibly identity-weak non-Jewish friends a reason to envy me precisely for the alleged strength of my identity.

A few months later, my anguish changed to its opposite—to a feeling of superiority and power. I had repressed the confusing, conflicting emotions, at least for the time being, and withdrew to a dispassionate space of analysis and intellectual insights. Here I could not overcome my split either, but here at least it could be observed. I myself felt it as progress. I liked myself especially in the role of the critical outsider, whose position between worlds sharpens the view of the environment. Maybe my future was in this romantic pose.

An opportunity soon arose to attack the problem of the split from this new perspective. I met an Israeli journalist who had been the assistant of a German television correspondent in Israel. A German television station had assigned him to make a documentary about Jewish youth in Germany. Now he was wandering around the country aimlessly, without access to either the subject or the youth. We talked one whole afternoon and then determined that we had both found what we were looking for. He had discovered somebody who could open and interpret for him and the German television audience the hidden, conflict-laden world of Jewish youth in Germany; and I was offered the chance to slip into the role of the border-crosser, express the unspoken, and thus gain a distance from my own conflicts. The following summer, we interviewed about a dozen of my Jewish and non-Jewish friends in Düsseldorf. The subjects were the unspoken attitudes and patterns of thought that determined relations between the groups. A year later, in the summer of 1971, the result, titled *Young Jews in West Germany*, was broadcast on German Television Two.

By the time the film was shown, the subject had lost its significance for me. I no longer maintained any contact with the Jewish community or Jewish groups, had resigned from the Zionist youth movement, and seldom met with my Jewish friends. I was now a student and belonged to a leftist group. In contacts with non-Jews, I had begun to factor out my Jewish identity completely. From now on, if I had to, I spoke of my Jewish origin or extraction. "Origin" meant that my Judaism represented a completed phase of my development, comparable to what my Catholic or Protestant contemporaries had absorbed in their parents' homes, before they also became apostates. "Origin" also established the desired relationship I wanted to develop with the conflicts I was exposed to as a Jew in Germany. I wanted to understand them as anachronisms, relics of the past, still perceptible in the present and future, but which finally had to die out completely. That suited my Marxist ideas that saw a person determined not by his ethnic or cultural origin, but by his social position and his role within the means of production. The left had become my new homeland, and in its conceptual world I felt at one with my non-Jewish environment.

In school and political activity, my Jewish identity still played a role, in a form in which it was still recognizable, but less vulnerable. I was interested in Jewish history and must have been the only one in the history department of the University of Düsseldorf in those years who was eager to work on the Jewish aspects of subjects discussed in the department. I wrote papers on the history of Jews in Germany in the Middle Ages, on the history of the Jewish labor movement in Eastern Europe, and on the discussion about the minority status for Jews after World War I. My teachers let me do what I wanted, but couldn't give me much help. Prior to 1933, German colleges had formed the center of scientific interest in Judaism, and a comprehensive scientific literature on Jewish history had been collected in German libraries. Afterward, literature and archival material, along with Jewish scholars, had been thrown out of the universities and libraries. Now, the articles, monographs, and source collections I ordered through interlibrary loan came back from abroad, reinforcing my sense of being involved with an esoteric science.

Important as it was to discuss the questions of my Jewish origin with my friends, it was virtually impossible. I still felt like an apostate, doubted the soundness of the path I had chosen and didn't dare admit my distrust of the environment, either to others or to myself. So it was easy to evoke my suspicion. A chance remark about some ethnic group was enough to set me speculating silently about the speaker's possible prejudice against Jews, his real opinion of me, and the survival of Nazi philosophy. I usually blocked out these thoughts on the principle of see no evil, hear no evil, speak no evil. It was probably just as hard for my non-Jewish friends to confront my Jewish origin and their identity as "German" after the Holocaust, but I didn't really know that. We didn't talk about it. As it turned out later, a lot was seething under the surface. One thing in particular was not clear to me then: as far as my future in Germany was concerned, I was on the wrong track. The path of repression I had chosen could not stabilize my life in Germany. On the contrary, the potential of a satisfying life in this country, which had accumulated during my childhood, now dwindled.

* 4 *

The ongoing political and military conflict in the Middle East kept my interest and emotional bond with Israel alive. Like many of my Jewish contemporaries who had joined leftist groups, I fluctuated between criticism, rejection, and solidarity, an ambivalence that also reflected the confused attitudes toward Israel widespread in West Germany in those years. Until the late 1960s, the State of Israel, its policies and its position in the Middle East conflict, had enjoyed seemingly unbounded, even enthusiastic backing among the German public. The establishment of Israel was considered a welcome compensation for the Holocaust, and anyone who was pro-Israeli and pro-Jewish, even thirty years after the end of the Nazi regime, could consider himself on the right side of German history. The displacement of the Arab inhabitants that accompanied the foundation of the State was seldom mentioned in public until then.

Only when the rest of Palestine was conquered in the 1967 war did the problems neglected since the establishment of the State in 1948 come to the fore again. The conquered territories were inhabited not only by millions of Arabs who had been robbed of their country by the establishment of Israel, but also by hundreds of thousands of refugees from Israel itself who had been waiting to return since 1948. The events of June 1967 radicalized both the Arab and the Jewish sides and globalized the conflict, not only with the terrorist acts of the Palestinian organizations, the airplane hijackings and the attacks on Jewish targets abroad, but also with the appeal of Jewish and Israeli organizations to Jewish communities in the world to support and defend the State.

I sympathized with the Jews of Israel and wished for a peaceful solution to the conflict, but moved to the opposite side in most political questions. The "right of existence" of Israel as a state of the Jews, approved by most Jews, but denied by the opponent in the conflict, formed the crucial political front line. This was an ambiguous slogan used by the various sides to propagate various ideas. Arab and Palestinian organizations demanded the dissolution of the Zionist "entity," as they called Israel, and supported the creation of a "secular" democratic state, which would have been dominated by Arabs because of their number. Especially ominous was the demand that the Jewish immigrants who had settled in Israel after a certain deadline would have to leave the country. All these demands were aimed at reversing the injustice caused by Jewish colonization and turning the clock back to the situation of 1948. Jewish organizations, on the other hand, spoke of the Jews' "right to live" in Israel, but not of the rights of the others who had suffered from Jewish immigration. Israeli governments never wearied of pointing out that the Arab side intended to throw the Jews into the sea and commit "genocide." I did not think that the injustice done to the Arabs should be answered with new violence. Therefore, the State had to continue to exist and had to be able to protect its citizens. What I did not consider worthy of preservation was the Zionist dimension of the State, those formal and informal elements in the political order of the country that made Israel the "state of the Jews" and discriminated against the non-Jewish population. As I saw it, only an Israel that rejected Zionism, compensated its victims, and turned into the state of all its citizens had a moral "right to exist." Given the militarization of the conflict and the continuing acts of violence, how this goal was to be achieved I didn't know. Only justice could lead to peace, but in a far distant future. In the meantime, the bloodshed had to stop.

After the war of 1967, I remember a sudden flood of leaflets, posters, and pamphlets released by Israeli organizations and the embassy in Bonn; rallies organized for older youths and students; and quite generally an atmosphere of siege and distress, which also led to a tangible revival of nationalist feelings. Typical titles in the repertoire of propaganda brochures distributed by the Israeli government were: "Twenty Questions and Answers to the Middle East Conflict," or "Argument Aids for Discussion among Friends and Colleagues." The material was intended not only for debate with critics of Israel but also to mobilize the Jews. Jewish communities in Germany represented an especially easy prey.

Support and donations to Israel promised relief for a community plagued by identity needs and guilt feelings.

Palestinians in Germany, most of them students, were also active. Palestine committees emerged in many universities and began distributing their own propaganda. I and many of my Jewish friends read and collected journals like *Resistentia*, later *Palestinian Revolution*, published by the General Union of Palestinian Students. These groups depicted the conflict as one between capitalism and revolution, between imperialism and the liberation struggle of oppressed peoples. As I saw it, these were general arguments that distracted from a concrete context. They left out the special relationship of the West to the Jews and to Israel, which had led to the support of Israel and to denying the consequences of the Zionist enterprise. As I perceived it, they missed a chance for a direct attack on the myth of the superiority of the Jewish claim to Palestine.

The debate about Israel and Palestine was conducted all over the world. In West Germany, there was also a debate about the relationship to Israel from the historical perspective of the Holocaust and Nazism that persisted into the 1980s and was certainly unique in the Western world. In the broadest sense, it was a debate about the character and identity of postwar German society and hardly needed an external impetus. It developed out of the increasing criticism of the persistence of authoritarian traditions in the education and justice systems and, because it was set in motion by the student movement, it was seen as a conflict between the war and the postwar generations. The question that emerged through the Middle East war was: What position can a society that produced Nazism and has to answer for the Holocaust take vis-à-vis the State of Israel and the Middle East conflict, whose emergence is directly linked with German history? Did German history oblige the support of Israel or didn't it necessarily produce solidarity with the Palestinians? On one side of the debate were the advocates of an unqualified pro-Israeli position: Germans had to support the Jews unconditionally and couldn't presume to criticize Israeli policy. This position emphasized the "special relation" of Germans and Jews produced by the Holocaust, and bordered on the "Philo-Semitism" of the Adenauer era. Its racist element made it fundamentally suspect for me and many others.

The intergovernmental variant of the "special relationship" was especially welcome to Israeli governments of the time. The supply of German armaments to Israel, stipulated in the German-Israeli treaty of 1953, established this special status: war goods were to be supplied in a region of crisis to a country at war, despite the justified protests of the Arab countries. The resulting decades of political support for Israel by an abstemious West German foreign policy may not have counted for much, but the very principle of the "special relationship" represented a great advantage in the international arena. West Germany appeared as a reformed, responsible partner of its former enemies, and Israel could represent the support of the Jewish State as a moral dictate produced by the Holocaust and obligating all countries, not only West Germany.

Another debate about Israel took place on the left, from the Social Democrats to the Marxists, and involved practically all the most prominent German thinkers. As elsewhere, the discussion split the left into two camps. One side viewed Israel as a bridgehead of imperialism and called for solidarity with the Arabs disenfranchised by the Jews; the other cited the traditional connection of the left with the Jews as a minority in Europe, which had produced an important impulse for the struggle for equality and social justice. The proponents of this view emphasized the threat to Israel's existence, accepting the Israeli argument that the readiness for war of their Arab neighbors in 1967 signified an intention to commit genocide, which justified the Israeli preemptive strike of the Six-Day War. For several prominent leftists, including Herbert Marcuse and

Jean-Paul Sartre, the decisive factor was that the Jews were clearly threatened with annihilation once again. The injustice inflicted on the Arabs with the establishment of the State of Israel could not be compensated by another, greater injustice, Marcuse argued a month after the Israeli victory of 1967. That was the view I adopted, too. It enabled combining two positions that were hard to reconcile—a basic criticism of Israel and an emotional solidarity with the Jews who lived there. The tacit assumption here, too, was that the territories occupied in 1967 would remain in Israeli hands only as a temporary bargaining chip in a future peace process.

It was apparently inevitable that the debate about Israel would bring to light latent anti-Jewish stereotypes that had been strictly taboo during Germany's recovery and the economic miracle. This taboo was, after all, part of the "anachronistic structures" of postwar German society the left was attacking. Dismantling these structures meant that Jews in West Germany experienced an unexpected and unpleasant confrontation with a side of German society they would also have preferred to deny. The German press praised Israel's military might, referred to the State as the "Prussia" of the East, and to Defense Minister Moshe Dayan as "Rommel" or the "Desert Fox," thus indirectly expressing pride in Germany's great military tradition, which had been taboo after 1945. Innuendos about the power and influence of the Jews also surfaced in the criticism of Israel by the left, reminiscent of the anti-capitalistic rhetoric of the past. Once again, there was talk of "Jewish" influence, "Jewish" interests, or "Jewish" sensitivity. "The Jews," as a collective, this nationalistic and racist notion, made an unchallenged entry into the discourse of the left and at the same time legitimized the anti-Jewish arsenal of the extreme right, which had previously remained taboo. Now, when somebody spoke of a "money mafia" in reference to Jews, it was no longer clear if the speaker was from the left or the right. Phrases like "a final solution of the Palestinian question" reflected the widespread desire for exoneration and role reversal and the relief that "the Jews" were not only victims but also perpetrators.

The anti-Semitic undertones surfacing in the debate evoked among Jews in Germany a wave of rage and indignation, which swelled over the years into a flood of journalistic attacks denouncing latent anti-Semitism among the left as well as among the general German population. Until this time, Jewish organizations and individual Jews had shown restraint. The desire to keep the Jewish profile in public life as low as possible was based on the realistic assumption that there were still a great many latent prejudices in Germany and that they could be kept latent with a strategy of invisibility. Along with realism, the tendency simply to deny undesired aspects of postwar society also played a role. Thus, astonished reactions among Jews to the indisputable resurgence of anti-Jewish prejudices among Germans, said just as much about the attitude of non-Jews as that of Jews. Many Jews sought to attach as little significance as possible to this unpleasant phenomenon. There has always been anti-Semitism, this group seemed to say; as long as it vented itself only in this way, it should be tolerated. Others tried to confront the resurgent anti-Semitism by mobilizing public opinion and seeking a direct debate with those who spread such stereotypes. Confrontations in the media brought even more latent prejudices to light, which in turn triggered new protests. Anyone who was biased against Jews could find new fuel for his prejudices in public pronouncements of Jews, and anyone who distrusted non-Jews had only to read the newspaper to have his opinion reinforced. Admonishers and critics on the Jewish side clashed publicly with apologists and critics on the non-Jewish side. In this way, not only the counterforces in the fight against prejudice mobilized. The debate also made it possible once again to divide the citizens of Germany into "Germans" and "Jews."

The debate and its repercussions had a considerable influence on me, albeit indirectly. It reinforced my tendency to deny the emotional aspects of my life as a Jew in Germany and thus contributed quite a bit to my later emigration. I was one of those who initially wanted to grant the anti-Semitic undertones little significance. I assumed that the Jewish minority in Germany had to put up with a certain degree of prejudice, as long as the political reforms after 1945 had not yet been consolidated. Direct attacks or discrimination seemed unacceptable to me, too, but I wasn't willing to get excited about every stupidity in the press. I was bothered by something else. Because the debate really revolved around the nature of postwar German society and in the broadest sense around German national identity after Hitler, "Jewish" and its alleged attributes appeared in their traditional function—as an identity-generating countertype to "German." Most affected by this renewed hardening of group identity was my own Jewish postwar generation. We were caught in the middle of an integration process that was difficult in any event. Now the conviction grew among us that integration had completely failed.

* 5 *

For a long time, the thoughts and feelings of late spring and summer of 1976, which led to my far-reaching and unexpected decision to emigrate, were incomprehensible. What always remained clear in my mind's eye was the practical part of my preparations, negotiations for the job offered, consideration of the many small details of dissolving the household, packing and moving. Much as I later tried to penetrate deeper into my motives and fathom the mood of this moment, my frame of mind at the time remained closed to me for a long time. Obviously, I had acted out of hidden impulses. Not until 1982 did I again have access to the mood of those months, when the Lebanese war and my situation once again threw me into a crisis about questions of identity, affiliation, and life plans. Only here did I again pick up the thread of that self-questioning, in which I tried to understand the social and cultural significance of my Judaism and growing up in Germany.

The simple facts of my emigration are soon told. It began with a visit of an Israeli trade union delegation I had to take on a tour of the Ruhr area, as part of my work at the head office of the German Trade Union Federation. I had found a job in the trade unions when I started school, to earn my room and board for the spacious two-room flat I lived in alone and didn't want to share with anybody. Over my six years of school, the student job turned into a serious position. Now I had my own office and a vague, unwritten job description that consisted of composing reports for the trade union press service, occasionally writing a speech for a member of the executive council, or doing some odd job in the chairman's office to which I was attached.

The group of visitors from Israel consisted of young people, up and coming managers in trade union enterprises and in kibbutz industry. I put together an itinerary that included the usual elements—a meeting with German colleagues in the cooperative sector, with representatives of the Employers' Federation, a visit to a steel plant, and to a coal mine. The Histadrut delegation was not the first I had had, but for the first time I stayed with the participants even after the official occasions. Perhaps I no longer needed the distance I often felt vis-à-vis Israeli visitors, perhaps it was only because they were all very nice. I enjoyed the evening conversations and the uncomplicated get-togethers, and when we finally parted I felt a longing for the untroubled relation and the ease with which I could join the group. It had been so relaxing and I was so off guard.

The experience confused me. Shortly after the delegation left, I had a feeling I hadn't known for years: once again I felt like a stranger in my German world. The significance of this feeling of not belonging had changed. Five years earlier, my vacillating sense of identity had seemed an inevitable symptom of Jewish life in postwar Germany, and I had accepted it as part of my self. Now I had considerably less tolerance for these fluctuations, for the suddenly invading feeling of alienation was extremely painful and upsetting. Much of what I had considered evident was in doubt. Should a few weeks with Israelis or Jews have had such an effect? I panicked.

Instead of taking my time to get to the bottom of the experience, I worked myself up into a situation of excitement and confusion. I diagnosed the experience as a result of denying my natural feeling of belonging with Jews and Israelis. This was my heart talking! What miserable and difficult constructions were needed, I told myself, to be able to feel at home in Germany!

About a week after the delegation left, one of the members, with whom I had become friendly, called me. He led an adult education program in the north of Israel and was a lecturer at Haifa University. He happened to hear that there was an opening at the university, a position that had been unfilled for some time, and my qualifications were perfect for it. They were looking for somebody who could teach German history and philosophy. The position seemed tailor made for me, he added. Two days and many phone conversations later, I sent my CV to Haifa. My professional future was still open anyway. Why shouldn't I try it there? There were enough arguments to convince myself that this was the right step. My life in Germany seemed to have no solid foundation. My parents had settled here without considering the long-term consequences for me. Now I had an opportunity to correct the mistake. As I was still debating with myself, I was invited to Haifa for an interview. I took a week off and flew to Israel. Had the dormant seed of my Zionist training risen?

I know only a little of my visit to Haifa in September 1976. And this memory is also steeped in the half dark the whole episode has for me to this day. The interviews in Haifa revolved mainly around one problem: I was to teach courses in the trimester beginning in mid-October, but I could not resign my German position so fast. After brief negotiations, we found a compromise. I was allowed to begin on January 1, and in exchange I was to teach two courses the following trimester, one for the colleague who substituted for me in the first trimester. I agreed. The appointment was limited to one year. I was assured I could count on tenure after that, but limiting the teaching obligation to the period from January to June was the decisive factor for me. I could take this risk. Whatever else came from this step, I was committed only until the next summer. With this feeling, I went back to Düsseldorf.

Even now, I was unaware of the strongly emotional impulses to emigrate. They were covered by a weave of rationality that grew denser with each decision. I had to resign my position in the German Federal Trade Union—hadn't I been dissatisfied there for a long time? My flat had to be given up—wasn't it time to move out anyway? Then I had to decide what to do with my household goods. At first, I had a plan that was both simple and practical: I wanted to cross to Israel by ship in December, take my car and my bags for a six-month stay, limited by what would fit into the car. I would store the rest somewhere. As soon as I called the Italian shipping company that ran the passenger service between Venice and Haifa, and learned that there was an especially favorable rate in winter for excess luggage—one cent per kilo—I came up with a better idea. Why not take everything at the same time, all the books, furniture, household goods? I might want to stay. Transport was cheap and if I wanted to return to Düsseldorf next year, I could wait for the winter rate to send it back. Thus I covered one impulsive decision after the other with the cloak of practical reason.

My Düsseldorf friends followed my preparations with amazement and criticism. They pointed to my waning interest in

Israel and the political questions of the Middle East conflict in recent years, and demanded an explanation for my sudden change of mind. Had I become a Zionist? I had worked out a formulation for myself that avoided questions of deeper motives and influences. I was tempted by the chance to participate in building a new society, I argued. That was where traditional Zionist ideas resonated with leftist utopianism. I emphasized the idealistic aspects of the decision, rejection of a life plan centered on materialism. I spoke of commitment and challenge. My friends reacted with skepticism. They reproached me with all the obvious reservations I myself should have had, and came to the same conclusion: I was quite obviously acting in the heat of the moment. My closest friends also felt a personal rejection in my sudden decision. I did my best to reassure them, to justify myself and to reconcile all contradictions. No wonder I longed to leave.

The day I left Germany for Venice, the change was complete. I secretly assumed I would never come back and was now leaving my life in Diaspora forever. My trip had become an emigration, my emigration had become "Aliyah." The romantic hackneyed phrases of the Zionist dream filled the void of my own history. I looked forward, because I didn't want to look back anymore. For my last night in Europe, I had reserved a room in a beautiful old hotel in Venice and celebrated the departure with a good meal. On a cold, rainy December evening in 1976, I sat alone in the almost empty restaurant and had become a lonely but proud emigrant.

Only years later did I begin to understand my motives. Obviously, at that moment, my decision had given free rein to long denied feelings of not being whole and not belonging, which emerged independent of one another both in my parents' home and in the environment, and had reinforced one another. When these feelings finally broke out, I could no longer understand them and could no longer integrate them into my life. They urged me to flee. What stood in the way of understanding, then as later, was the masking of an individual experience by a similar one in the social sphere, an interplay that kept the deeper wounds concealed for the time being. My feeling of being excluded and my fears of rejection by non-Jewish society could easily be traced back to the political and historical constellations of growing up in the post-war period. In fact, in the years before my emigration, I kept denying these fears more strongly. But they were also part of those experiences of all Jewish youth at this time. The other, domestic dimension of the feeling of rejection, remained closed to me for a longer time and was opened to me only when I myself became a father. I now understood that, in the economic depression of the early 1950s, my parents had gotten into an even more difficult situation because of my unplanned birth than they were already in after years of persecution and immigration. I began remembering my parents' comments and my feeling that my birth had not been welcome, at least in those first, difficult years. Here was the deeper layer of my feeling of homelessness, which spurred me to a lifelong search for a place of safety and acceptance.

* PART 3 *

6

* EVEN A STRONG NATION IS SOMETIMES SAD *

The Holocaust and the Israeli Myth of Origin

* 1 *

My work as an historian in the Israel Defense Forces began with a trip. After a day of introduction and speeches at headquarters, I was sent to lecture at a base I didn't know, in a place I had never heard of, to a group of people I knew nothing about. I knew only the subject of the lecture. This obscurantism was not due to the constraint for secrecy nor the distrust of a newcomer, but to that overpowering combination of false assumptions and good intentions, shame, shyness, and zeal, which I displayed excessively on that first day in the army. I knew so little about the army, its procedures and conventions, that I didn't even know what questions to ask. Despite my nervous vigilance that day and the great excitement I tried painfully to hide, all I really understood of the instructions for my first official trip was the admonition to hold on to my expense receipts. That was familiar ground. The rest consisted of a torrent of acronyms I didn't understand and the names of bus stations where I would be picked up. That was enough for me for the time being.

The exact subject of the lecture had been left up to me. It was to be about anti-Semitism and the Holocaust, persecution and resistance under Nazism. Major Wechsler, my boss for the next twelve months, had sketched the circle of subjects with these five keywords and a broad circular motion of his hand alluding to the extent. I nodded, he nodded back, pleased, and we went on to discuss my other duties and tasks in the department of "Battle Heritage." Despite the extremely terse description of the subject of my lecture, Wechsler could assume that I grasped the core of the matter immediately. In Israeli public consciousness, the Holocaust, ushered in by centuries of discrimination and anti-Semitism, seemed both the culmination of Diaspora history and its turning point, leading to the establishment of the State of Israel. The details of this teleology were left up to me. Every child knew the most important components of this interpretation—the natural and irreconcilable character of the hatred of Jews; the obsequious victims, who were led like sheep to the slaughter, despite the many warnings; the few exceptions, of those who warned and those who resisted; and finally the tragic heroics of the resistance itself, which was condemned to failure from the start, but was done nevertheless to defend an even higher good than life—the faith and honor of the nation. Those were the hazy but still present outlines of the myth, cited every day in the schools, the media, and the political and historical discourse of the country, and to which Wechsler now referred me with that circular gesture.

This was a modern, nationalist myth that drew its force from both secular myths of history and from the Bible and the traditional culture of the Jewish religion. At the core of the teleological view of the Holocaust are the eternal conflict between Jews and their archenemies and the promised redemption through metahistorical forces. The Israeli writer Karl Shabbetai expressed this idea as a reaction to the Eichmann trial in his 1962 book, *As Sheep to the Slaughter*, placing the Nazis in the long chain of enemies of the Jewish people and the Warsaw Ghetto uprising in the series of resistances beginning with the revolt against the Egyptian slaveholders four thousand years before. He devoted his very popular little book, translated into many languages, to the "Jewish victims who fell in the eternal battle with Amalek." Amalek, descendant of Esau and progenitor of the Amalekites of the Negev desert, epitomizes the foe of the Jewish nation. It was the Amalekites who prevented the tribes of Israel from taking the country after the Exodus from Egypt, and Amalek who was beaten by the Israelites after long battles, but wasn't destroyed.

Shabbetai also cast Jewish resistance against the Nazi machinery of annihilation in a mythical light by placing it against the background of the tradition of martyrdom, "Kiddush Ha-Shem." In certain cases of threat to belief or the nation, this ethical principle demands choosing death as a public acknowledgment of God. Thus, acts of rebellion, flight, or obstruction aimed at saving life appear as self-referring actions, undertaken with awareness of futility, for the glory of God and the nation. Gideon Hausner, the prosecutor in the Eichmann trial, also drew on this myth when he wrote in the foreword to Shabbetai's book: "Jewish armed resistance was a genuine miracle. Where did these starving, debilitated, and humiliated people get the strength to confront the military superiority of the Nazis? It is an enigma. They formed the only resistance movement that went into battle without any hope or prospect of success." In the teleological scheme, martyrdom comes before redemption and divine intervention, and thus in the modern myth of the revival of Israel as a nation, a corresponding place is attributed to the Holocaust and Jewish resistance.

It was no accident that complex experiences were transported from the confusing scenery of political and historical reality to the clear landscape of biblical legends. The first generations of Zionists read the Bible as a national epic, it fired their imagination and their rhetoric, and they traveled throughout the land carrying the Pentateuch as a guidebook. They recognized themselves in the biblical stories—as those returning from exile, as conquerors of the promised land, and as founders of the nation.

The Bible, which emerged in another period of crisis and longing for Zion during the Persian exile in the fifth century BCE, not only provided the nineteenth- and twentieth-century reader with a dramatic and romantic history of the rise of the nation, but also lent modern ideas like the "Jewish nation" and the "ingathering of the exiles" an historical quality and the certainty of a predestined fate. But above all, it glorified the necessary means for that—taking the land, expelling the Arabs, and the accompanying militarization of the Zionist movement. Hence, the outcome of the eternal struggle with the archenemy seemed predestined: "And the Lord said unto Moses, Write this for a memorial in a book, and rehearse it in the ears of Joshua; for I will utterly put out the remembrance of Amalek from under heaven" (Exodus 17:14); "The Lord will have war with Amalek from generation to generation" (Exodus 17:16). The struggle against Amalek is on the threshold of forming the first nation; the Holocaust is on the threshold of the second. All this seemed buried deeply in the "historical memory of the Jewish people," that store of nationalistic myths from which Zionism eagerly drew. What place could an historian and his frame of reference originating in conventional historical research have in this teleological scheme?

My activity for the next twelve months was to consist mainly of writing educational material on the pre-State "battle heritage," on which the army, established in 1948, could build. This meant primarily the exploits of the precursors of the Israel Defense Forces, the Jewish militias that had operated in Palestine since World War I. Recently that had come to include the partisans, ghetto fighters, and participants in the concentration camp uprisings, whose model was to be integrated into the "battle heritage" of the Israeli army as well. Ever since Begin had come to power, "Holocaust and Heroism," as it was called officially in curricula and ceremonies, had been gaining more momentum publicly as a political and ideological point of reference, and thus the army also received appropriate directives. My most important assignment was shaping and inserting this new subject into the army's educational material. Along with this regular activity, I also had to deliver lectures. Major Wechsler compiled a list of subjects with me for which I could be requested by the units—anti-Semitism, Nazism, Holocaust, armed resistance—but immediately calmed me with the prospect that they were not taken very seriously. The units would express wishes, but ultimately I had a free hand with the lectures. His facial expression spoke an even clearer language. He grimaced as if he had just bitten a sour apple. This was apparently to let me know that this subject was tedious and I could count on his sympathy. His cavalier approach to this part of my assignment surprised me. Did Wechsler want to convey to me that, despite its great significance in Israeli public life, the Holocaust was not considered so important in the Israeli army? Did the subject itself provoke indignation or resistance? Or was the traditionally leftist education unit submitting reluctantly to new material outside its normal political and military history purview imposed by the first right-wing government under Menachem Begin?

Major Wechsler, who was promoted to lieutenant colonel shortly after, then told me a little about himself. He had begun as a professional officer in the tank corps and had ended up in the education unit after a wound ended his career as commander of a fighting unit. Now he directed the department and, whenever he had time, he wrote educational material himself. He had just completed an essay on his old corps. The pamphlet dealt with the tank battle on the Golan Heights in the first days of October 1973, that desperate, legendary defensive battle of small Israeli units against the surprise attack of five Syrian divisions. The small brochure he immediately pressed into my hand also mentioned the feats of a young lieutenant, who had single-handedly wiped out sixty enemy tanks. Wechsler pointed to this place in his work and mentioned that he knew the man well: "A blond guy, the son of Holocaust survivors."

In Hebrew, the word is not "survivor," but "rescued" or "saved," a term that emphasizes the passivity of the survivor in his own salvation. Wechsler's tone made it clear that this ostensibly casual mention of the fate of the parents in connection with the soldierly achievements of the young lieutenant was meant to contrast the activity of the child and the alleged inactivity of the parents. He thus alluded to one of the most important national myths—the transformation of the weak Diaspora Jew into the strong Israeli, the salvation and liberation of the Jewish people by Zionism. I myself was the child of parents who had just barely escaped annihilation and felt stunned by this tacit assumption about the behavior of the survivors. That notion, widespread mainly in Israel, that most Jews had behaved somehow shamefully and ignominiously during the Holocaust because they could be made into victims, indicated great ignorance and insensitivity. Here the most unpleasant side of the Israeli reception of the Holocaust became apparent to me—the division of Holocaust history into an idealized and an undesirable aspect, into glorious and inglorious, strong and weak, acceptable and unacceptable behavior of the victims.

At the end of my first day in the department of "Battle Heritage," Wechsler also talked about my origin and had asked me if I would be willing to give lectures on my own experiences as an immigrant, on life in Germany and the reasons for my "ascent." The story of immigrants motivated the troops and raised morale, and a Jew from Germany was an interesting case. So, for example, I could talk about the question of how strong anti-Semitism still was in Germany, or how much the German national character, which had produced the Holocaust, still played a role. The prospect of this premium did not excite me. After a few years in Israel, I had begun to react with irritation and aversion to the subject of Germany. The skein of ignorance and prejudice I usually faced could hardly be unraveled. Understandably, the image of Germany was still populated by Eichmanns and Hitlers. But it was complemented by several ostensibly positive associations—famous soccer players and certain German consumer goods, whose glory had also penetrated Israel. This mishmash was accompanied by speculations seeking causes of the special nature of the Germans in personality, culture, and language.

It was also unpleasant to be identified with that. Many Israelis regarded me, a "Yekke," a German Jew, as a cultural type whose qualities were not always flattering. These judgments seemed independent of the level of education. "German" meant competent, authoritarian, devoid of feeling and humor; "Israeli," on the other hand, meant sloppy but lovable. A well-known Israeli psychologist, author of books on theories of personality, once got me involved in a serious discussion of the thesis that the lack of autonomy of the German individual had to lead to the disaster of Nazism. Israelis and Jews, on the other hand, she asserted, because of their great individuality, were immune to authoritarian usurpations by the collective. Behind all these opinions and theories was the need to create an idealized self-image. This desire for differentiation by identifying generic traits in perpetrators was common to many other groups. If the crimes of Nazism could be traced back unequivocally to one genetic anomaly in the German *corpus publicum*, all others would be immune to it.

The enormous significance of the Holocaust in the self-image of the Jewish society of Israel inhered not least in its power to grant identity. It had made people with complex national and cultural identities into "Jews" again and Israel into their obviously only safe homeland. If Israel was the opposite of Auschwitz, the land of salvation, then Israel's existence as a Jewish state had to be sacrosanct and warding off Arab claims was a holy mission. The army also recognized the enormous impact of this myth. The preservation of military "morale"—the readiness for battle, discipline, and loyalty vis-à-vis superiors, army, and state—was based on cohesive, identity-granting notions prevailing in Israeli society. All these notions had to be translated into a specific ethical code that referred to the activity of the combat units and the troops as a whole. The most important component of this "fighting morale" was a positive self-image—pride of the individual, the regiment, the brigade, the branch of the service, the whole army for their own acts and the history of the state. Israel's complete lack of a national tradition and the rejection of the Diaspora made this mission of the army educational unit especially significant and explosive. What should a soldier or a citizen use to draw a positive self-image? In 1948, the army had been a violent godfather to the nation and had thus become both the source and sponsor of national pride and of the collective self-image taking shape. But, according to its own myths, Israel's origins lay to a large extent in that territory of persecution, death camps, and national disaster that in Israel looked almost like the battlefield of a lost war. How could a positive image be achieved from that? The negative aspects of the history of the Holocaust that demolished the positive self-image had to be split off. The Holocaust could thus become the model of both contemptible and exemplary Jewish qualities, the stage of national weakness and ignominy as well as the symbol of resistance and autarchy.

The army tried to educate its soldiers in the facts of the Holocaust the same way it permeated the troops with its own meager military traditions—by a process of trimming and honing the tradition into simple, edifying, or deterrent models. In the end, the recruits were to gain the same soldierly self-image from studying the Holocaust as from studying the history of the Israeli wars—that of the strong and proud Israeli who ultimately triumphs in the just struggle against superior forces. General educational goals that could have been derived from the history of the Holocaust—like tolerance, the reinforcement of democratic and humanistic attitudes, rejection of nationalism and militarism—were not considered opportune, at least not for the time being. Nor did human identification with the victims or solidarity with other persecuted minorities, basic elements of the culture of commemoration maintained in the Diaspora, fit the scheme. Not until the first and second Intifadas, when the inhuman behavior of individual soldiers in the occupied territories raised concerns, was there a change of heart. Education officers recognized that bifurcating Holocaust history could also lead to identifying with the perpetrators.

At the time I began my army service, the Holocaust happened to be the focus of a passionate public debate, not as an historical event but as a subject of the mass media and the developing culture of commemoration, caused by the recent American TV series *Holocaust*. In the U.S., to which Jewish society in Israel and the army began to refer more strongly in those years, the Holocaust also entered political discourse and the national self-image. At the first American Holocaust memorial day, introduced by law the previous year on the day it was commemorated in Israel, President Jimmy Carter had just announced the creation of a Holocaust memorial and a national Holocaust museum in Washington. Carter enumerated the reasons that made the Holocaust an event of fundamental significance for U.S. citizens, too: the foremost reason, the President noted, was that it was American troops who had liberated many of the death camps and helped expose the horrible truth of what had been done there.

This moral protection of the nation's self-image and its military came just at the right time. A few years earlier, the American army had ignominiously pulled out of an extremely controversial war. Images of American soldiers in Da Nang and My Lai and the fall of Saigon were still vivid. By linking the memory of the Holocaust with the acts of the U.S. army, Carter conjured up images of the liberation of Dachau and saving Europe from the Nazis instead of those of Vietnam. The U.S. Holocaust Museum, which opened in 1993, staged this connection impressively. Visitors were greeted at the entrance with enormous photos from 1945 showing U.S. soldiers before the mountains of corpses of the liberated camps. The fight against Nazi Germany became the universal shorthand for the "just war," and the Israeli military now appropriated the symbolic force of this struggle.

*** 2 ***

I traveled to the base in nervous speculation. My lecture had been arranged on short notice, the list of my lecture subjects had been in circulation for only a few days, so I assumed that the invitation wasn't due to my repertoire but to the cancellation of another lecturer.

At the bus stop was a vehicle with red military license plates, a small Renault, driven by a mid-level officer. The envoy of the unit who was waiting for me was a major, and introduced herself by her first name, as usual in the army. On the way, Rachel gave me information about the subject and purpose of my trip. My audience was to be a dozen participants in a course for education officers, and so were part of those several hundred, mostly female noncommissioned officers in all army units who gave courses, guided field trips and museum visits, and were responsible for all educational and informational needs of the soldiers. The lecture gave me an opportunity to learn something about their expectations and the precise context for subjects like the Holocaust or armed resistance.

The education branch of the Israeli army went back to the cadre schools of the small, ideological, and party-oriented militias of the mandate period. The Jewish militias had emerged from the two main Zionist currents, the Zionist Labor movement and the anti-socialist Zionist Revisionists, and served as a forge of the political elite. While the Zionist Left still had the trade unions and the kibbutz movement as a recruiting and ideologizing stage, the Zionist right, for all intents and purposes, had only the underground militias and the youth movement, Betar. In the Haganah (Defense), the underground army dominated by the Labor parties, as well as in the rightist nationalist militia, the Irgun Zwa'i Le'umi (National Military Organization) and its splinter group Lohamei Herut Israel (Israeli Liberation Fighters), the unit commander was both educator and political officer. Instruction in philosophy and weaponry went hand in hand, with ideological armaments often more significant in view of the rudimentary weapons. Willingness to sacrifice, complete devotion to the cause, and an unconditional will to fight were the minimum requirements for members of these cadres, which expanded with the formation of the State into bigger, socially and politically heterogeneous units.

The young women, hardly twenty years old, who showed up for my lecture were in this tradition even if they themselves clearly didn't know much about it. There were worlds of difference between these education officers of a modern army and the Zionist underground cadres. Where awareness of an explicit ideological mission and a concrete historical task once prevailed, now the individual could hardly perceive anything ideological behind the facade of military professionalism. Where various Zionist trends once competed, the education officer now carried only a single message—the defense of State and Zionism. Just as the army was considered an ideal reflection of Israeli society, so the education unit wanted to be considered an idealized reflection of the army—as kind, caring, nourishing, as the "maternal" side of an organization that was otherwise not so squeamish about the body and life of its members. By the early summer of 1948, when the first hastily recruited newcomers to the country were thrown almost unprepared into the fight against the Arab armies, that special blend of indoctrination and integration had taken shape that determines the purview of the army education unit to this day. The predecessors of these young noncommissioned officers instructed the newcomers of 1948–1949 not only in Zionist history and the political geography of the country but also in the Hebrew language and elementary civics, without which the recruits could not even have completed simple weapons training or survived the first encounter with the enemy. These nonmilitary functions still dominated the self-image of the education branch. If the Israeli army was the melting pot of the nation, the women in the education unit were the spoon that stirred it.

The presence of the women also fulfilled another function. Photos of female soldiers armed with machine guns had gone around the world in the 1950s and 1960s and contributed a great deal to the transfigured image that both Jews and non-Jews made of the new State. The pictures stood for the emancipation of woman in Israeli society and hinted at other humanist and socialist ideals ostensibly being realized by Zionism in the State of Israel. The image of the armed woman also contained a message about the nature of force used by Israel. Here armed citizens or civilians fought, temperate in their aggression and willing to show mildness and leniency toward the enemy. But above all, the image of female Israeli soldiers contradicted the idea of the weak Jew. Nothing could have expressed the break with the past any better. This image gave the State an extremely effective symbol. The image of the woman in uniform spread the Zionist argument better than a hundred brochures, but above all, it did one thing—it feminized and eroticized the image of the soldier and thus trivialized the violence that really came from the Israeli army.

While the army might have been useful as an instrument for the ideological impregnation of Jewish immigrants and their political integration into a homogeneous settler society, as an institution to fill the Zionist promise of gender equality it had to fail. Right at the creation of the army in 1948, women were removed from the battle units they had served in during the underground period, and assigned to perform traditional female functions—welfare, education, administration. Just as the equality of women in the army remained a fiction, equality in the society as a whole was also an unfulfilled promise. The reasons have to do with another goal of Zionism that contradicted the equality of women—the fastest possible growth of the Jewish population of Israel, which had to hold its own in the demographic competition with the Arabs. Only about half of the able-bodied women were conscripted. Anyone who was married or who got married during her military service was immediately released from the army and given the opportunity to comply with the national duty to reproduce.

The use of women in battle units encountered reservations, anyway. As long as women were used in typically female roles, they kept intact a counter-stereotype that was still essential for the army and male soldiers in the first decades of the State—that of the strong, bellicose man always ready to fight. Reservations about women began to diminish only with the change of the soldierly image from a fighter to a technician. But even when women did undertake functions in battle units, masculine and feminine domains still remained separate. The army was primarily a fighting organization. It had to be revolutionary only in one area—strategy and weapons techniques. Otherwise, it had to be socially conservative. Hierarchies and differences were cultivated; distinctions between front and rear, between elite and supply units, fighters and providers, between air force and infantry, typically Ashkenazi and typically Sephardi brigades, between typically male and typically female tasks were to promote the sense of cohesion and esprit de corps, and thus enhance fighting morale.

* 3 *

During the lunch break, Major Rachel, the leader of the teachers' course, began to pump me for information about my origin and private life. This fit the familiar tone of intercourse in Israel and the informal, friendly forms of intercourse of the education branch, which always amazed me. I liked the personal tone, even if I still bristled at exposing my domestic and financial arrangements to a stranger. The army was unknown and hostile terrain; I was in a bad mood and needed a conversation about ordinary things. I only hoped that nobody knew my secret—that I had fought to the bitter end against doing my military service. In Israel, the citizen did not have the right to refuse service in the army, and exceptions were made only for Orthodox Jews and Arab citizens, the non-Zionist segments of the population. Refusal was considered betrayal, and the very few recruits who took this step at the age of seventeen had to count on imprisonment, social contempt, and major disadvantages in later life. Even those who were physically unfit were stigmatized. If you didn't want to accept that, you had to emigrate. In addition, there were also a few, albeit seldom-used back doors—simulating psychological illnesses or making informal "arrangements" about non-combat service or release from service in the occupied territories. Such an arrangement had led to my assignment in the education branch.

I had gotten advice from a few older colleagues who were known for their pacifist position. These were three prominent former members of "Brit Shalom," the Peace Alliance of the

Mandate period, who still had good contacts in politics and academe. These men were not opposed to the principle of refusal to serve and were willing to help me. The director of my institute, who had an important position in the religious peace movement, also wanted to pull some strings for me. After a while, I was advised to apply to the education unit, where somebody had apparently put in a good word for me. But, as so often in the system of "protektzia" so popular in Israel, here too the outcome remained vague. Up until a few weeks before my entrance into regular military service, nobody knew if the intervention would work. So I had to decide if I wanted to use the only alternative still open—to leave the country immediately. I decided to stay. This paltry manifestation of my own will in the face of coercion now helped me disregard the feelings of humiliation and impotence of conscription and intake. I was still on guard, but began to react less hostilely to my new military environment. I had to find a way to get through the next twelve months of my regular duty without too many crises. In the past year, as a member of the academic reserve, I had finished my basic training during the semester breaks and learned that a measure of conscious and unconscious adjustment and self-denial was inevitable. My previous experiences with the army were limited to offices and training camps, to that wasteland of human relations every recruit and novice has to go through. The personal, hardly military tone of relations in the education branch now brought a refreshing change and the prospect of getting off easy.

Rachel had asked me to talk about the development of Nazi policy toward the Jews, that is, the process that began with depriving German Jews of rights in 1933 and ended with the mass murder of the European Jews by Sonderkommandos and the industrial killing in concentration camps. That was a subject that was not easy to talk about. Even a great deal of routine and the greatest possible sobriety in representing phases and turning points on the way to the Holocaust could not help depressing the audience and me, too. The education officers now listened silently to the explanations and then wandered to the dining hall in a somber mood. But recalling the past caused not only sadness. In treating this subject, a wave of rage sometimes overcame me, too, along with violent fantasies about the perpetrators and a need for revenge. I assumed others felt the same.

After the lunch break, a discussion was to take place and I waited tensely for what reactions the subject had evoked. First, a young woman stood up and said, "The recruits will laugh at us if we come again with the Holocaust." For a while now, Israeli students in both primary and secondary schools had gotten lessons in "Holocaust and Heroism," as it was officially termed, and a certain aversion to it was now obvious. Another participant reported on the obscene behavior of soldiers during the visit to Yad Vashem, the national memorial for "Holocaust and Heroism" in Jerusalem, which is part of the basic training of the army. The Holocaust was considered a matter of European Jews, she said, and left the Oriental Jews cold. "For them, Holocaust Memorial Day is an Ashkenazi holiday." This referred to a common anonymous saying. I don't know if an Israeli of Oriental Jewish origin really would have characterized Holocaust Memorial Day as a holiday of European Jews. But there was clearly a problem. Another participant in the teachers' course said that, in a discussion, a soldier of Oriental-Jewish origin had characterized the Jews of prewar Europe as a rich, morally corrupt group who were too partial to money and business to summon up enough self-respect and strength to stand up to the Nazis. The same could also be observed in Israel. The Ashkenazi upper class had become too fat and comfortable to impose their will on the Arabs. The speaker did not take offense at the anti-Semitic stereotypes she was citing. They must have seemed to her to be a close relative of the Zionist notion of Diaspora Jews. Instead, the speaker lamented the threatening ethnic split. Emphasizing the fact that the Holocaust had affected Ashkenazi Jews could undermine fighting morale. An external enemy couldn't harm Israel, she said; the nation could be defeated only through internal strife, which was why she criticized the attitude of the soldiers. She was expressing a widespread opinion: The war with the Arabs saved Israel from a civil war between the various Jewish groups or classes.

In the early 1970s, a social protest movement emerged that put the poverty of and discrimination against Oriental Jews on the agenda. In reply, the threatening image of a split, even a civil war, was projected by the European-dominated public, but it wasn't clear if that was meant as a warning to the Oriental groups or as an admission of guilt. The increasing political use of the Holocaust must have alienated Oriental Jews and looked like a diversion from their social problems. Moreover, the Holocaust as a symbol of the common identity of all Jews must have appeared to many Orientals as a demand to give up their separate cultural and religious identities and accept solidarity with the dominant Europeans. What made everything even more confusing was that the Holocaust was used politically by a European Jewish party of the right, which owed its election to the Oriental Jews and their dissatisfaction with the European Jewish establishment of the left. But in one respect, the Holocaust ethic encountered general agreement also among the vast majority of Oriental Jews, when it legitimized stronger action against the Arabs.

The ethnic conflict between European and Oriental Jews jolted the self-image of the education unit. For a long time, the education unit had derived a sense of pride and self-confidence from its social mission, the education of recruits from socially marginal groups who had had an inadequate formal education. Now this task expressed more the concern about a lack of loyalty and discipline. The focus was increasingly on protecting the army from the results of the cultural and social conflicts that had erupted in the country.

But it was hard to defend the "non-political" status the army claimed for itself. More than half the recruits now came from Oriental Jewish communities, while the European Jewish part of the population still dominated the professional army, the officer corps, and the military leadership. It was easy to understand that the Oriental Jewish protest movement of the 1970s saw the army as a pillar of the society that oppressed them. The one-sided cultural integration processes, which were also supported by the army, and the introduction of the Holocaust as a point of reference of the military self-image had to inflame ethnic conflict.

I could also have contributed an anecdote that illustrated the situation. During my basic training, I shared a tent with a man my age from Morocco who had wound up as a child in one of Israel's notorious "development towns." The government had steered the great streams of North African immigration of the 1950s to these new towns, which became a synonym for poverty and backwardness, in order to Judaize the southern part of the country and the Negev Desert. For reasons I didn't know, my fellow recruit had managed to avoid military service, an attitude that was much less offensive in his cultural milieu, and he was now with me and other somewhat older newcomers. He told me about his work and I told him about my study of the development of anti-Jewish legislation in Nazi Germany during the 1930s. On guard duty together one night, when we were very tired, he suddenly tried in vain to remember my name. We often forgot names and it was common to identify somebody by his profession or hometown, as the "baker from Kiryat Gat," for example. But how could he describe me? To general amusement, he finally found a way out. He simply called me "the Eichmann from Jerusalem."

Rachel concluded the discussion that afternoon with a sentence I was to keep hearing in the coming years in various contexts. "Even a strong nation is sometimes sad," she said, clearly to reconcile the attendees with the idea of Jewish suffering in the

Holocaust. Later, I heard this phrase more often, at the funeral of a soldier or civilian who had been killed in military actions or attacks. The optimistic basic current of Zionist culture, the rejection of the supposed tragedy of Jewish life and the trust in the solution of the establishment of the State, had to be reconciled with the portents of persistent hostility to Jews that clearly still remained and had to remain to legitimate Israel as the heir to and savior of Jewish culture. That was the paradox Zionism created in its split attitude toward Jewish history.

* 4 *

To get in the right frame of mind for my work in the department of "Battle Heritage," I took home a long list of monographs and articles about military history, the Middle East conflict, and the operations of the Israel Defense Forces, and spent the next weeks in the National Library improvising to cover the weakness of my explicitly unmilitary professional knowledge. In another respect, too, the subsequent weeks served as my introduction to military culture. At the very beginning, I was struck by the informal tone in the headquarters of the education unit in Tel Aviv. To my great surprise, when I arrived I was taken first to the commanding general who had the title of "Chief Education Officer," the designation of the entire education branch, until it was changed into a corps a few years later. The general, who was lodged in a modest cubbyhole, introduced himself by his first name, pulled up a chair for me, and offered me a cup of coffee. Then we chatted about my future work. Here, in the green barracks of the education unit, the aura of the egalitarian settler society was still present, of the kibbutzim and cooperatives, the spirit of those better times before the coming of the "others," the Oriental Jews, when the pioneers of the Zionist community of Palestine had still been by themselves. It was a time many now longed for, that world of supposed selflessness and social harmony, embodied in the legends of the briefcase, which I heard in many versions over the years with different places and protagonists. The core of the story was that a briefcase was forgotten in the morning by its owner on a bench or some other public place in the middle of town (Haifa or Tel Aviv) and was still in the same place, intact, that night.

Many officers in the education unit wore the field or B uniform of rough, wrinkled cotton. Their contempt for the A version, worn by a "jobnik" rushing to his office job, was an expression that they too—warding off the intellectual dangers of people and state—were to be considered a fighting collective, even if their fighting was limited to the hostility of Tel Aviv traffic. Here, in the education unit, the scions of the settler society set the tone, at least for the time being, and were clearly willing to accept me into their community. Of the three departments of the education unit—training, education, and entertainment—the last two were considered a refuge for intellectuals and artists, who could perform their military and reserve duty here in a relatively free atmosphere. The nostalgia that was palpable in the department was aimed at a definite tradition—socialist Zionism—and conjured up primarily the figures of the socialist Zionist Pioneers and activists. This type—farmer, educator, and soldier all in one—stood for contempt of the bourgeois lifestyle, for the renunciation of materialism, and for that strange nationalist spirituality that developed to the sounds of a harmonica or accordion and reminded me of the German *Wandervogel* youth movement and other branches of Bundist youth. Even older civilian lecturers in the army seemed to be beholden to some outer characteristics of this tradition: the beret and the open-necked white shirt, whose collar was worn over the jacket. Breeches and knee socks had died out, but the open collar worn over the jacket seemed to have found its last refuge in the education unit of the Israeli army. This yearning for the beginnings had become more intense and urgent because of the most recent political development—the historic defeat of the leftist parties in the 1977 elections.

In the past, the brigadier general in charge of the education unit had usually been close to the left wing of the Labor party, or the socialist Mapam. Like many former generals, two former colonels in the education unit had gone into politics and become well-known peace activists. Their political positions on current issues and the conciliatory attitude toward the Arabs gave the education unit the public reputation of an enclave of progressivism within the army, a reputation it didn't deserve, since here, too, political opinions on current affairs remained private. All that changed when I began my service. The new political values of the governing coalition under Menachem Begin were now palpable in the army as well, and new slogans now entered the departments of the education unit. It was still led by a general of the old guard, but his discharge was approaching and that stronghold of Labor Zionism threatened to become the bulwark of rightist Zionist Revisionism. My first assignment was already a result of this change of power. The idea seemed to come directly from a Revisionist wish-list given the education unit by the Likud party after they won the election: I was assigned to write a lesson plan on the contribution of the Revisionists to the illegal immigration of the Jews in the 1930s, which had long been neglected, and for which there was no educational material because, until now, "Battle Heritage" reflected the perception of history and the historical positions of the Zionist Left.

* 5 *

Aside from their brief participation in a national unity government in 1967, the Zionist Right had stepped out of the opposition and into a position of power for the first time, and now they clearly had old scores to settle. It was not by chance that the "Battle Heritage" received an assignment on the history of illegal immigration. During the mandate period, the issue of immigration had been a flashpoint of political debate between the Zionist groups and had been in the center of both political and military conflicts between Jews, Arabs, and the British. It led to the first split of the Zionist camp and to the establishment of an opposition, "New Zionist Organization." Here were the origins of the Revisionist movement.

The Union of Zionist Revisionists was established in 1925 in protest against the policy of the Zionist Organization under Chaim Weizmann, by his former fellow board member in the Zionist Executive, the Russian Jewish journalist Vladimir (Ze'ev) Jabotinsky. What Revisionism wanted to revise was the pragmatism that had descended on the Zionist movement with the establishment of the British Mandate for Palestine and the beginning of the actual nation building, to limit Zionist goals to what could be achieved at the moment. The liberal pragmatist Weizmann followed a strategy of small steps, the conquest of Palestine "dunam by dunam" (quarter acre by quarter acre), thus complying to a large extent with the interests of the Zionist protector, Great Britain. In 1922, London had divided the territory and removed the area across the Jordan River from Zionist construction. Because the Jewish population in Cisjordan (Palestine) at this time was only 10 percent of the total and in Transjordan (later the kingdom of Jordan) there were no Jews at all, the Zionist Organization accepted this division. The Revisionists, on the other hand, insisted on maintaining the Zionist claim to the entire area. The slogan of the movement, referring to the territorial claims to both the right and left banks of the Jordan, thus became: "On both banks!"

Jabotinsky's predilection for Italian Fascism, his friendship with Mussolini, and his negotiations with the Ukrainian nationalist Petlura and the Polish nationalist Beck, made him anathema to his Zionist opponents as an anti-democrat and a fascist. The polished style of his articles and the brilliant rhetoric of his speeches were widely admired. The Jews of Eastern Europe, among whom he traveled nonstop to recruit for his party and paramilitary organization, still remembered his appearances years later. Even my father, who had seen him in the early 1920s in Vienna, still heard Jabotinsky's voice ringing in his ears more than four decades later. Above all, Jabotinsky was the kind of nationalist produced by the movements of "national re-awakening" in Eastern and Southern Europe, a national revolutionary for whom issues of Liberté and Égalité, political freedom and social equality, were in second place, and Fraternité, brotherhood, came last. Thus, his policy and that of the Zionist Labor movement differed not only in the aims but also in the methods allowed to realize national goals, and mainly in the methods in relations with the Arabs.

From the start of the Zionist-motivated immigration at the end of the nineteenth century, relations between the small Jewish community of Palestine and the Arab majority had worsened. With the British defeat of the Turkish rulers of Palestine in 1918, they took a catastrophic turn. At the urging of London, which had adopted the goals of Zionism for its own policy in 1917, the League of Nations in 1922 mandated Great Britain to establish a Jewish national homeland, but set limits to the number of immigrants. The key to that was placed in the hands of the Arabs: "The administration of Palestine, while ensuring that the rights and position of other sections of the population are not prejudiced, shall facilitate Jewish immigration under suitable conditions," stated the crucial passage in the League of Nations resolution. Thus, the most urgent goal of Zionism in those days, the largest possible immigration of Jews to Palestine, was at least indirectly contingent on the agreement of the Arabs. In violent protests in 1920 and 1921, they had announced their fundamental opposition to the pro-Zionist Mandate and the European immigrants.

A committee of inquiry on the anti-Zionist riots of 1920–1921 established by the Mandate government summarized the problem thus: "The fundamental cause of the Jaffa riots and the subsequent acts of violence was a feeling among the Arabs of discontent with, and hostility to, the Jews, due to political and economic causes, and connected with Jewish immigration, and with their conception of Zionist policy as derived from Jewish exponents." The Zionist Labor movement wanted to stem this fundamental conflict—that put the entire Zionist enterprise in question—through dialogue and compromise, or at least to declare their willingness to do so. However, it never came to a dialogue with the Arabs and the only partner for dialogue and compromise were the British. Jabotinsky did not believe in the possibility of a compromise. In 1923, he stated that the Arabs quite obviously "will resist alien settlers as long as . . . there remains a solitary spark of hope that they will be able to prevent the transformation of 'Palestine' into the 'Land of Israel' . . . Zionist colonization, even the most restricted, must either be terminated or carried out in defiance of the will of the native population."

"In defiance of the will of the native population," was the motto of Revisionist strategy that from now on informed its attitude toward immigration. As Great Britain curbed the immigration of the Jews because of the Arab protests and introduced a system of a quarterly setting of visa quotas, the stage was set for the conflict with Great Britain and a clash between the Zionist parties. Allocating "immigrant certificates" was determined by a complex formula of the country's absorptive capacity in both political and economic terms. As long as the number of certificates and the number of voluntary immigrants remained relatively small, each of the Zionist parties tried to bring its own supporters to reinforce its own groups and institutions in the country. The Zionist self-administration organs of Palestine, dominated by the Labor parties, negotiated every three months with the Mandate authorities about the number and categories of certificates, and at the same time used all legal and illegal avenues of the system to bring in as many immigrants as possible over the quotas, while trying to limit their conflict with London. Jabotinsky and his supporters, on the other hand, were not afraid to provoke the Mandate power. They rejected the quota system on principle, condemned British policy as anti-Zionist, demanded an immediate mass immigration and a rapid establishment of a Jewish state, and openly established a militia to take over the military defense of the Jewish settlements from the British.

In the fourteen years from 1919 to 1932, altogether 130,000 legal and illegal Jewish immigrants came to Palestine. The annual quota vacillated strongly for political reasons, but also because of the lack of jobs and the chronic economic depressions in the country. With the Nazi rise to power in 1933, pressure began mounting. In the next six years, 235,000 Jews, including 65,000 illegals, flowed into Palestine, which severely aggravated the conflict with the Arabs and the British. Despite the quota system, the Jewish population from 1918 to 1939, when the outbreak of World War II put an end to immigration for all intents and purposes, had increased tenfold—from barely 60,000 to 600,000. The portion of Jews in the population of Palestine had risen from under 10 percent to just 30 percent.

All participants in the settlement and creation of a Jewish "Homeland," both British and Zionists, saw the local Arabs as hardly more than an obstacle that deserved attention only when it turned out to be really troublesome. This was true of almost all Zionist currents of the time, both left and right. In the eyes of all Zionists, even the most progressive, the Jewish settlement of Palestine stood for the beginning of the inevitable process of modernization of a backward province on the margins of Europe and the superimposition of European economic and social structures on those of the Arabs. Most Jews in Palestine were as convinced of this civilizing mission as other colonists in other places. Zionists and their Western sponsors regarded Arab resistance as directed against the current of time and history. Jabotinsky, who considered the resistance of the Arabs against the civilizing gift of Zionism as "natural" and inevitable, saw violence as the only means left. The Revisionist banner said it clearly: Against the background of a silhouette of the "Land of Israel," which included both banks of the Jordan, was a raised arm holding up a weapon. The motto read: "Only thus!"

* 6 *

I was keenly interested in my assignment from Wechsler. I finally had a chance to deal with an historical subject whose consequences for the future had always concerned me. I got busy on the historical literature and the few extant official documents of the Mandate period, but was quickly disillusioned. It turned out that I could not expect quick and reliable answers to my questions. Most previous descriptions of Palestine and the pre-state history of Israel had either a propagandist, party political, or autobiographical strain, or both. The archives were not yet accessible and historical research on the history of the emergence of the State had not yet begun. What had appeared so far was still shaped by the sharp debate between Arabs, Jews, and British and the bitter war of 1948 that had indeed led to the Jewish State, but also to the destruction of Arab Palestine and the slim hopes for a peaceful settlement of the basic conflict. Up to now, the propagandists and mystifiers had had the field to themselves. So many products of Jewish authors reported to the world the amazing events of a state in the making in a breathless, melodramatic tone more suited to a magic show. The victory of Zionism was unparalleled and nobody wanted even to imagine the political consequences for both sides of the Arab loss.

The illegal immigration of both left and right was organized and carried out in secret, and aside from the memoirs of the participants, the first phase, from 1932 to 1939, had left hardly any written traces. Everything that had been uncovered by the British administration, by police and army, could be roughly reconstructed. The rest was primarily legends. But many of those who had participated in organizing the illegal immigration were still alive. An army assignment opened doors to me everywhere and I now used that. In ways that apparently had to remain just as secret, I got names and phone numbers from activists in the party and the Revisionist youth organization "Betar," who had been involved in the illegal efforts of the 1930s. Thus I came to Moshe Galili, who, in his youth, had been one of the first organizers of the Revisionist underground. As soon as I sat down at his kitchen table with my tape recorder, he declared: "There was no 'illegal' immigration. How could the return of a Jew to his original homeland be illegal?" He claimed that he had started up the organization of the illegal immigration in 1936, after a few years of standstill, all by himself. His story unexpectedly took me back to the period of youth groups, hunting knives, and campfires.

In the early 1930s, Galili went from Palestine to school in Italy. Since 1929, he had been a member of Betar and had been committed to party work even before. In Italy, he was influenced by Fascism, as he spoke for my tape recorder: "I envied my Italian friends. They had a fatherland and a flag. We had nothing. For us there was only one solution: to create a Jewish majority in Palestine as fast as possible, no matter how." Like Jabotinsky, Galili admired Il Duce. If Palestine was to be the fatherland, Fascist Italy was the motherland of the Revisionists in many respects. Here, the party held its congresses and here Jewish youth of Palestine and Poland were trained for Jabotinsky's "Jewish Legion." In November 1934, more than 130 Betar members were admitted for training in the notorious "Scuola marittima" of the Fascist Black Shirts in Civitavecchia, and Mussolini himself appeared at their graduation in 1936. They all came from East or Central Europe. Italian Jews were hardly interested in Zionism at all. Similar Revisionist training centers also existed in Poland, where over 250,000 members of Zionist youth organizations waited for emigration, including some 10,000 in agricultural or paramilitary training camps, the "Hakhsharot."

Galili's story was like an adventure. During a trip to Paris in the summer of 1936, he came upon a group of Jewish youth from Poland who did not want to return to their original homeland, but could not settle in France either. Some were drawn into the Spanish Civil War, "in order to have something to do," as Galili described their aimlessness. Such young men must have seemed useful to him. He appealed to the French Jewish aid organization, which was taking care of the youth to establish a training camp for them with the means now "squandered" for their support in Paris, and to send them to Palestine at an opportune time. But the plan failed. On the way back, in Vienna, he met Wolfgang von Weisel, the treasurer and Eastern European emissary of the Revisionist "New Zionist Organization," and proposed a plan to him: instead of smuggling Jewish youth into Palestine individually and circuitously, he wanted to try the direct illegal transfer by ship.

The idea wasn't new. In 1934, a Polish Zionist youth organization had brought 350 immigrants to the coast of Palestine for the first time and had smuggled them into the country unnoticed with the help of the Haganah. Betar, whose supporters were waiting impatiently for emigration in Eastern Europe, organized its own ship, which landed 117 youths on the Tel Aviv coast a month later. The third attempt failed. When the first ship, the Vellos, returned in September 1934 with a second load of 350 immigrants, the landing was interrupted by a British battleship. Fifty passengers reached the coast, the rest remained on board. The Vellos, christened a "ghost ship" by the press, wandered from port to port with 300 passengers for ten weeks and finally had to take the immigrants back to their starting point.

The fate of the Vellos shocked the Jewish society of Palestine. The Jewish leadership, confronted by the resolve of a world power like Great Britain, backed down and prevented all further attempts to smuggle people into Palestine by ship. In late 1934, given the persecution of Jews in Germany, London began to loosen the limitation of visas and promised to raise the quota to 42,000. A few hundred illegals now seemed insignificant to the Jewish leadership under David Ben Gurion and not worth a fight with Great Britain. The Revisionists saw things completely differently. They anyhow rejected British policy and a possible division of the country, an idea first discussed at the time, and felt that they had always been discriminated against in the distribution of certificates. After the split of the Zionist Organization in 1935, the Revisionists were hardly able to fill the ranks of their Palestinian party cadres. Consideration of either London or the Arabs of the country, was not a profitable strategy for them.

In 1935, immigration reached the highest level of the Mandate period: in that year, more than 66,000 Jews came into the country. This flood of immigration led to a third wave of Arab protests and violence, lasting until 1939. The British government again reacted by appointing a committee of inquiry, which in turn indicated the wish for independence among the Arabs of Palestine and their total rejection of the Zionist enterprise and immigration. The committee recommended dividing the country and in the meantime, an annual quota of 12,000 immigrants as a politically feasible maximum. As a result, in 1937 immigration was limited again for the first time and sank to 10,000. Another consequence of the so-called "Arab Revolt" of 1936 was a closer cooperation between British security organs and the Haganah, the underground Zionist army controlled by the Labor movement. In a reciprocal agreement, Haganah members could be recruited as special constables in the British police. For the British, this meant saving staff: the Jews could protect their settlements and establishments from the Arabs by themselves. For the Haganah, the cooperation brought the welcome opportunity to subject their volunteers to a military training in broad daylight, in the likely event that the Zionist dream would be realized only with the help of the military. For the Revisionists, who had meanwhile established their own militia in Palestine, the Irgun Zwa'i Le'umi, this cooperation meant another setback in the internal Zionist struggle.

Thus, somebody like Galili came just in time. Wolfgang von Weisel checked on him and when it turned out that the young man was not a British spy, he came right to the point. If Galili was to organize the illegal immigration, who was to be smuggled into the country and who was to finance it? Galili got a payment of 300 Austrian Schillings and was sent to find suitable candidates for the first transport, while emissaries of Vienna started collecting money in East European community organizations. As for the candidates, the local Revisionist party echelons set conditions. Only Austrian passport holders could participate in the first attempt since, if things went wrong, they could go back home. After almost a year, Galili assembled fourteen young people, most of them still underage. To avoid raising suspicion, the youths were sent individually to Piraeus. There they boarded a decrepit fifty-ton coastal motor ship, which Galili had bought cheaply on condition that it would be returned gratis to the captain and crew after the successful end of the mission. The rest of the story, which Galili told in the tone of a Zionist heroic epic, could have been the script of a slapstick comedy.

In March 1937, the trip began in stormy weather along the coasts and the Greek islands. After a stop in Cyprus, the group undertook a first attempt to land on the coast of Palestine. The advance ceased because of high seas, and the ship had to return to the open sea. A storm of several days finally forced the group to an unplanned maneuver—the ship sought refuge in the port of Haifa, where it weighed anchor surrounded by British patrol boats. When the British demanded information, the storm was claimed as an excuse: the boat was in distress and would put to sea again after the weather improved. But how were the passengers to get to land? After a three-week trip, they were a hundred meters from their destination, but this short distance seemed unbridgeable.

They needed outside help. Galili had a letter of recommendation from the Vienna Revisionists to party members in Palestine, but he didn't know anybody in Haifa. As the only one on the ship with a Palestinian passport, he rowed at night to the tip of the jetty and slipped into the city. After straying through the night streets, he reached a Revisionist sick fund clinic where he finally found a familiar face, a nurse, who immediately summoned the local Irgun Zwa'i Le'umi representative. A few rowboats were organized for the next night and a stone with news of the plan was tossed to the group remaining on the ship. The next evening, a party member, who was an engineer at the Haifa Electric Plant, switched off the current in the harbor; the illegal immigrants climbed into the boats in total darkness and came to the country undiscovered. Then it was celebrated. "I still had some money in my pocket and invited them to eat sausage," Galili told me. "That was then the style in Palestine."

The successful landing of the illegals was the beginning of the Revisionist "convoys," as they were called in a dramatic exaggeration. With the help of the Irgun and Betar, Galili set up a better organized enterprise, which subsequently landed five more ships with Betar members successfully on the coast of Palestine. The left-oriented youth organization, "He-Halutz," organizer of the Vellos, thereupon resumed their smuggling operations, too.

With the events of 1938—the annexation of Austria and Czechoslovakia, the Evian Conference, and Kristallnacht—the illegal immigration reached a new stage. In view of the now apparent massive expulsion of the Jews by Nazi Germany and the political change of heart of the British concerning immigration quotas, the Labor party also gave up its resistance to illegal immigration and entrusted its underground militia, Haganah, to implement it. The Haganah created the "Mossad le Aliyah Bet," the Organization for Illegal Immigration, in Tel Aviv, opened offices in Paris and Geneva, and replaced the arbitrary and unplanned activity of its predecessors with a tight network all over Europe. The demographic composition of the illegal immigrants also changed. In place of young Eastern European party activists who had been smuggled into the country to reinforce their own units and paramilitary organizations, came refugee families. Now, as in the past, candidates were selected according to criteria like health and fitness, but the catastrophe overtaking the Jews left less and less room for that as well.

After the outbreak of war in 1939, only a few ships succeeded in landing their passengers undiscovered. Most were captured and the immigrants interned for the duration of the war in British camps, often far from Palestine. More than a thousand illegals were killed in these and similar campaigns. After the war ended, the Mossad, with financial support from American Jewish federations, began the more comprehensive transport through land and sea of survivors, refugees and DPs from parts of Europe formerly occupied by German troops. These were spectacular campaigns increasingly aimed at world opinion, which were later glorified in books and films and determined the image of the illegal immigration in the world. Only with the declaration of the State on May 15, 1948, did the status of the ship transports change from "illegal" to "legal." Of the roughly 115,000 people who had come to the country illegally since the time of the Vellos, according to the statistics of the Jewish Agency, Haganah and Mossad later claimed 105,000, the Irgun 24,000—irreconcilable numbers hinting at the continuation of their political rivalry into historical research.

* 7 *

Other activists of the 1930s also gave me interviews. Most had taken part in the rear of the Revisionist "struggle for immigration" and described political, organizational, or financial aspects of the illegal campaigns. Their descriptions roughly followed the myth of origin of the State and the Revisionist version of history of the struggle on three fronts—against the anti-Zionist British, the anti-Jewish Arabs, and the soft Zionists of the Ben Gurion type. Moshe Galili's story was the only one that dealt with a concrete campaign told from the perspective of the main character and had a little drama, fitting the scheme of the materials published by the "Battle Heritage." Measured by the high standard of the Zionist heroic epic, Galili's campaign seemed hardly spectacular or extraordinary. But within the Revisionist universe, it had now assumed the character of a path-breaking pioneer feat. Aside from the involvement of the Irgun in landing the illegals, his story had no military elements, but Galili was the typical idealistic volunteer, whose spirit of sacrifice, enterprise, and strength of will could serve as a model for youth, even where the goals were not so sublime or clear. His tale also illustrated another aspect of Zionist teleology—the way from a "crazy idea" to its realization, the triumph of the will over power and reason. Theodor Herzl had already caught this myth in his slogans "Where there's a will, there's a way" and "If you will it, it is no dream," thus elevating the incongruity and incoherence of Zionism to a virtue. All those were tones that had resonated in more than one national movement, but in the ears of a Zionist they sounded as fresh and new as many others in this act of the fairytale-like resurrection of a nation.

My assignment was to write a "workbook" about the contribution of the Revisionists to the illegal immigration, and I made Moshe Galili's narrative the core of the text. He had told his story to me as an isolated dramatic event, and thus his tale took on the special force of a saga or legend. As an historian, on the other hand, my assignment was to show the contexts, to explain and analyze them. But how was I to describe the problem of the immigration and the positions of the British, Jewish, and Arab sides? It was not hard to describe the details, the circumstances, method and scope of immigration during the Mandate period. I drew diagrams and selected tables. But what was I to write about the internal Zionist debates and the policy of the Revisionists? What position should I take with regard to the political and ideological aspects of the subject, and how could I control the subsequent use of my description? What latitude did I have within the boundaries of the army education unit?

The illegal immigration occupied an important place in the myth of origin of the State. Its legendary episodes emphasized the idealism and devotion of the Pioneers, glossed over the methods of the Zionist agencies and parties that began radicalizing and militarizing around this issue, and distracted from all important political issues. Narratives like Galili's trivialize the colonization forced on the locals. As I saw it, the stories and materials I had collected testified to the ruthless pursuit of Jewish immigration and to the unscrupulous and disastrously naïve attitude toward the Arab inhabitants of Palestine. But how was I to express my judgment?

As an historian I had to approach the subject of immigration independently and objectively, but the prevailing view among the Jews of Israel was extremely one-sided. If I wanted to contribute to a more objective view of history and to a better understanding of Israel's origin, my text had to be a corrective. In the Zionist camp, there had also been those who sought other solutions and were willing to limit strongly or even stop Jewish immigration for a peaceful coexistence of Jews and Arabs. In the 1920s, under the slogan of "bi-nationalism," these Zionists propagated an alternative to the violent suppression of the Arab resistance and for a few years promoted their ideas in "Brit Shalom" (Peace Alliance) among the Jews and Arabs of Palestine, but with very little success. This political trend of the Mandate period was now known only among historians and I decided to include some of their contemporary statements in my text. In terms of the minimal importance of Brit Shalom in the politics of the Mandate period, mentioning their immigration policy in the few pages I had for this aspect was extremely exaggerated. But, by referring to this alternative, I could incorporate the Revisionist position into a broader political and moral spectrum of the time and comment more subtly. So I defined my assignment as that of a generous supplier who supplied more than was ordered, and hoped that a few education officers and their students would draw their own conclusions about it. It suited my purpose that the Zionist mainstreams had argued passionately about the issue of immigration in the past and were still concerned with the historical interpretations. In this pluralistic scheme, perhaps there was also room for another point of view. It was my first work for the Battle Heritage, and I was not at all sure that even a single sentence of my text would remain intact.

Wechsler had agreed with my concept even before I drafted it and received the manuscript without comment. He liked to call people with whom he was in constant communication "Jew" or "Yid," a habit from Yiddish culture of Eastern Europe that reminded me of the custom of American blacks to take the sting out of the discriminating "nigger" by using it themselves. Now he said only: "This Jew here has brought us something." He thus appealed to my tribal loyalty, which now certainly seemed dubious to him, and to my guilt that did in fact plague me. I was already working on a new assignment when I was finally called to Tel Aviv for a discussion about the workbook. To my great satisfaction, the anonymous editors had hardly changed my text. Only the passages about the spectrum of political opinion of the time were abridged except for the description of the Zionist mainstreams, but my exaggeratedly nonpartisan summary of Arab attitudes toward the pro-Zionist Mandate and Jewish immigration, on the other hand, was unchanged. That is where I had expected the most objections. I indicated that I had granted so much space to the political debates of the time in order to reconstruct the consciousness and horizon of decisions of the 1930s and thus to make the illegal immigration comprehensible in its time. That was, naturally, an academic argument. The concept of the Battle Heritage consisted precisely of the subjective and arbitrary linking of the past with the present, but I didn't want to let my text be cut without any resistance. I asked for a postponement and prepared a second version, making the cuts myself, without changing the content. The next meeting, at which my second version and the first almost identical reworking by the anonymous editor were on the table, brought nothing new. Wechsler listened politely to my protests, but it was clear to both of us that the first editing was the last word and was a really acceptable compromise for both sides. I had to give in. This was the army and not a civilian environment.

Nevertheless, I was still uneasy. I had gone into the education unit to avoid armed service and an assignment in the occupied territories. Now I was cooperating in the indoctrination of the troops, reinforcing fighting morale by distributing Zionist myths of history. Wasn't the difference only subjective? In conversations preceding my decision to submit to military service, one of my wife's relatives had confronted me with the argument that it was precisely somebody like me who should serve in the occupied territories. He was an architect in Jerusalem and served a month every year as a reserve officer in a paratrooper unit in the occupied territories. Everybody knew his critical attitude toward the occupation, security controls, and searches, the violation of human rights and the daily suppression of all civil rights for which his brigade was responsible. "How can you do it?" I asked him. "Isn't it better for somebody like me to lead a mission that might lead to friction with the civilian population?" was his reply. "It's precisely in these positions that you'd like to have an officer who respects the 'purity of arms,'" he said, referring to the still unwritten, vague code for the use of firearms that distinguishes between good and bad, permissible and impermissible force. So he went along only to prevent worse things, as they would say in another context. Was that an excuse for his participation in politically and morally questionable acts he didn't want to oppose openly? Or had his presence really prevented infringements? There might be Arab civilians in the occupied territories who owed their life or their health to the fact that he—and not some other officer—had led a certain action.

I didn't kid myself. Even if I could have done more good in the occupied territories, I preferred to serve in the education unit. During the various stages of my military training, I had seen enough of that—the daily misery of the population in the occupied territories, the coarse manners of the occupation troops, the mutual hatred, the dangers, the stress. I was not in the education unit to prevent worse things, but for my own peace of mind. But what applied to my relative also applied to me. The political and moral questions were everywhere and every day I had to find another concrete answer.

* 8 *

In the following months, I continued working on the history of the underground militias. I taped more history interviews and wrote educational material about the beginnings of the Mossad prior to the establishment of the State in 1948. Only then did I get to my real assignment, describing the armed resistance against the "Final Solution of the Jewish Problem." As in the first project, this enterprise was also announced in a directive from Jerusalem. I was summoned to a discussion and told of the government plans for the fortieth anniversary of the Warsaw Ghetto uprising, on April 19, 1943. The Israeli cabinet, led by Menachem Begin, had decided to use the milestone anniversary to pay tribute and present to the world the "Jewish struggle against the Nazis," as it was put. This time, the government wanted to honor not only the former partisans and ghetto fighters among the Israelis, as had been usual since 1967, but also the Jewish citizens of other states, veterans of the Allied armies who had fought against the Wehrmacht. From now on, their military service was also to be counted as the "Jewish struggle against the Nazis." According to the directive, the government wanted to integrate the Jewish soldiers of the Allied armies into a total view of the Jewish "war effort" and to show the world the considerable scope of this effort. Thus calculated, a few thousand partisans, ghetto fighters, and resisters were joined by some 1.4 million Jewish soldiers in the Allied armies, more than half of whom came from areas where the genocide was carried out. Thus, went the reasoning, it was legitimate to consider their participation in the war as a direct contribution to the Jewish struggle against the Final Solution. In this way, almost a million people would have been involved in the "Jewish struggle against the Nazis."

For the anniversary itself, a parade at the Wailing Wall in Jerusalem was planned. The government would invite Jewish veterans from all over the world to the capital, where they were to receive the medal of "Fighter against the Nazis" in a military ceremony broadcast live on television. The medal would be pinned on them by Prime Minister Menachem Begin in person. The education unit now received instructions to prepare fitting events and publications to pay tribute to the medal and the anniversary within the army.

I was speechless. This total perspective of the "Jewish struggle against the Nazis" was pure fiction and so was the attempt to make Allied soldiers who could be identified as Jews, regardless of the motive and area of their war service, retrospective participants in a mythical "struggle of the Jews" against the Nazis, a struggle visible only from a Zionist perspective. The government thus usurped the Jewish origin of the soldiers and "Zionized" their motives. Granting an Israeli army medal to foreign veterans was to equate the "just war" against Nazi Germany with Israel's campaigns and the Israeli army. The army entered the tradition of the morally unambiguous fight against unquestioned evil and claimed for itself the position of the partisans and resistance fighters, who fought a superior enemy. But Israel was occupied neither by German nor by Arab troops, and the situation of 1943 was not that of 1981. After the peace treaty with Egypt (in 1978), a conventional war with the armies of the Arab neighbors became unlikely and the external threat to Israel had diminished significantly. What remained was the core of the Middle East conflict, the dispute with the Arabs of Palestine over territory and sovereignty. It seemed to me almost as if Israel wanted to wrap itself in the mantle of the resistance fighters and partisans quickly before somebody on the Palestinian side came up with the idea of comparing their own much more similar situation to it.

Other implications of the thesis of the pan-Jewish struggle against the Nazis annoyed me just as much. Here the mythic view of Jewish history as a single nation, going back to historians like

Graetz and Dubnow, went too far. If the Jewish nation had been at war with Nazi Germany and the Jewish legions had been formed of individual Jewish soldiers in the Allied armies, what role was assigned to the victims of the genocide? Were they the civilian victims of a German-Jewish war? This was once again an attempt to change the "defeat" and shame of the Holocaust into a victory. Who was waiting for proof of a comprehensive "Jewish war effort"? The whole thing reminded me of the "Jew census" in the German military during World War I, which helped to refute anti-Semitic charges of Jewish cowardice and disloyalty during the war. Were Jews now to be counted for the same reasons? Only this time, the issue was not a proof of loyalty for the German homeland but for the Jewish fatherland.

I was assigned to prepare two publications. The first was a historical survey of the *Armed Resistance of the Jews During the Holocaust* and a bibliography the education officers could use as a basis for educational, informational, and memorial events in the units. The second was an anthology of reports and memoirs of Jewish fighters. The anthology had to draw as wide a perspective as possible and deal with the campaigns of the Allied armies as well as feats of the resistance and "underground" in the West and the partisans and ghetto fighters in the East. It was to be published by the Israeli army publishing house. I had to select the reports, provide them with an introduction and commentary, and produce a general survey with maps and tables. This historical collection was to illustrate for the readers the scope and intensity of the worldwide Jewish struggle against the Nazis. The deadline for the manuscript was the end of the year. That was the army; this was an order to change history.

I had so many objections that at first I kept my mouth shut. Above all, I felt the nationalistic perspective of the two volumes was extremely problematic. The survey was to include all areas where Jews had participated in the resistance. The criterion was the Jewish origin of the resister. Naturally, I could investigate if and under what circumstances Jews in various countries joined individual resistance organizations or had formed specific fighting units, but that was not the issue. The perspective to be created here was that of a mythical historical space to accommodate both the Holocaust and the current struggle against the foes of the Jewish nation. Would it not have been much more sensible to limit ourselves to publishing a few examples of "Jewish resistance," that is, to organizations and activities that had emerged among Jews, and were directed at the special situation of Jews under the rule of the Nazis and their allies? The same was true of the collection. How could I reduce the war experience of a Jewish conscript in the British army to a common denominator with the memoirs of a concentration camp inmate who had taken part in a revolt? Aside from these misgivings about content, I was also horrified by the large scope of the work. I had seven months to come up with the manuscripts, by the end of the year, when my year of duty ran out and I would be a reservist again. Until that time, the army did have unlimited access to my labor and could use me twenty-four hours a day, seven days a week, but the assignment was not kitchen duty. How much archival material or literature could I process in a day, how many pages could I write?

I waited for an opportunity to do a few laps around the barracks with Wechsler. I wanted to discuss the matter first with him, to explore in private how much latitude I still had before I decided on a strategy. At a cigarette break, I pulled him outside. He seemed just as bewildered by the issue and listened attentively to my objections. But in the end, he only passed on the orders of his superiors and finally summarized his position thus: "I don't understand enough about these things." He told me that in this project, an "advisor" would back me up, one Ephraim Weichselfisch, a member of the central committee of the ruling Likud party and an acting member of the board of Yad Vashem. Weichselfisch, a veteran of the Red Army and a leading member of the World Federation of Jewish Fighters, Partisans, and Camp Inmates, would write a foreword for the anthology and contribute his own story. I was to meet with him as soon as possible. Wechsler hinted that only after this meeting would we know whether the assignment could still be changed. From Wechsler's behavior, I concluded that I was being sent to a kind of political commissar, who had to supervise my work.

Soon after, I received an invitation to lunch with Ephraim Weichselfisch and his wife at their Tel Aviv flat. Weichselfisch introduced himself as a former officer of the Red Army. Even without this unexpected introduction, the décor of the apartment and the memorabilia on display would have indicated the outstanding place this glorious past occupied in his life. He came from Lodz, a city with a prewar Jewish population of more than a quarter million. When the city was occupied by the Wehrmacht in the fall of 1939, annexed by Germany along with the western part of Poland and renamed Litzmannstadt, the twenty-year-old Weichselfisch fled to eastern Poland, occupied by the Soviet Union. In 1940, along with many other Polish refugees, he was conscripted into the Red Army, trained as an officer, and assigned in 1941 to the Kosciusko division, composed of Polish exiles. He took part in the march to Berlin, was badly wounded, and saw the conquest of the capital in 1945. Two years later, he came to Palestine as an illegal immigrant.

It was soon clear that Weichselfisch wanted to set his own priorities. He was interested most in one thing in the planned publication: the contribution of the Jews in the Red Army, especially in national units like the Czech, Lithuanian, and Latvian divisions, in which Jews constituted up to 50 percent of the manpower. He had already written his own memoirs of the fight for Berlin and the "assault on the Reichstag." He wasn't especially interested in the rest: a great many Jews had fought against the

Nazis, and it was high time to show clearly that Jews had been neither cowards nor weaklings. As with so many other members of his generation who had been involved in the war as boys or young men, the experiences of those few years seemed to overshadow their subsequent life. Despite the horrible scenery that formed the background of his experiences, the traumatic events and the severe wound he had suffered in the war, his memories were stamped with the spirit of adventure. This blend of heroism, trivialization, and suppressing the emotional essence of his own experience also gave his descriptions that aura that always drove young readers to long for military adventures and regret not having been present at that great hour.

* 9 *

At that moment, I knew little about the history of the national units in the Soviet army. I did not believe, though, that the high percentage of Jews in these regiments and divisions indicated a particular fighting spirit of these groups, even if the desire for revenge or retribution played a role for individuals. Some 150,000 Jews had served in the Polish army before 1939, and some were taken into the newly created exile army in the east. The same held for the Czechoslovakian Legion that had emerged in Poland after 1938 and formed the nucleus of the Czechoslovakian units in the Red Army. It was true everywhere that Jews in their native lands conquered by the Wehrmacht had to fear the worst and could expect hardly any help from their non-Jewish compatriots. This was the main motive for the Jews' flight eastward to the territories under Soviet rule; this was the main reason for the high percentage of Jews among the refugees and among those recruited by the Soviet army. For the Soviets, their hopeless situation in their homelands made them the most reliable and hence desirable elements of the exile units. A large part of the troops, those that had not fled as units after the defeat, had been conscripted. Moreover, Jews had only reluctantly identified themselves as Jews. All this contradicted the thesis of the volunteer Jewish war effort against the Nazis or of special Jewish motives, or of a participation in the war driven by a national pride, which could justify a comprehensive perspective of the "Jewish Struggle against the Nazis."

Weichselfisch's intention to represent these people in his foreword as idealists, who had willingly thrown themselves into the struggle against Germany, seemed inappropriate to me. The orientation of the collection mystified the position of Jews during World War II strongly enough in any event, and so I wanted to try to counteract this tendency at least in the accompanying texts. I immediately began searching for descriptions and source material, but came up with only a few studies and one anthology published in Israel. Both treated events completely in the Zionist vein and attributed national motives and goals to the actors a priori. Other publications containing source materials were not to be found. The reason for this scanty result was that Israel had no relations with the Eastern Bloc countries. There was only what had accidentally come to Israeli libraries from immigrants or through other channels, and the archives of Eastern Europe were not open to local scholars.

As for the material, I soon got lucky. An historian friend pointed me to unpublished autobiographical reports in the archive of Yad Vashem and also told me that his own father had served in the First Czech regiment, formed in the Soviet Union in 1942, composed of 70 percent Czech Jewish refugees. The father, whom I knew and esteemed as one of those survivors who had integrated their experiences into their lives "afterward" by studying and writing about them, had also recorded this episode in an article. I could start there. Most reports I now came upon in the archives would all fit under the headline "My Part in the Victory over the Germans." The point of view of the narrator remained close to his own experience and was limited to the nearby vicinity, but the tone was idealistic and the conclusions global. The depictions dealt with episodes between 1940 and 1943, but had all been composed after the war, when the scope and radical nature of the Nazi annihilation campaign against the Jews came to light. I had to assume that this belated knowledge had influenced the writing and was responsible for the many sharp contrasts between the relationship to the German soldiers and their own Jewish identity. In addition, all the reporters had immigrated to Israel and their war experiences had assumed a Zionist hue typical for Israel, although to various degrees.

The Jewish content of the reports was rather conventional. There were descriptions of Jewish army worship and the constant, sometimes obtrusive, sometimes discreet, but seldom waning references to the Jewish origin of an officer or soldier, who had distinguished himself with special courage. The anthology was for the army and the army publishing house and what the descriptions lacked in cultural and social detail was made up for by the great variety of tanks, planes, and artillery mentioned. As I saw it, there was hardly anything more boring than a battle described from the point of view of a soldier taking part in it, where the view only seldom goes over the trench and the reader waits in vain for events to be placed on a political or military map. My assignment was now to select the best pieces and provide them with introductions and explanations, mostly comprehensive texts to supplement what the autobiographical reports lacked in references to contexts. I selected a depiction of the Lithuanian division, the Czech regiment, and two memoirs of the Polish exile army—one by Ephraim Weichselfisch, the other by a refugee living in France who had joined the Sikorsky Army, established in London in 1939 by the French government and the Polish government-in-exile and recruited in France.

From the tone of this report, the Polish refugee seemed to have waited impatiently for his chance to throw himself at the enemy. In June 1940, shortly before the ceasefire took effect, he and a group of Polish Jews had become German prisoners-of-war and were taken to a labor camp in Germany. There, he immediately came up with the idea of escape, which he described thus: "The fighting spirit was still strong in me. I was willing to sacrifice my life for the chance to get out of the camp and carry on the struggle against the enemy." That was the tone an Israeli soldier was to identify with, the desired counterimage of the victim led submissively to the slaughter.

After some preparations before I went to work, I had to negotiate with Colonel Wechsler about my conception of the two publications. The *Survey of Jewish Armed Resistance During the Holocaust*, the ponderous title I gave the booklet, was to give a differentiated view of the extremely varied circumstances and preconditions that had furthered or impeded the resistance of Jews. For example, the partisan war in the East organized very quickly from Moscow represented an important strategic factor that had no equivalent in the West, where hardly any fighting took place between the summer of 1940 and the spring of 1944. Thus, the organized armed actions of the Jews in Eastern Europe corresponded to the general pattern of the fights between occupiers and occupied in this region, while the many forms of obstruction, sabotage, and civilian countermeasures and rescue operations in the West fit the completely different situation in these countries.

In Eastern Europe, there was a "Jewish resistance," organized by Jewish groups growing out of prewar Jewish associations or parties. Such groups were the exception in the West, where Jews joined general groups as individuals, communist resistance cells as communists, for example. All these trends reflected local conditions and were seldom specifically Jewish. Moreover, in terms of persecution until 1941 and the subsequent implementation of the Final Solution, about fifty different areas of Europe had to be differentiated, where anti-Jewish measures were applied in different ways, with different goals, and at a different pace. Thus, the sudden invasion of a German firing squad into a White Russian village left the local Jews very few alternatives, while the deportation of the Jewish population in Western Europe was prefaced by months and even years of bureaucratic sanctions that left the affected groups and their environment much greater latitude. I had to mention all that in my introductory and survey chapters in order to counteract the simplifying and sweeping political myths.

I suggested to Wechsler that, aside from "armed" resistance, other manifestations of resistance, rescue attempts, and the disruption of administrative measures should be included in the summary as well, at least marginally, to show the reader that it was not only the armed person who was brave, it was not only "fighters" who took a risk, and that the preconditions for some form of active resistance were generally not available. Wechsler was willing to accept my suggestions, as long as I depicted the "core of the issue" in detail, the ghetto uprisings, the struggles of the partisan groups, the concentration camp revolts. He would have preferred to get from me a simple enumeration of the events, fitted out with inspiring quotations, roughly divided into a few simple categories. He considered everything else unnecessary.

I went to work with a double warning to myself: not to take my assignment more seriously than necessary, and not to fall into the opposite tendency—to refer too much to manifestations of dignity, initiative, and the will to live and thus indirectly confirm the thesis of the somehow defective attitudes of Jews during the Holocaust. Above all, I also had to resist the penchant for sweeping statements. Jewish history was the history of individual groups whose development had been extremely varied, and that also applied to attitudes during the Holocaust. The discontinuities and diachronisms in the history of the Jews were not transformed into the history of a single race or a single nation even by the common threat of annihilation and the racist logic of Nazism. Jews had not reacted as a nation to this unparalleled challenge. The political and cultural traditions of the country they lived in, the social class they belonged to, the special development and position of the Jewish communities, the attitudes of the general population toward the occupiers—those were the factors that said much more about individuals or groups than the generality "Jewish."

* 10 *

With his allusion to the "core of the subject," Wechsler had again indicated to me the canon of "Holocaust and Heroism" in Israeli public opinion. Unlike the Diaspora, in Israel it was the struggle in the ghettos and the partisan war of Eastern Europe that was considered the epitome of Jewish resistance. There were several reasons for this. Eastern Europe had the biggest prewar Jewish population and hence the most victims. The familial and cultural roots of the Jewish community in Israel were also in Eastern Europe, and after 1945 and 1948, many more Jews of Eastern Europe had chosen to immigrate to Israel than Jews of other regions. Another continuity formed an even more important factor: almost all Jewish fighting units within the ghettos and partisan groups grew out of local Zionist groups, so many leaders of the Jewish resistance in Eastern Europe had attained position and authority in Israel. Two kibbutzim, one established by veterans of the resistance, maintained museums and educational centers devoted to the ghetto fighters.

The Zionization of the history of Holocaust and resistance had even gone into the design of Yad Vashem, the Jerusalem memorial center. There, the "Square of the Warsaw Ghetto" formed the central forum where annual parades of the memorial day for "Holocaust and Heroism" took place. The square was bordered by a symbolic ghetto wall with two very different sculptures. One was a gigantic group of figures dominating the square, titled "Revolt in the Warsaw Ghetto," and showed the "armed men, women, and children in the heroic struggle against the background of the burning ghetto." The other, essentially more modest sculpture was a small black relief at the edge of the square. It was called "The Last March" and depicted the path of the Jews in the death camps. Both sculptures conveyed the proportions of the two elements of "Holocaust and Heroism" in the public mind.

In schools and in the mass media, the history of the Warsaw Ghetto uprising was also the focus on memorial day. The constantly repeated descriptions and interviews with survivors concentrated on the course and result of the actual fighting. The prehistory and the debates between the individual Jewish groups about the formation of the resistance in the ghetto after the first big deportation of 300,000 Jews in the summer of 1942 were not discussed. That would have had a special resonance among Israel's political parties and their adherents. The conflict about the form and goal of a common defense organization in the ghetto had lasted almost a year and reflected the split between the ideological currents among Polish Jews. Representatives of various socialist Zionist groups, the Revisionists, and the anti-Zionist Bundists and Communists clashed with one another and were incapable of developing a common strategy. This hardly edifying but realistic model of a common Jewish undertaking formed another reason for thoroughly mystifying the past.

The uprising could count as the greatest and most significant act of Jewish resistance against the Final Solution, and as one of the very few that demanded major military countermeasures from the Germans. Its significance was not in the number of lives saved or annihilation campaigns prevented, but in the psychology of the moment. The armed resistance played its greatest role only in retrospect, in the national mythology and the political and historical self-image of the State, where the Zionist parties and the army made the manifest Jewish "willingness to fight" into a legacy. However, transferring the "Battle Heritage" of the ghetto to the situation of Israel raised some problems and this was probably why the army had not adapted this model in the past. In the process of mythologizing and popularizing the Holocaust, those acts of resistance were invested with the stigma of "Kiddush ha-Shem," martyrdom, the self-sacrifice and acceptance of one's own inferiority and weakness. The fighting in the ghetto was considered an act of affirmation, as a saving of national pride and dignity in the face of certain defeat, but not as a rational use of military means to achieve a concrete goal. Models for courageous behavior in the face of certain death belong in movies or novels, but were not suited to motivate flesh-and-blood soldiers. The army could train for nothing but belief in the rationality of force, in the military superiority of your own side and belief in victory. The idea of "Kiddush ha-Shem" did not fit this scheme, certainly not as model behavior against a superior opponent. Moreover, the story of Jewish resistance had to fit the constructions that Zionism made of Diaspora history. Jewish heroism during the Holocaust had to contain the tragic features of ineffectiveness and futility, so it could serve as a precursor of the national solution, as the last stage in the metamorphosis from weak Jew to strong Israeli.

How was I to account for these myths and ideas of history in my work? As in the projects on the Mandate period, there was as yet hardly any research or scientific debate, but rather an excessive amount of ideology and legend-forming, and a superfluity of memoirs tinged by party politics. Like many other historians before and after me, the one-sided and ideologically informed reading of Jewish history and the history of the emergence of Israel pressed me reluctantly into a position of corrector and revisionist. At any rate, I could not fulfill this function adequately under the circumstances of my military service.

In the first part of the "survey," I presented examples of resistance in eight different ghettos in White Russia, the Ukraine, Lithuania, and Poland. My strategy here was to temper the simplifying tendency of the project a little by emphasizing the complexity and variety of the situations, indicating the differences of Jewish reactions and the extremely narrow bounds of action and judgment for deciding on armed campaigns. The second part dealt with the history of the underground in Auschwitz, Sobibor, and Treblinka, with the escape attempts, revolts, and sabotage. I also described the attempts to gather proof about the industrial killing, to smuggle reports to the outside world, and other equally important activities of the "underground" in the concentration camps, where an office formed the backdrop to heroism. The third part discussed the partisan groups and the conditions under which Jews had joined existing formations or had formed their own groups, and the fate of the refugees who found shelter in partisan family camps. The last part surveyed all other areas and regions of the resistance of Jews, in southern and southeastern Europe, in Belgium and France, and Algeria. In this way, I attempted to sketch a "total picture" of Jewish resistance.

I turned in the manuscript of the survey with very mixed feelings. I had described the Holocaust from an odd perspective hardly suited to deepen ideas and knowledge of the subject. I would much rather have written directly about the history of the individual communities at that time, about what happened to people, and about the great variety of reactions and attitudes in the face of imminent disaster. Now I felt I had not done justice to either of those subjects.

Nevertheless, I could not decide on any other procedure for the anthology either. The documents I selected for the collection—reports, journals, and contemporary materials, including those that had survived in hiding, as well as memoirs written in retrospect—were to give a differentiated image of life under inconceivable conditions and reflect especially the political and moral constraints imposed on the leaders of the resistance. Beside the reports of Jews in the Allied armies, I selected autobiographical documents of the ghetto revolts and chronicles of the resistance in the concentration camps. The third part of the book presented four former partisans in Eastern Europe and two members of the Resistance in Paris. A member of the underground in Algeria contributed the wonderful story of the Jewish sport club "Salle Géo Gras," whose innocent scenery covered preparations for the "complot of Algiers," which allowed the Allied landing in Algeria in November 1942. In the last part, I put the memoirs of two soldiers in the "Jewish Brigade" and the "51 Commando," British units that had been recruited in Palestine during World War II. The 51 Commando consisted of half Jews and half Arabs and British, and was used against Italian and German troops in Africa. In contrast to the survey, I concluded the work on the collection with a sense of satisfaction. The variety of perspectives and standpoints, the range of activities and positions of the participants, and the natural variations in personality and temperament of the reporters gave the book a multifaceted nature that contradicted the myth of the national struggle.

I delivered the manuscript shortly before the end of my year of compulsory duty and my discharge. As I waited with considerable tension for the examination of my work and the concluding discussion, I prepared to return to civilian life. I had been spared the usual circumstances of military service with the normal limitations of personal freedom. But the restrictions and constraints on my work as an historian had turned out to be just as oppressive. Despite the almost unlimited freedom of movement and the nearly complete control over my time, which I had spent almost exclusively in archives and libraries and at my desk at home, I felt abused and humiliated. I had "served" against my will and it was this omnipresent constraint that rankled, despite my relative independence.

Now, shortly before the end, I felt for the first time an intense disgust at my own role in the Battle Heritage and everything connected with it. As long as I was at work, I had reached a modus vivendi with the circumstances, even if pugnaciously, but always aiming at compromise and the possible. Now, I preferred not to know any more about my maneuvers. The compromises I had found seemed hardly more than an excuse designed only to ease my conscience. The unit and Colonel Wechsler had not treated me badly and, just like me, had avoided direct confrontations. My doubts about the Zionist construct of history, my penchant for relativizing historiographical positions, and my basic skepticism, attitudes that would have been considered normal and desirable in other contexts, must have seemed bizarre and extravagant to Wechsler and his colleagues. The army education unit was one of the most important distributors of Zionist myths and thus could hardly react to this kind of dissent with anything but amazement.

When I finally got the news that the anonymous editors had finished their assessment of my manuscripts, for the first time I wanted to fake illness to avoid having to show up for the discussion. I had only ten more days as a soldier, and I would gladly have missed my last appearance. But, once more, I put on the uniform that had hung in my closet for most of the last twelve months, and went to headquarters in Tel Aviv. There, it turned out that the editing of the collection had not yet been completed because the translation of some parts into Hebrew and Ephraim Weichselfisch's foreword were still missing. The editing of the survey was done. It didn't take me long to find many places where the editor had plied his red pen. Almost every description of the external conditions and the milieu of the resistance was deleted. Here and there, a few euphemisms had survived the editing and now spoke of unexplained "circumstances" or "factors" that had enabled or impeded an action. Mentions of other, nonmilitary forms of resistance were also omitted. Only one single sentence in the introduction still referred to this broader perspective. Everywhere, the reader came upon the phrase the "Jewish struggle against the Nazis." It had appeared instead of the countless nuances I had taken such pains to work into the text. I pretended to look through the manuscript to the end, but only leafed through it mechanically. Even if there had still been a possibility of rescuing some formulation or other, I had lost the will for further arguments. I gave up. A few days later, I returned to civilian life.

* 11 *

Twenty years later, for the sixtieth anniversary of the Warsaw Ghetto uprising, in 2003, the Israel Defense Forces held a special commemoration of the Holocaust and Jewish heroism. This time, the event took place in Poland. In the past twenty years, a new, very popular form of national memorial had developed there, aimed mainly at Israeli students in the upper grades of high school just before they enter military service, and since the 1990s, at Jewish youth of other countries as well. This was the "March of the Living," a secular, nationalistic pilgrimage of Israelis and Jews to Auschwitz. The march, a paramilitary event, was held on Israeli Holocaust Memorial Day and followed the traces of the "death march" from Auschwitz to Birkenau. Young people wrapped in Israeli flags, delegations of the Israeli army marching in formation behind the banners of their units, politicians from Israel, Poland, and other countries wanted to demonstrate that "the nation of Israel, the nation of Israel, the nation of Israel is alive," as in the variegated lyrics of a popular song in Israel. After the march, the foreign youth in their blue uniforms, made especially for this occasion, were flown to Israel, where they took part a week later in the Memorial Day for Israeli soldiers who fell in the Middle East conflict. Connecting the Holocaust and the Middle East conflict could hardly have been shaped more subtly by the Israeli creators of this "March of the Living." In this way, those who fell in Auschwitz and those who fell in the Gaza Strip were both declared martyrs of the nation.

The chance to create the special military memorial act of 2003 had been offered by accident. The Polish air force, which had maintained friendly relations with its Israeli counterpart and the Israeli aircraft industry ever since the fall of Communism, celebrated its eighty-fifth birthday. The climax was a gala event in late August planned for the air force base in Radom, some 250 kilometers from Warsaw, where air forces from all over the world were to show their skills and weapons technology. Israel announced that it was sending a fleet including a squadron of F-15 fighter jets to perform air acrobatics over Radom. The subsequent conversion of Israel's participation in a conventional military air show into a national ritual can serve as a model for the appropriation of the Holocaust by Israel, the linking of the Holocaust with the campaigns of the Israeli army, and the emergence of a new element in the symbolic language of Israeli memorial culture. Involved in creating this new ritual were the supreme command of the Israeli air force, representatives of the government, and members of the board of Yad Vashem.

Appearances of Israeli officers and uniformed soldiers at Auschwitz-Birkenau go back to 1992, when the chief of staff and future prime minister, Ehud Barak, who led the first army delegation to Poland, linked the catastrophe of Auschwitz with the achievements of the Israeli army in a simple formula: "We are fifty years too late." That visit also took place against the background of increasing bonds of the military and the military industry. Since then, the Israeli army has drafted a special program for the visit of members of the military, the "witnesses in uniform." In the summer of 2003, 140 officers were scheduled to visit Auschwitz in the framework of this program. But Poland's invitation posed a question for the Israeli air force: Was it enough to send the personnel to visit the Auschwitz Museum or could the air force show respect for the dead in its own way?

Ever since the victory parade in Jerusalem in May 1968, celebrating both the twentieth anniversary of the State of Israel and the enormous victory of June 1967, the Israeli air force had not staged any more air shows. In 1968, it had been French jets that had thundered low over the houses of Jerusalem, drawing Stars of David with blue and white smoke in the sky; now it was American F-15 jets that were to testify to Israel's superiority and destructive ability. But was it appropriate to demonstrate Israel's military might over Auschwitz in this way? In Israel itself, since 1968, the demonstration of military equipment in parades was taboo, but for appearances abroad, it was the opposite. Here, participation in such performances was desirable both to increase national prestige and to promote export.

Aircraft electronics, guided weapons systems, and other products of the government-owned Israel Aircraft Industries IAI, the weapons development authority Rafael, and the electronic company Elbit, developed and produced in Israel, constituted a growing portion of total Israeli exports. The new NATO members and the threshold nations of Eastern Europe formed an especially attractive target for Israel's expertise in conversion and rebuilding older aircraft and weapons systems. Poland was one of the first countries of this region that had had older weapons systems of the Eastern Bloc updated by the Israeli military industry in the early 1990s. Thus, the Air Show Radom 2003, as the celebrations of the eighty-fifth birthday of the Polish air force were called, was considered both by producers and participants primarily as a demonstration of the achievements of the civilian and military aviation industry.

The leader of the Israeli contingent, Brigadier General Amir Eshel, announced the plans of the air force in a newspaper interview shortly before the flight to Poland in late August 2003: "We will fly past over Auschwitz and we will show the most powerful might of the IDF where the most awful tragedy happened to the Jewish people. This symbolizes so much where we come from and where we are going." The three F-15 fighter jets were to reduce their speed over Auschwitz and fly as low as possible over the railroad tracks, the former ramps, and the guard tower with the entrance gate. Eshel explained that he had chosen reservists and veterans of Israeli wars for the mission who were to represent the whole nation. The grandparents of one of the pilots had survived Auschwitz and had migrated to Israel. Another was the son of resistance fighters. Captain Shai, the child of Sepharadi parents from Morocco and Iraq and assigned to one of the jets as a navigator, explained to the press: "I am a member of the Jewish people and that serves as my connection to the Holocaust. This is also very important for me because it shows our might today. We are returning from a position of strength to a nation where there was an attempt to vanquish the Jewish nation. Not only will we be remembering the six million murdered in the Holocaust, but this flight has great importance today since it shows the vitality, versatility, and might of the Air Force. For us to come back in an F-15, the greatest symbol of the Jewish nation's strength, will characterize the whole route our people have taken. I will feel very proud."

After tough negotiations with the Polish authorities, who initially showed little enthusiasm for the idea, September 4 was set as the day for the overflight. Shaping the ceremony more precisely was transferred to the board of Yad Vashem. Here the idea emerged of linking the overflight with the people who had been murdered in Auschwitz on that day. Yad Vashem announced: "During Yad Vashem's computerized search in its Hall of Names, it was discovered that all of the victims from September 4 arrived at Auschwitz from a transport from Drancy, France, that had departed two days earlier (September 2, 1943). 661 of the individuals were sent to their immediate death in the gas chambers within hours of their arrival. Fourteen of the names taken from Yad Vashem's Hall of Names will be read at the ceremony. The actual Pages of Testimony will be in the planes that will fly over the ceremony at the same time."

Representatives of the Polish National Museum of Auschwitz-Birkenau protested the planned overflight: "It's a cemetery, a place of silence and concentration," they argued. Nevertheless, the ceremony took place as planned. Two hundred Israeli soldiers and officers stood at attention on the grounds of the former concentration camp Auschwitz II-Birkenau as the names of the victims were read out and the jets flew low over the tracks, the blue Star of David, emblem of the air force, visible from the ground. The Israeli ambassador to Poland said that the ceremony was "to honor the ashes of their fathers and grandfathers."

With the military ceremony, the Israeli army joined the memorial traditions of the two world wars, the commemoration at military cemeteries and the rituals at memorials to the Unknown Soldier. The use of Israeli fighter jets over Auschwitz represents a new climax in the process of reinterpreting and transferring the conflict with the Arabs into that mythical space of history, where the Jewish nation continues to defend itself against Amalek.

7

* A REST STOP IN THE COUNTRYSIDE *

Jews, Palestinians, and the Expulsions of 1947–1948

* 1 *

Halfway between Jerusalem and Tel Aviv, on the side of the highway, is a small rest area established by the Jewish National Fund and named Canada Park after the homeland of the donors. Here, Israelis often stop for a picnic or a rest in the countryside as they drive between the two cities or come to recuperate on the Sabbath from a hectic workweek. On the big brown wooden sign at the entrance, identifying the park as a creation of the Jewish National Fund, the organization responsible for purchasing and settling land, is one of those magical formulae of Jewish solidarity that decorate the walls of hospitals, schools, and cultural institutions: "Canada Park has been developed through the Generosity of Joseph & Faye Tanenbaum, Toronto, Ontario, Canada."

I still remember precisely the day I stopped in Canada Park for the first time on a trip through the foothills of the Judean Mountains. Until 1967, the border between Israel and Jordan had been in this area, as still indicated by the old, badly maintained roads leading nowhere. From the park, a few buildings could be recognized on the slope of a nearby chain of hills. The biggest was a European structure in that romantic style of the late nineteenth century the Europeans called "Oriental," identified by an inscription on the gable as an establishment of the "École biblique et archéologique française." Not far away was a small medieval church and a field with excavations. I asked an Arab attendant for information and learned that I was standing before the ruins of an early Christian basilica, built on the remains of a Roman villa, which had once been part of the biblical city of Emmaus, well-known in both Jewish and Christian history. The attendant showed me around. In the end, he talked about the history of the post-biblical period. As the Arab village of Imwas, the place had continued to the present with almost two thousand inhabitants and was destroyed after the 1967 war. Now, ten years after the destruction, there was no longer any trace of the most recent history or of the Arab inhabitants. The attendant could tell me only that the inhabitants along with their neighbors from two other villages had been ordered by the Israeli army to leave the village within a few hours and all the buildings were then blown up and any remnants were bulldozed. Later I heard—at that time, there was no written information on it—that more than a hundred thousand Arab residents of the conquered cities of Tulkarem and Kalkiliyya and the refugee camps in Jordan had also been expelled by the Israeli army in 1967, apparently because their houses had been too close to the borders.

For a long time, I was haunted by the idea that I had stood on the flattened grounds of a village whose population had been expelled ten years before. Hiding the traces with a park and establishing a rest area for the Jews seemed cynical to me and indicated a measure of insensitivity and indifference to the suffering of the previous inhabitants that still surprised me at that point in time when I had just immigrated. There must have been many other such places in Israel, even hundreds of them, which had been erased from the landscape in 1948 after the flight or expulsion of almost a million people. The custom of going into the country-side on the weekend to find rest and relaxation in nature was destroyed for me. I soon realized that the Jews of the country had to live in a special relationship to their environment. Their relation to the landscape was based on a selective view that emphasized the traces of Jewish history in the country, avoided those of Christianity, and completely overlooked those of Arab history. The villages and Arab inhabitants of the country, who had defined the landscape until 1948, had been almost completely deleted from consciousness. Nowhere, until then, had I discovered an indication that a majority of the six hundred or so agricultural settlements, kibbutzim or moshavim in the Israeli heartland, their fields and groves, plantations and woods, stood on the grounds of Arab villages that had been leveled to the ground after the expulsion or flight of the population.

In the agricultural settlements that had emerged since the beginning of the Zionist immigration in the 1920s, this peculiar relationship to the environment could also be read in another way. They were often placed on hills or strategic sites, in order to dominate the surrounding area. Their plan and architecture did not adapt to the environment, but often created a deliberate contrast. The little houses where the members lived were mostly handsome and pleasant with their red roofs and simple, clear lines, and were reminiscent of Central and Eastern European villages. The community buildings, the multipurpose halls, dining rooms, stables and barns followed a modernist aesthetic that referred neither to the history nor the tradition of the country, but rather to all the new things—the new era, the new inhabitants, and their new ideas of Jewish history. The feeling of disconnection was reinforced even more by the omnipresent sloppiness and indifference vis-à-vis the environment. Thus, many of the collective settlements, with their machines, tools, junk, and garbage lying all around, did not give the impression of a village but of a hastily erected and gradually dilapidated industrial plant. The only exception was the residential area of the members and the grounds set aside for tourists, where a geographically indeterminate "paradise" had arisen.

All kibbutzim and most other settlements I visited were surrounded by high fences and barbed wire and had a guard post at the gate. This sight oppressed me. In the Jewish settlements in the occupied territories, I could imagine the reason for it; but in the villages in the heartland, these cautionary measures seemed exaggerated. How must a child feel growing up behind barbed wire and unable to play outside in field or forest because an enemy could be lurking there? Later, when I began to discover the hidden layers of the Israeli landscape, I learned more about the origins of these defense installations. Of the 370 settlements originating between 1948 and 1958, 350 were on Arab land or former Arab villages. Most of the former inhabitants had wound up in refugee camps, often only a few dozen kilometers from the new borders. Almost everywhere, Arab families tried to return to their fields and groves or to their houses, to seek their belongings or simply to check on their property.

The Israeli army's expression for the exercise of this elementary need and human right was "re-infiltration." The fences were erected for fear that the exiled or refugee inhabitants would return. After the 1967 war, the borders of the 1949 cease-fire were abolished and many inhabitants of the refugee camps tried for the first time to visit the houses and property they had then left within a few hours. That provided a new reason to renew and improve the fortifications. The bombings, terror attacks, and Israeli retaliatory measures that began with the occupation of the rest of Palestine in 1967 provided another motive for an increased protection of individual Israeli settlements, indeed the whole area of Jewish settlement. In 2004, construction of an impregnable security strip with fences, walls, and watchtowers began, to surround the heartland, Jerusalem, and the big settlements in the occupied territories, in fact, to fence in the areas still left to the Palestinians. Thus, the events of 1948 go on shaping the landscape of Israel.

* 2 *

The war that produced the State of Israel is known by various names. The Israelis call it the War of Independence or Liberation, the Palestinians call it al-Nakba—the catastrophe. Almost a million people, more than half the Arab inhabitants of Palestine, fled or were driven out of the area of the Jewish State within a short time. They left whole towns and neighborhoods empty, along with houses, shops, plants, and hundreds of villages. Even during 1948, the villages were destroyed, the land and the crops ripening in the fields and groves were taken over by their Jewish neighbors, and the houses of whole towns and neighborhoods given to Jewish immigrants. In the Jewish society of Israel, these events are wreathed in powerful, ubiquitous myths. Along with the Israeli interpretation of the origins and results of the war of 1948–1949, they're part of that comprehensive myth of the origin of the State, widespread not only in Israel and the Jewish Diaspora but also in a large part of the Western world, where Zionism and the idea of a state for European Jews in the Middle East have always enjoyed a great deal of sympathy and practical support.

For a long time, the question of responsibility for or cause of the tragedy of the Palestinian people was answered unequivocally in Israel: the catastrophe was caused by the Palestinian-Arab leadership and the governments of the neighboring Arab countries themselves and resulted from the civil war of November

1947–May 1948, provoked by the Arabs, and the subsequent first Middle East war, which began with an attack by the neighboring Arab states on Israel and ended with Israel's triumphant campaign in the Negev Desert in 1949. According to this version, the flight of the civilians was the spontaneous escape of the Arabs from the fighting, encouraged by the Arab leadership who wanted to bring the civilians to safety behind Arab lines temporarily. Since the Arabs had tried aggression to prevent the implementation of the U.N. Partition Plan for Palestine, they had to bear sole responsibility for the war, the resultant wave of refugees, and the emergence of a refugee problem. Israel has always rejected its obligation under international law to take back the refugees after the end of the war, an obligation that exists regardless of the causes of the flight, with the argument that the exercise of this right would jeopardize the "Jewish character" of the country. Safeguarding the "Jewish character" does not mean guaranteeing freedom of religion or further development of a secular Jewish-Israeli culture, but rather maintaining a clear demographic superiority of Jews vis-à-vis Arabs. Thus far, Israeli governments have been able to call on this prerogative successfully, despite the far-reaching consequences for the refugees and the rights of the non-Jewish citizens of Israel, because this principle is legitimated by the League of Nations Mandate of 1922, the U.N. Partition Resolution of 1947, and other decisions of the community of nations.

This assertion of innocence for the Palestinian catastrophe is of fundamental importance for the Jews of Israel. The system of justifications and accusations Israeli society created for itself in the form of "Hasbara," public relations, aimed at the Jewish Diaspora and the world, depends on it. The feeling of moral superiority and integrity, underlying the population's willingness to sacrifice and the army's will to fight, along with the support of Jews abroad, stands or falls with it. In Israeli domestic politics, this thesis is so firmly established that it leaves hardly any latitude for foreign policy. Every agreement to Arab demands produced by the catastrophe of 1948—the return of refugees, restitution of property, or payment of compensation—is not presented to the Israeli public as a moral or legal obligation, but rather as accommodation and possible reward for concessions on the other side. The gap between the Israeli and the Palestinian versions of the history of the conflict is so wide that all negotiations with neighboring countries and the Palestinians sink into it. Every attempt to jolt the basic assumptions of the thesis is immediately disavowed and resisted in the Israeli public.

Along with the quasi-official Israeli version of the history of the rise of the refugee problem, there are Arab and independent representations that assume more complex causes or even a planned expulsion of the Arabs by the Israeli army. What was common to all versions until the late 1980s was that they could not be supported and were based only on the memories of the participants on one side or the other. The research that started after the opening of the Israeli archive began to paint another, much more differentiated picture, that completely contradicted the current thesis of innocence. When the "New Historians" tried to revise or objectify the mythical view of the period, other historians counterattacked, imputing political motives to the New Historians and dismissing their conclusions as anti-Zionist propaganda. There was certainly enough in the material from the official archives to jolt the established view—the minutes of the meetings of the Israeli war cabinet, the war journals and written orders of the military authorities—but the oral sources, the witness accounts of Arab refugees who often provided the only information on the conquest of hundreds of villages, remain by their very nature ambiguous and less reliable. Thus, some of the research, the reconstruction of expulsions, acts of violence and massacres carried out by the Jews is tarnished with the stigma of bias and partisanship. Critics of the New

Historians also charged that, in fact, some of these historians were known critics of Zionism.

The research of the New Historians barely resounded in the Israeli public. As for the mass media, as in the case of a recent M.A. thesis on a massacre of the population in an Arab village in 1948 apparently based on false information, only the historian's alleged political motives were discussed. The content of the work seemed too absurd to be taken seriously. Thus, the Israeli public persists in the idea that the flight of the native population was triggered by the confusion of war and the incitement of the Arabs. One prominent Israeli historian and defender of the prevailing view of history formulated this simply in June 2002: "A la guerre comme la guerre," war is what it is.

Investigating the events of 1948 is not the only way to approach the question of the displacement of the Arabs. With the thesis of a "land without a people for a people without a land," the local population had already been displaced intellectually. In the very beginning of Zionist settlement, their humanity was ignored and their claims were trivialized. Therefore, the result of 1948, the disappearance of 90 percent of the non-Jews living in the future state of the Jews, can hardly be considered an accident arising in the chaos of war. The question of the fate of the Arabs must start with the plans and attitudes about Arabs and the "Arab question" prevailing among Zionists since the 1920s.

* 3 *

Despite the great resolve with which the Zionist movement settled the Jews, built the economy, and created a modern infrastructure in the country, the core question of Zionism remained unanswered for a long time: the creation of an independent Jewish state in a country inhabited by another people. Jewish settlement had begun pragmatically—wherever a piece of land was for sale, it was bought, built, and settled, while the leadership didn't care much about the long-term perspective. Thus, the first Arab protest in April 1920 triggered a shock. The German-Jewish economist Arthur Ruppin, who had guided colonization in Palestine for the Zionist movement since 1908, wrote in his journal on April 7, 1920, one day after a lull in the two-day protests: "A few days have been enough to change the image of Palestine and the view of our work. As of this evening, six Jews are dead, and several wounded are still hovering between life and death. Under the impact of these events, Weizmann has collapsed completely and at a meeting this morning seemed to say that Zionism had come to an end."

A year later, on May 1, 1921, Arab citizens of Jaffa used a May Day celebration of Jewish workers as an excuse for another protest against the Zionist Mandate and the unlimited immigration of Jews. On May 1, Ruppin noted in his journal: "For me, it is especially depressing that these incidents really indicate such an anti-Jewish mood of the Arabs that one must almost despair of an honest reconciliation between Jews and Arabs." In subsequent days, the protests spread over the whole country and claimed many victims. Ruppin saw immediately that "an honest reconciliation" was not the only way to deal with Arab resistance to the coming of the Jews. On May 5, 1921, he noted: "Many experts say that [a consistent policy of reconciliation] toward the Palestinian Arabs is inappropriate and that they can only be won over with a 'strong hand.' Yet, I am determined to withdraw from my leading Zionist position if it turns out that one must resort to a policy of force." Since Arab resistance did not slacken, in fact, the "policy of force" was that of the future.

In 1923, Ze'ev Jabotinsky, the Revisionist leader, began to expound the ethics of force in a series of articles titled "The Iron Wall": "Every native population in the world resists colonists as long as it has the slightest hope of being able to rid itself of the danger of being colonized. . . . We cannot offer any adequate compensation to the Palestinian Arabs in return for Palestine. And therefore, there is no likelihood of any voluntary agreement being reached. So that all those who regard such an agreement as a condition sine qua non for Zionism may as well say 'non' and withdraw from Zionism. *Zionist colonization must either stop, or else proceed regardless of the native population* [emphasis in the original]. Which means that it can proceed and develop only under the protection of a power that is independent of the native population—behind an iron wall, which the native population cannot breach. In this matter there is no difference between our 'militarists' and our 'vegetarians.' Except that the first prefer that the iron wall should consist of Jewish soldiers, and the others are content that they should be British."

After the outbreak in 1936 of the most violent unrest so far, the idea of dividing the country arose for the first time, proposed by a British commission of inquiry on the armed uprising of the Arabs. This first partition plan of 1937, which was adopted by the United Nations in a different form ten years later and led to the establishment of the State of Israel, also raised the problem of the two population groups living in close proximity. By that time, the scattering of Jewish settlements had made it impossible to draw a clear line of separation between the groups. For the most part, that was the result of a deliberate policy of destroying the contiguity of Arab space. Parcels of land were purchased in areas densely populated by Arabs later to justify the claim to include these areas in the Jewish State. Thus, already in an early stage of settlement, the seed of the gradual displacement and the motive for a later expulsion of the Arab population was planted. In the first partition plan of 1937, a solution was proposed for the problem of the mixed areas of settlement: the "transfer" of the Arab population out of the mixed areas into pure Arab regions. The Zionist leadership reacted positively to the proposal. In July 1937,

Ben Gurion wrote in his journal: "The compulsory transfer of the Arabs from the valleys of the proposed Jewish state could give us something we never had, even when we stood on our own during the days of the First and Second Temples. . . . We are being given an opportunity which we never dared to dream in our wildest imaginings. This is more than a state, government and sovereignty—this is national consolidation in a free homeland."

A few months later, he was already preoccupied with the practical implementation of the proposal. On October 5, 1937, David Ben Gurion wrote to his son Amos: "We do not want and do not need to expel Arabs and take their places. Our whole desire is based on the assumption—which has been corroborated in the course of all our activity in the country—that there is enough room for us and the Arabs in the country and that if we have to use force—not in order to dispossess the Arabs from the Negev or Transjordan but in order to assure ourselves of the right, which is our due, to settle there—then we have the force." This could not be expressed publicly, even in the Zionist committee. In the Zionist Executive, "legal" transfer was discussed. The idea of the transfer of population on the basis of international treaties was not unknown at the time and after World War I, it was considered repeatedly in the solution of ethnic conflicts in various parts of Europe, but was not implemented. In answer to a question of one of the participants as to whether he would consider a transfer of population by force, at a meeting of the Jewish Agency on June 7, 1938, Ben Gurion said: "[No.] The Jewish State will discuss with the neighboring Arab states the matter of voluntarily transferring Arab tenant-farmers, laborers, and *fellahin* from the Jewish State to the neighboring states."

Even before the outbreak of the war, the British government restricted Jewish immigration because of Arab pressure. Thus, during the Holocaust, Palestine was closed to the Jews of Europe as a refuge. The dwindling hope that a demographic superiority could be achieved quickly through free immigration led to a radicalization of Zionist attitudes, which shaped the events of 1948 and still influences the policy of the State of Israel today: a piratical aggressiveness coupled with diplomacy to reach compromise and peace. This paradoxical behavior has its roots in the widely differing political attitudes within the Jewish community in Palestine but also reflects the isolation and colonial nature of a settler society that had no long-established contacts, no clear borders, and no firm place in the power structure of the region. The enormous dependence of the Zionist enterprise on a protective power —first Great Britain and later the U.S.—dictated a cautious procedure oriented toward negotiations and treaties. The political and military weakness of the Arab population and the neighboring countries, on the other hand, enabled a strategy of expansion and faits accomplis. These two elements determined the dynamic that led to the Arab catastrophe of 1948.

In 1946, the change in political strategy came to the surface. Chaim Weizmann, the humanistic and liberal leader of Zionism in the first decades, lost out to the "pragmatic" Ben Gurion. Ben Gurion immediately set in motion a massive, secret campaign to purchase weapons in the West. Almost thirty thousand battle-experienced Palestinian Jews, who had entered the British army during the war at the urging of the leadership, now joined the Jewish underground army, the Haganah, established during the Arab unrest. The two-pronged strategy of violence and diplomacy took shape. Military actions against British and Arab targets and against the blockade of immigration ships went in tandem with diplomatic efforts in England and America, to move the great powers to take further steps toward a Jewish State.

The question of transfer and the relationship to the Arab population was no longer discussed publicly. While an Anglo-American commission visited the country in 1946 and once again raised the question of the future of the region, the Jewish leadership formulated a first, detailed plan: Plan May. In case the British withdrew, it planned the takeover of the Mandate administration by Jewish organs and assigned the underground army, the Haganah, to protect the Jewish area of settlement, which included a large Arab minority. The plan was based on the assumption that the British army would not interfere in the struggle between Arabs and Jews and would leave the Haganah a free hand.

The Zionist leadership correctly predicted both the British decision to withdraw and its policy of non-interference two years later and began preparing for it. That was a crucial advantage. At the same time, the Arab leadership proceeded on the opposite assumption: that the British would not give up the Mandate, would not withdraw the army, and would not allow the Jews to take power by force. At any rate, most of the Arabs were neither willing nor able to engage in a military confrontation, while a divided and unpopular Arab leadership pursued, as one critic wrote, "a completely naïve and unrealistic policy." The different expectations and preparations explain the extremely unequal power balance between the two sides at the end of 1947. If it came to a direct confrontation between the militias of both sides, most neutral observers expected a defeat of the Arabs.

On December 3, 1947, four days after the U.N. decision on partition, Ben Gurion gave a speech to party members about the problem of the Arab minority. In the planned Jewish state, along with about 600,000 Jews, there were also to be 400,000 Arabs. "This must be viewed in all its clarity and sharpness. With this [population] composition, there cannot even be complete certainty that the government will be held by a Jewish majority. . . . There can be no stable and strong Jewish State as long as it has a Jewish majority of only 60 percent. [This] requires a new approach, [new] habits of mind to suit our new future."

Just a few weeks later, the "new habits of mind" were to have concrete results. But it was not the vague expectations and hopes with respect to the "Arab problem," nor the secret intentions or plans of the Jewish side that might or might not have existed at that time that triggered the beginning of the exodus and expulsion. In late October 1947, an agent of Haganah intelligence wrote about the mood among the Arab population: "The *fellah* is afraid of the Jewish terrorists . . . who might bomb his village and destroy his property. The town-dweller admits that his strength is insufficient to fight the Jewish force, and hopes for salvation from outside. The moderate majority are confused, frightened. . . . They are stockpiling provisions and are being coerced and pressured by extremists . . . all they want is peace, quiet." At the same time, the Arab chairman of the Jaffa Chamber of Commerce, Za'fer Dajani, explained to another agent: "If it comes to war, we will lose. But the struggle will go on for decades, centuries, until the Islamic world will defeat the Jews, just as the Crusaders in the Middle Ages were finally defeated."

The reaction of the Arab leadership to the Partition resolution of November 29, 1947, was to create a civil defense in the cities and villages, and to recruit a few militias, a troop of about twelve thousand badly trained or untrained men with simple weapons, who were to operate at their own discretion under the command of local defense committees or associations. Given the generally known military weakness, all hopes were trained on the troops of the neighboring Arab countries who were to march into Palestine after the British withdrew and prevent the establishment of a Jewish State.

The first step toward the Arab catastrophe happened shortly after with the announcement of the British government that they would pull their troops out between spring and summer 1948. The Mandate government didn't think it could guarantee the peaceful and orderly implementation of Partition. The use of troops would remain limited to ensuring the smooth withdrawal of British personnel and the safety of the retreat. This decision triggered great fear among the Arab population. The Zionist leadership reacted differently. In a speech to the Jewish National Assembly, Ben Gurion declared: "We must show the world and the U.N. that we will carry out the Partition Plan, that, from this moment on, the beginning of the transition period, we are willing and able to function as a transitional government ourselves in place of the withdrawing British administration."

Less than thirty years after immigration began, the Jewish minority was ready to take power in Palestine. Ben Gurion's announcement looked like a declaration of war to the Arabs of Palestine. The Jewish State was to be created by force—against the will of the Arab part of the population and despite the threat of war from the neighboring countries. The Zionist movement had promised the U.N. to follow a policy of tolerance and equality toward the Arabs, but many doubted the sincerity or feasibility of this promise. The intentions, desires, and plans of the Jewish leadership were at least ambivalent.

* 4 *

The day after the vote on the Partition Plan in New York, Arab youths seized two buses near the airport in Lydda and plundered a Jewish market in Jerusalem. A three-day protest strike against Partition was called. The first skirmishes between the militias of both sides took place on the border of Jewish and Arab quarters in Haifa, Jerusalem, and Jaffa. The first day ended with seven dead on each side. The British High Commissioner reported to London: "The unrest is not the beginning of an organized attack against the Jews, but rather spontaneous protests against the Partition decision." The Jewish leadership, on the other hand, declared to the world: "The war of annihilation against the Jews has begun." In a meeting of the defense committee of December 10, the assessment sounded different: "The outbreak should not yet be seen as the start of planned, systematic and organized Arab aggression. The Arab population does not want a disruption of peace and security, and there is not a decision [by the Arab countries to go to war]."

The Haganah was ordered to limit itself to retaliatory strikes, so as not to expand the "circle of violence," and involve more Arabs. Nevertheless, the circle of attack and retaliation did spread. In mid-December, the Jewish leadership feared that the defense strategy could be construed as weakness. In the meeting of the defense committee of December 18, the leader of the Sephardi community in Jerusalem urged "wiping out" the Arabic suburb of Abu Kabir as a deterrent. The mayor of Petah Tikvah protested that the suggestion reminded him of Lidice, and that should make the members of the defense committee think.

In Haifa, inhabited by about 70,000 Arabs and an equal number of Jews, Arab traders began selling their wares at a 25 percent discount. Arab shops closed and the exodus of the Arab middle and upper classes began. According to estimates of the Mandate Authority, by mid-December 15,000 Arabs had left the city. Many went to nearby Lebanon, to Beirut. The population of Jaffa, too, the most modern Arab city of Palestine at that time, with almost 80,000 inhabitants and the center of the famous Jaffa oranges, then in Arab hands, was affected by the spreading civil war. Six weeks of hostility on the border of Tel Aviv had led to an almost complete collapse of life in the city. On January 6, 1948, members of Menachem Begin's extreme right wing Irgun militia blew up the city hall of Jaffa with a car bomb. With that, the exodus of the middle and upper classes began here, too. Most closed their homes and businesses, hoping to return in a few months—after the invasion of Arab troops from neighboring countries.

In Jerusalem, inhabited by some 50,000 Arabs and 100,000 Jews, the political and military situation was different. The Partition Plan granted the city an international status. Jerusalem, unlike Haifa and Jaffa, was in the middle of a region densely settled by Arabs. Access roads were controlled by the Arab militias, which—as everywhere in the country—resorted to interrupting traffic between the scattered Jewish areas of settlement. Jerusalem was one of the very few places where Jews had to flee from besieged neighborhoods of the city. The tactic of the Jewish militia was accordingly more aggressive here. In December and early January, the Haganah and the Irgun carried out repeated attacks on Arab suburbs on the road to Tel Aviv. After the conquest, Jewish officers ordered the population to evacuate the places. One town, Sheikh Badr, was plundered the next day by a Jewish mob. On February 5, 1948, Ben Gurion issued an order to conquer the Arab neighborhoods in West Jerusalem and to settle Jews in the vacated areas. Ben Gurion described the result at a party meeting on February 7: "If you drive into Jerusalem today—through Lifta, Romema, Mahaneh Yehudah, King George Street and Meah Shearim—there are no strangers anywhere. 100 percent Jews. Since Jerusalem's destruction in the days of the Romans, it hasn't been so Jewish as now. In many Arab areas, not one single Arab is seen. I do not assume this will change."

Ben Gurion concluded with a comment that gives the first, still indirect indication of a gradually hardening resolve under the impression of the past weeks: "What has happened in Jerusalem could well happen in large parts of the country—if we hold on. And if we hold on, it is very possible that in the coming six, eight, ten months of the war, there will take place great changes—not all of them to our detriment. Certainly there will be great changes in the composition of the population of the country."

In January and February 1948, in the coastal plain, the rural areas of the Galilee, and the areas south of Tel Aviv, a slow, constant exodus of Arab villagers began. In these areas, an increasingly violent struggle took place for the roads. In most cases, the inhabitants fled after attacks or retaliatory actions of the Haganah and Irgun, or out of fear of such attacks. In a few cases, whole villages were deliberately expelled, moved to flee by intimidation, or evacuated by order of Arab militias. The great majority of these refugees, particularly the urban population, counted neither on permanent exile nor permanent refugee status.

In the first four months after the Partition decision in New York, 75,000 to 100,000 Arabs fled. This first mass exodus was not the result of a general policy of expulsion, but rather of attacks and retaliatory strikes by the Jews to defend their own areas, and the fear and vulnerability of the Arabs. The extent and rapidity of the exodus surprised everybody. Among the Jewish leadership, they led to a new strategic thinking.

At this time, Joseph Weitz, one of the directors of the Jewish National Fund, traveled throughout the country, made notes, and wrote reports. In January, he spoke with the staff about the problem of the Jewish land in the Galilee leased to Arab farmers, and noted: "Isn't now the time to get rid of them? Why continue to keep these thorns in our midst when they pose a danger to us. Our people are weighing up [solutions]." When he heard that the Bedouins south of the Kinnereth had begun moving across the border to Jordan, he wrote: "It is possible that now is the time to implement our original plan: to transfer them there."

In early March, he organized with a few kibbutzim near Haifa to evacuate and destroy nearby Arab villages. In late March, he urged Ben Gurion to expel all the Arabs living in the future area of the State. Ben Gurion and the political leadership refused. Such a plan would be against international law and obligations. The British were still in the country, along with the international press and representatives of Western governments. All events would be closely observed. In relations with the Arabs, the future state leadership could not allow anything that could not be explained as the undesired and tragic results of the war. An open policy of expulsion was impossible in terms of both domestic and foreign policy.

Given the civil war, the Jewish political parties had formed a big coalition that included the religious parties, Ben Gurion's Labor party, Mapai, and the leftist socialist Mapam. In this war coalition, which formed the first Israeli government after the Declaration of Independence on May 15, only Mapam advocated an Arab-Jewish coexistence and protested the "voluntary" and involuntary exodus of the Arabs. The existence of this internal opposition was one of the factors that led to shifting all important decisions about the Arab question to a smaller war cabinet. Here, provided with dictatorial power, Ben Gurion, as prime minister and defense minister, along with the chief of staff of the army, acted without any real democratic or political control.

In March 1948, the British withdrawal was far advanced. The neighboring Arab countries had not formally decided on intervention, but all sides assumed that the civil war between the militias would very soon expand to a war between the armies of Israel and the neighboring countries. The Arab armies had to wait at least for the formal abolition of the Mandate and the complete withdrawal of the British, who would not allow foreign troops to invade Palestine. The Jewish leadership thus had one or two months to secure the interior of the future state where now only the weak Arab militias operated, and gather the scattered Jewish settlements into a defensible entity. The high command of the Haganah presented a plan for that—Plan D—in early March. Parts of this plan were later introduced by Arab historians as proof that at this point in time, a planned and systematic expulsion of the Arabs was intended. A close analysis of the operations and orders carried out under this plan, only a small part of which were in writing, gives a more complex picture. In fact, however, for all intents and purposes the defensive actions under Plan D in March through June led to an almost complete depopulation of the Arab areas. The interplay between military operations and a frightened Arab population ready to flee, had already been demonstrated.

Plan D anticipated a gradual takeover of British areas, as well as their military and civilian institutions. In these areas, the Haganah was to carry out "operations against enemy settlements which are in the rear of, within or near our defense lines with the aim of preventing their use as bases for an active armed force." Settlements were to be surrounded and searched for weapons and militia members. In case of resistance, enemy forces had to be destroyed and the inhabitants expelled from the area of the State. In case of peaceful surrender, the towns were to be disarmed and a garrison left behind. Should that not be possible, the villages were to be destroyed by burning, demolition, and mining of the ruins.

The Haganah wanted to take no risks. During the expected fighting with the Arab armies on the external borders, the internal areas of the country had to be secured. For all intents and purposes, all Arab towns within the future State were declared military targets.

* 5 *

Military operations anticipated in Plan D began on April 6, 1948, in Jerusalem. The objective was to abolish the almost complete cordon and siege of the western part of the city held by Jews. Within two weeks, dozens of Arab villages on the access roads were attacked and the militias expelled. The entire population of these towns fled either before or during the attacks. A few empty villages were completely destroyed; in others all the houses not needed for defense were blown up. This first big campaign of the Haganah, whose results would be partly reversed in later battles, had a shock effect on the Arabs. The case of one village, Deir Yassin, had such an effect that many Arabs and Jews saw this episode as the most important psychological factor in the events of the following months.

To this day, the Arabs consider the massacre of Deir Yassin symbolic of the Arab catastrophe. On the morning of April 9, the town on the western edge of Jerusalem was attacked by units of the two extreme right-wing Jewish militias, Irgun and Lehi. After a long, inconclusive exchange of fire with the Arab defenders barricaded in the village, the Haganah, which had reluctantly agreed to the action, had to come to the aid of the Jewish militias. They bombarded the village with mortars and thus drove out the last of the armed defenders. After the Haganah withdrew, members of Irgun and Lehi went from house to house and systematically killed the civilians hiding there, old men, women, and children. A few dozen men were driven together by the Jewish militiamen and executed in a stone quarry at the edge of the village. It was only the appearance of Orthodox Jews from the nearby neighborhood of Romema, who approached the village with loud shouts of protest, that put an end to the bloodbath. Some two dozen survivors were loaded onto open trucks and paraded through the Jewish quarters of the city and then expelled to the Arab part of Jerusalem, then the village was laid waste. The representative of the International Red Cross who entered the village shortly after reported some 200 victims, who had been killed "without any military reason or any provocation." The few houses of Deir Yassin that weren't blown up are now inhabited by Jewish citizens of Jerusalem. The former village school is part of a Jerusalem hospital.

Israel's political camps still argue about the number of dead in Deir Yassin, the course of the battle, and the question of whether it really was a massacre. The Likud party, historically associated with the two Jewish militias, the former commander of the Irgun and future prime minister Menachem Begin, as well as the former commander of the Lehi Militia and future prime minister, Yitzhak Shamir, claimed that the high rate of civilian casualties resulted from the violent battles. The attackers had done everything to prevent losses among Arab civilians.

Whether the massacre was planned or arose from rage at the failed attack is not clear even today. The tactic of intimidation used by Irgun and Lehi in later operations indicates that in Deir Yassin, too, the population was to be panicked by terrorist acts and driven to flight. The supreme command of the Haganah immediately condemned the crime of the rightist militias, but observed the effect of the massacre with great interest. Deir Yassin may have been the model and starting point of the "psychological warfare" used in later attacks by the Haganah and the Israeli army formed in May by the three militias. In this strategy, Israeli officers used a "whisper campaign" to inform the civilian population of the villages surrounded or designated for conquest that the Jews had carried out a massacre in the area or that they wanted to. In most cases, these communications made the entire village population flee.

News of the events of Deir Yassin, which were immediately condemned by leftist Jewish parties and the leadership, reached all villages and towns. The concrete threat and intimidation represented by the massacre influenced events in Haifa and Jaffa, which were attacked two weeks later by Jewish troops behind the withdrawing British.

At that point, Halid Mansur, who has lived in the big refugee camp in the West Bank town of Jenin since 1948, was a member of the Arab militia in Haifa. In an interview in the summer of 1997, he remembered the mood among the fighters in Haifa and the fear among the civilians: "Seven Arab countries persuaded us that the Jews were weak and couldn't defeat the Arabs. We were to hold out. We got weapons from the Arab countries and believed we could hold out until the liberation of Palestine by the Arab armies. It didn't happen because the British protected Israel and the Jews. We held out, but the majority fled because they thought: What happened in Deir Yassin will also happen to us."

One of the opponents of Halid Mansur and his people was young Haganah officer Gershon Gilad, who had come to Palestine from Germany as an illegal immigrant in 1933. In 1997, still living in Haifa, he described the situation in Haifa at that time: "For years we of the Haganah had prepared our army. It was a very strong army, very well organized. We had to bring weapons into the country illegally—and we were successful. But all that was not aimed at conquering or driving the Arabs out of the country. It was defense. The fighting began because the Arabs disrupted the roads, shot at buses and cars, and killed people here and there by shooting from their neighborhoods into ours. That's how it started."

The Jewish attack on Arab Haifa began hastily. On the night of April 20–21, the British had unexpectedly retreated to the beach and the port. The Haganah acted to fill the vacuum. At noon on the 21st, Jewish troops began by conquering strategic access roads, in the evening with an attack on the Arab quarter. The so-called battle for Haifa, which brought a total catastrophe for the Arabs, lasted about 24 hours. Some five hundred Jewish soldiers took part in it and twenty were killed. Halid Mansur remembered: "The battle began at about six in the evening. Tanks and artillery bombarded us. We were at home, defended our houses, our land, our children, sisters, mothers. A few people hid their valuables. At four in the morning, we heard that our fighters had run out of ammunition. We couldn't do anything against the British, against British cannons and tanks. Against the Jews, yes, who were weaker than we were. Then we fled to the port, in great fear."

The grenades Halid Mansur heard came not from the British, who observed the conquest of the Arab quarters of the city from nearby, but from Haganah mortars. They had placed their bets on causing the greatest possible shock and surprise, and thus bombarded the center of Arab Haifa, the market, without ado. Cut off from supplies, all Halid Mansur and his people could do was follow the others. "Our commanders informed us that we had nothing to defend ourselves with. If we had stayed there, they would have killed us as in Deir Yassin. So we were forced to go to the port. In the east, the English blockaded us; in the west, the English and the Jews. There was only one way out: the port. The English opened the gates, all inhabitants of Haifa came down to the port, and the English guaranteed them protection. On the way, many were killed. The Jews shot down at us from Hadar HaCarmel, at women and children. There was one woman who started shouting on the boat: 'My son! My son!' In her haste, she had grabbed a pillow instead of her baby."

The story of the baby mistakenly left behind comes up in many reports of refugees. It is part of collective formulas depicting the event and expression of loss, which has led most Israeli historians to a wholesale rejection of these Arab oral sources.

The Haganah attack on Haifa's Arab quarter followed the logic of Plan D: hostile or potentially hostile localities had to be pacified by surrounding and shelling them and, if unavoidable, by conquest. The mass flight triggered by the mortar shelling was not an effect initially intended, as Gershon Gilad recalled in 1997: "We had only a few mortars. These weapons were not used much; some were even homemade. I don't remember if there was a real artillery attack on the Arab quarter, the market. What I do remember is that, during the battle on May 22 or 23, we shelled the market to break the remaining resistance, to use our advantage, because their resistance began to collapse. If a few mortar grenades hit them, they would give up faster. But we didn't mean to say: Pack your things and get out of the city."

The shelling of the market put not only 1,500 Arab militiamen to flight, but also almost the entire civilian population—50,000 people. Mansur recalled: "There was great fear and sadness. We went down to the port. The British brought landing craft. It took a week to bring everybody to Akko, two or three hundred each time. The dead lay on the streets. Only seven days later did a ship come to take those wounded in the last fights from Haifa to Akko. The people said we had lost Palestine. We were lost. Where were we to sleep, get food? Where to find work, a place to live? We had lost our home and our country. Shopkeepers had lost their shops, workers their work. We were lost as a people. It was hopeless. A few wept because they had lost their sons or had not heard from them. Maybe they had been killed or wounded on the way, maybe taken prisoner by the Jews. It was a horrible tragedy."

After the fighting ended, Gershon Gilad visited the Arab quarters. "I felt uneasy. I had never seen anything like it. Not even in a dream had I imagined such a thing could happen. We were glad. Maybe glad isn't the right word. We were satisfied that it was over."

The Arabs of Haifa, who had been taken by boat to Akko, did not find a lasting refuge there either. In the same week, the Haganah began shelling the old port city, and two weeks later, Akko was conquered. Of the more than 40,000 people in the city, 90 percent fled over the border to Lebanon and Syria or to the West Bank of the Jordan.

Three days after the battle for Haifa, the attack on Jaffa took place. That was the biggest Arab city of Palestine, which was to belong to the Arab state as an enclave in the Jewish territory. This city adjacent to Tel Aviv, surrounded by Jewish settlements, was not regarded as a threat by the Haganah, who planned to use a blockade to force the militia in Jaffa to give up. But the Irgun, led by the right-wing opposition, saw it as an opportunity to send a political signal.

The attack on Jaffa began at dawn on April 25, with shelling by heavy mortars stolen from the British. The Irgun needed three days to take the well-defended city. For seventy-two hours, the inner city quarters were under grenade fire. Among the defenders was seventeen-year-old Emile Toubassi, who recalled in an interview in 1997: "The people in Jaffa knew there was no more hope. Panic prevailed also because of the massacre in Deir Yassin. Everybody prepared to emigrate. There was the way through the sea, to Port Said or Alexandria in Egypt or Beirut, and the way by land from Jaffa to Ramallah. You couldn't get to Jerusalem because of the siege." Weeks earlier, Emile Toubassi's father had gotten a visa for Egypt, but the only Egyptian ship in Jaffa took only Egyptian workers on board. The next day, the family heard that a Swedish ship bound for Beirut was in the harbor. Emile Toubassi reported: "We needed a visa for Lebanon. I still remember the line of people that stretched more than five kilometers, all of them wanting a visa. It was April 26, 1948. The consul was a friend of my father. We were lucky. When we came to the ship in a boat at night, the ship was already too full. A few boats had capsized. Corpses were swimming in the water. We had to go back."

The Swedish ship left without the Toubassi family. A few days later, the British, who had again stayed out of the fighting, also organized the evacuation of the remaining inhabitants. Toubassi: "We were given five days. Then we went to Ramallah in a convoy of twenty to thirty cars with one British tank in front and one in back."

Fakhri Geday, who lives in Jaffa, was studying in Beirut in the spring of 1948 and had no news of his family in Jaffa. In 1997, he described how he was one of the very few who was able to return to his family in Jaffa two years later. Of the roughly 80,000 original inhabitants of Jaffa, only 3,000 were left: "In 1950, I got a letter from the Red Cross about a plan to unite families. My father had attempted to get permission for me to return. When I returned, Jaffa was full of Jewish immigrants. Bulgarian Jews, Romanian, Polish. Jaffa was full of people from all sorts of countries, very cosmopolitan. In Beirut, I had gotten more than ten keys from people who wanted me to look in on their homes. My father only laughed. Throw the keys away, he said. All houses are now inhabited by other people. In fact, a house with three or four rooms was occupied by three or four families." The story of the keys taken into exile, symbolic of the loss and sudden homelessness, is another collective formula that appears in many refugee memoirs.

What Fakhri Geday found on his return to Jaffa in 1950 was the result of a policy that began to take shape in late April 1948. In Joseph Weitz's journal, we find references to this new attitude, which, for good reason, was not put into writing. In the meantime, the Haganah and the Irgun had conquered not only most Arab towns in the territory intended for the Jewish State, but also additional territory. On April 21, Weitz noted: "Our army is steadily conquering Arab villages and the residents . . . flee like mice [when] during the night a few shells will whistle over them. Villages are steadily emptying, and if we continue on this course—and we shall certainly do so, as our strength increases—then villages will empty of their inhabitants."

In mid-April, for the first time, Ben Gurion gave a direct order to "cleanse" an entire rural region southeast of Haifa of Arabs, despite an offer of a cease-fire by the Arab militia. The leftist coalition partner, Mapam, protested. Ben Gurion accused his cabinet colleagues of hypocrisy: "The ideology of the Jewish-Arab brotherhood was one thing, strategic necessities another." Our troops "face a cruel reality," he said. "[They] saw that there was [only] one way and that was to expel the Arab villagers and burn their villages."

Since early April, an additional group of almost 200,000 people were forced to flee. On May 14, two weeks after the fall of Jaffa, the British concluded their withdrawal. The State of Israel was declared and the Jewish immigrants, who had waited for the opening of the borders, were finally let into the country. This combination of factors—the reinforcement of the strategic position of the Jews by incoming waves of immigrants and the flight of the Arabs in the face of the Haganah attacks—led to the policy of targeted expulsions. On June 15, Israeli Foreign Minister Moshe Sharett wrote to Nahum Goldmann, president of the World Jewish Congress: "The opportunities which the present position open up for a lasting and radical solution of the most vexing problems of the Jewish State are so far-reaching as to take one's breath away. Even if a certain backwash is unavoidable, we must make the most of this momentous chance with which history has presented us so swiftly and so unexpectedly."

* 6 *

With the intervention of the neighboring Arab countries on May 15, the civil war changed into a confrontation between armies. But here too, forces were extremely unequal. The Arab countries, released from the colonial yoke, underdeveloped and impoverished, sent a troop of 23,000 men into battle against the just established Israeli army with more than 35,000 soldiers in fighting units. Only the Arab Legion of Jordan was regarded as a serious opponent by the Israelis. But, on the basis of secret agreements between the Jewish leadership and King Abdullah of Jordan, the Legion limited itself to defending areas designated as Arab under the Partition Plan that Abdullah wanted to annex to his kingdom. The secret talks the previous year had not brought agreement about Jerusalem or the link to the coast. Only here the Legion and the Israeli army fought one another.

After the first cease-fire on June 11, the cabinet dealt with the question of whether the refugees could return. Ben Gurion saw the return as the seed of a new war. Too many Arab villages and towns had been destroyed and plundered in the meantime. Moreover, room had to be made for the Jewish immigrants. On June 16, this position became official Israeli policy. On June 17, 1948, the government explained to U.N. negotiator Count

Bernadotte, who demanded that more than 300,000 refugees be taken back: "This question cannot be discussed while the war was going on. The government has not yet fixed its policy about the ultimate settlement of the matter. Proprietary rights would certainly be respected." Thus was a policy formulated, which is still in effect. In July, the foreign minister telegraphed instructions to the Israeli U.N. delegation containing the key arguments the Israeli government would also use in subsequent decades to absolve itself of all guilt:

1. Arab exodus direct result folly aggression organized by Arab states.
2. No question allowing Arab return while state of war continuing. . . . Exceptions only in favor special deserving cases compassionate grounds. . . .
3. Question of Arab return can be decided only as part peace settlement with Arab states. . . .

But the first phase of the Arab tragedy was not yet over. In brief military operations following the first cease-fire, new territories were conquered between the summer and winter of 1948—in the north, the whole of the Galilee, in the south, the Negev Desert and a broad strip of land between Tel Aviv and Jerusalem, which included the Arab cities of Ramle (now Ramla) and Lydda (now Lod, where Ben-Gurion Airport is located). In July 1948, only a single company of Jordanian troops, some hundred-fifty soldiers, was ready to protect it, expecting that the Israeli government would stick to the secret agreement with Abdullah. But for the Israeli government, the two towns outside the designated territory of the State, but barely twenty kilometers from Tel Aviv, represented such a great threat that they assigned several brigades to conquer them. The orders read: the defenders are to be overpowered as quickly as possible and the population moved to flee.

On July 10 and 11, the cities were bombed from the ground and from the air. Part of the population fled. On the night of July 12, the Jordanian troops withdrew. At the same time the city council of Lydda signed the surrender. The document guaranteed protection for the life and property of the population. Israeli troops entered Lydda at dawn and interned the male population in the mosques and churches of the city in order to conduct an unimpeded search for weapons. Only in the police station was there still a handful of Jordanian soldiers and militia.

Engineer Aspeer Monayer volunteered to take care of the victims of the air raids of the previous days and spent the night in the hospital. The next morning, Israeli soldiers drove him and all the staff into a mosque. At ten thirty, the women and children present were ordered to leave the city and go to "King Abdullah," to Jordanian territory beyond the front. Christian men were separated from Moslems and interned in churches. At 11 a.m., Aspeer Monayer, a Christian, persuaded an Israeli officer to let the clinic staff back into the hospital. In an interview in 1997, Monayer remembered: "On the morning of July 12, things were quiet. Suddenly, at noon, we heard shooting and explosions everywhere. We didn't know why. We thought the city had been taken already. Then from the balcony, we saw people running, falling, shot. At two o'clock, everything was quiet again. Then we heard that many in the streets had been shot, in the mosques too, that everyone in the mosques had been shot. Later we learned that Jordanian armored vehicles had penetrated the city to liberate the Jordanian commander and had then withdrawn again."

In the confusion caused by the entry of the armored cars, a massacre began whose precise course is still controversial. Apparently, some of the inhabitants considered the exchange of fire with the Jordanians as a signal to resume the fighting and started shooting at the Israeli soldiers from the houses. Others tried to flee. Panic erupted among the relatively small Israeli occupation force, some three hundred men in a city of more than 60,000 inhabitants. The soldiers shot everything that moved. In a few mosques, the interned Moslems were killed. In the end, some three hundred Arabs lay dead in the streets.

Two days later, Aspeer Monayer was ordered to bury the dead: "We had to carry the corpses to the cars. Then we had to bury them in graves, open graves. Two days later, we couldn't lift the corpses anymore. The arms and legs fell off the bodies. I had to throw up and was sick. I couldn't go there anymore. It's very very hard when you know the people, when they're friends."

As Christians, Aspeer and his family were treated differently from their Moslem neighbors. In the conquest of Nazareth and other Christian-Arab towns in the north, too, distinctions were made between Christians and Moslems. The Israeli government had just decided to exempt the Christians—a small, mainly urban minority among the Arabs—from the expulsion, either in consideration for public opinion in Christian countries or with the expectation that Christian Arabs would be less hostile to the Jewish State. In any case, Aspeer and his family were spared the fate that now struck the Moslem population.

The baker Mahmud Ali Jassen, who has lived in Ramallah since his flight from Lydda in 1948, shared the fate of the Moslem part of the population. He had survived the bloodbath on the second day after the conquest, because, as a baker, he was allowed to leave the mosque before the massacre to bake bread. On the third day after the conquest, soldiers came to his bakery and expelled him. In 1997, he said: "They told us: Go to the mountains, everybody go to the mountains. To Barfiliyya. They put an Arab in a jeep with a megaphone and drove all around the city. The city was big. Those at one end didn't know what was happening at the other end. The news went from mouth to mouth. It took three or four days until everybody was gone. After we had left the city, we had to walk another four or five kilometers. It was summer, July, and we were fasting because of Ramadan. The people wanted to drink, but there was no water. The water was as far as from here to Beit Hanina. If somebody came back with water to give it to his family, others attacked him because there was no water. An old man lay on the side of the road. He asked for water. But who could give him water? He lay there and died. Four or five people died like that. We carried them into a wheat field and covered them up. They died of thirst." Ali Jassen and the fifteen members of his family survived the march and reached the Jordanian-occupied West Bank at dawn.

After Israel conquered this part of Palestine, too, after the 1967 war, Ali Jassen and his three children went back for the first time since 1948 to visit his house in Lydda. The house was now inhabited by an Israeli of Polish origin who had been given the house by the government in late 1948.

A second cease-fire in July 1948 gave the Israeli army an opportunity to clear the interior of the Jewish territory and the front lines of hostile or "potentially hostile" Arab inhabitants. This time, the attacks on the still intact villages south and southeast of Haifa provoked protests abroad. The U.N. decided to investigate and U.N. envoy Count Bernadotte called the conquests unjustified, especially "in view of the willingness for negotiations," and condemned Israel for the "systematic" destruction of villages. The attacks of July through October put about 100,000 more people to flight.

After fighting resumed on October 15, the Israeli army conquered more territory: the upper Galilee, the coastal strip south of Tel Aviv, the foothills of the Judean highland, and the northern part of the Negev Desert with the Arab city of Be'er Sheba. By the end of December, another 100,000 to 150,000 Arabs had fled.

During operations in October, a series of atrocities took place against prisoners and Arab civilians. The leftist Mapam party began collecting witness accounts. In one village, Ad Dawayima, the Israeli conquerors carried out a massacre on October 29. One Jewish participant reported to the party: "The first [wave] of conquerors killed eighty to a hundred men, women, and children. The children were killed by breaking their heads with sticks." The rest of the population was locked in the houses without food or water. One of the officers ordered a soldier to blow up the houses. The soldier refused. Others carried out the order. One soldier boasted that he had raped a woman and then shot her. One woman with a newborn baby in her arms was employed to clean the courtyard where the soldiers ate. In the end, they shot her and the baby. . . . Cultured officers had turned into base murderers—not in the heat of battle, . . . but out of a system of expulsion and destruction. The fewer Arabs remained—the better. This principle is the political motor for the expulsions and atrocities."

In November, Mapam called for an official investigation of the "Nazi actions," as one party leader put it. The cabinet finally assigned three government ministers to investigate the incidents. Their report, presented to the cabinet in early December, is still classified. Several officers and soldiers were discharged or imprisoned. In late December, for the first time, the army received guidelines for relations with the Arabs, but the measure came too late.

In the final weeks of the war, the Israeli army conquered the entire Negev as far as Eilat, and expelled most of the Bedouins living there. As the year ended, only 100,000 Arabs remained in the territory of the Israeli State, where there had originally been about a million. Yitzhak Pundak, born in Poland in 1913 and immigrated to Palestine in 1933, had just been promoted to brigadier general in the new Israeli army. As commander of the southern sector, he had cleared out hundreds of villages during the war. In 1997, he was asked how he now endures the injustice done to the Arab population under his command. "The population of two hundred villages fled. We destroyed the villages. You can say that's an injustice. But the greater injustice was done to the Jews in the Holocaust. A hundred thousand Jews were waiting to come to the country to find a homeland. Their only homeland was Israel. Nobody wanted to take them. Europe. France, England, the United States—nobody wanted them. They were seeking a homeland, and the only refuge was Israel. So, where could we settle them? In Tel Aviv? We needed land to take in the people, to build settlements for them. So, naturally we were happy the Arabs fled."

Thus ended the first chapter of the Palestinian catastrophe.

* 7 *

The next chapter began with the refusal of the Israeli government to take back all or part of the refugees. The obligation to take back refugees from war zones after the end of the fighting is enshrined in international law and weighed heavily on Israel. At the end of 1948, the U.N. and the supporters of Israel there demanded unequivocally that the government agree in principle to take back all those who wanted to return. It was assumed that not all former Arab inhabitants would want to live in the Israeli State. The relevant U.N. resolution of December placed no term on the return and spoke only of the "earliest possible point in time." Nevertheless, the Israeli government refused. The neighboring Arab states, who had provided asylum for the refugees, declared that they were unable economically to keep all the refugees in their countries in the long run. Nevertheless, the Israeli government turned down the possibility of a peace treaty that had surfaced during the Geneva peace negotiations in the spring of 1949. The Israeli strategy, which remained in effect until the 1990s, was expressed by the future Foreign Minister Abba Eban in July 1949: "[There is] no need to run after peace. An armistice is sufficient for us. If we run after peace, the Arabs will demand of us a price: borders or refugees or both. We will wait a few years." A few years turned into decades. The Arab countries that were initially willing to integrate some of the refugees, soon recognized them as the only means of pressure they could use against Israel. Thus began the next chapter of the catastrophe: a continued existence as refugees in the dreadful conditions of the camps.

At the end of the war of 1948–1949, the new borders of Israel encompassed almost 80 percent of the whole Mandatory territory of Palestine. By the summer of 1949, some 200,000 Jewish immigrants came to the country. Sixty percent of them were lodged in deserted Arab houses. Jewish settlements, kibbutzim or moshavim, arose on the ruins or near destroyed villages. According to a U.N. study, about a quarter of all housing stock was in the deserted Arab towns. Thus, the abandoned property of the Arabs guaranteed the economic survival of the young state. While Israel profited from the flight and expropriation, the Arab society of Palestine collapsed. Most of the refugees and their offspring still live in refugee camps in the occupied territories or on the borders of Palestine. The rest have found a new home in Arab countries, Europe, or America. Many of the refugees still dream of returning to a homeland of which nothing remains.

8

* AN END, A BEGINNING *

* 1 *

On a rainy November day in 1983, in the second year of the Lebanese war, I joined the members of my lecturers' unit at a Tel Aviv cinema. We had come here from all over the country to meet the new commander of the education corps and to attend his lecture explaining the new slogans. Many considered the new man regular army and an adherent of that ubiquitous Orwellian idea of "security," which, in Israeli usage, covered the disturbingly broad span from basic human need to the radical methods used to satisfy it. The mood in the unheated, damp cinema rented by the army for that day wasn't exactly cheerful. The Lebanon war had opened a deep credibility gap between citizens and government, and relations between the various levels of command in the army were troubled.

In the very first month of the war, when a shocked population and, as is maintained to this day, a shocked majority in the cabinet became aware of Israel's complete war aims in Lebanon, a protest had risen against the invasion. Hardly three weeks after the beginning of the invasion on June 6, 1982, the protest movement "Peace Now" held a meeting in Jerusalem attended by several hundred people, including me. One week later, the first mass demonstration took place in the center of Tel Aviv. For the first time in the history of Israeli wars, there were public protests in the middle of the war itself, a breakdown of the national consensus, and it had the effect of an earthquake. At about the same time, barely a month after the beginning of the invasion, in a letter to Prime Minister Begin, eighty officers and soldiers asked to be relieved of duty beyond the 1967 borders: "Too many of us have been killed, too many of us have died in Lebanon," said the letter. Shortly after, the education corps put on the emergency brake. Lectures of the reserve unit were stopped for fear that the Left could "sabotage the war effort," as Defense Minister Sharon put it.

A few colleagues had drawn far-reaching conclusions from the invitation to the meeting: the new commander clearly planned to abolish the exceptional position of the education corps and finally turn us into a normal military unit, where deviant behavior wouldn't be tolerated. Ours was an outfit that considered itself not the least important in the country. Thus, the new general had to contend with the easily offended vanity of a group whose members had been pulled out of their normal activity solely to give the new man an opportunity, as many expected, to strut around before us with a presumably unimportant and badly formulated speech. Announced by his deputy, when he strode stiffly out of the wings to the lectern in dark red paratrooper boots and roared "Good morning," all the fears seemed confirmed at one fell swoop.

The unfortunate greeting was followed by an equally ill-fated meeting. The new commander, an infantry general, began with a maneuver that revealed him immediately as a distinguished strategist: before he began to inspire us and spur the unit to new achievements, he engaged in a far-reaching criticism of our previous work. In sharp, undiplomatic terms, he accused our unit of laxity and unprofessionalism and blasted the frequent cancellations and excuses we apparently used to shirk our reserve duty. He didn't list numbers, for such things should not reach the ears of the enemy. In fact, the system of requisitioning us to the unit for one or two-day stints of lectures and appearances lent itself to abuse. We had to fill a certain annual number of service days, but nobody could or would check whether a lecturer's refusal was justified by illness, family, or professional obligations. The system was based on trust and the assumption that the desire to stay in the unit acted as a curb on abuse. Taking my own cancellations in the past twelve months as a gauge of the "fighting morale" of all reservists in our unit, the lecturers must have missed about half their assignments.

Today's assignment was evidently more popular. Of the more than five hundred members of the unit, about three hundred had made it to the cinema. These scholars and lecturers in Israel's colleges submitted to the military hierarchy on this day, and listened silently to the general's tirades. Even the leader of our unit, Major Krauthammer, who sat unmoving in the first row of the auditorium, seemed to endure the inevitable with iron discipline. The general explained the measures he planned to take to rectify the problem. From now on, the education corps would insist that we satisfy 100 percent of our reserve duty. Since the members of the lecturers' unit now fulfilled only half their annual duty, the unit could get along with half the lecturers in the future. The other half were to be transferred in subsequent months to other departments of the education unit or transferred out of the corps to other troops. That sounded like a threat, was meant to be, and was taken as such by those present. Reserve service in the education corps was considered the best lot a scholar in the humanities or social sciences could draw. Unlike colleagues in medicine, natural sciences, or engineering, the education corps offered these scholars the only possibility of doing reserve duty under civilian circumstances in their own field. Since annual reserve duty covered about thirty days and lasted until the age of fifty, the place and circumstances of the assignments remained important.

An outsider would easily have dismissed the general's criticism and the problem of shirking duty as an inevitable result of the special structure of the Israel Defense Forces: along with the small professional army and basic military service, half the army consisted of reservists. Without the citizens who left their civilian life behind for a month year after year, the army and the State could not exist. For the Zionist part of Israeli society, military service was considered the highest civic duty, the epitome of Israeliness; and membership in a particular unit or branch of the service formed an important part of one's personal identity. Among able-bodied young people, the army was even so popular that the ranks of combat units could be filled exclusively by volunteers. In hardly any other state did the military and civilian realms mesh so closely, in hardly any other society were the borders between citizen and soldier so indistinct. The result was a society militarized from the bottom up. Sometimes you couldn't tell whether the Jewish inhabitants of Israel were soldiers in civilian clothes or civilians in uniform. That made the defense policy of the State into a private matter, but it also made the political opinions, fears, and desires of the citizens into a military matter.

This amalgam of the military and the civilian led to a marked conformity in questions of "security." A citizen could hardly feel free in civilian life to reject a specific policy if he had to risk his life for it as a soldier. Hence, political and social debates in the society submitted to a certain discipline, while the army had to show a certain tolerance for the political opinions of the citizen soldiers. For reservists, this blend of forced conformity and freedom was often confusing, but most learned quickly what the issue really was: the individual would be granted a certain degree of freedom as long as his loyalty remained basically guaranteed. While in uniform, the citizen was not allowed to agitate, but was permitted to express his political problems with concrete orders. The venting of political concerns ultimately provided for the internal cohesion and functioning of the unit. As soon as there was any doubt about whether aberrant opinions were conducive to cohesion, political expressions were immediately banned. The new general also referred to this code of behavior. His criticism of us aimed not at the small quota of reserved duty filled, which presumably had always been at such a low level, but rather at our slack attitude concerning discipline and our unreliability in questions of politics and ideology. Even if his reproaches were formulated indirectly, the reaction showed that the reasons for his reprimand were correctly understood.

In the framework of our military meeting, criticism of Israel's actions in Lebanon could not be expressed directly. This time, officers and soldiers had a special reason for criticism that went far beyond the general dissatisfaction in the population. In the first days of the invasion, the general staff, the sector commanders, and the commanders of the battle groups that moved into Lebanon, those ad-hoc divisions with which Israel made war, had left the lower-ranking officers in the dark about the real purpose of the invasion. From the company commanders up to the battalion commanders, everyone was deceived. This maneuver concealed political motives. Because the defense minister and the war cabinet—the "Government Committee for Security Issues"—could not rely on a general cabinet agreement to the full objectives of the war before the invasion began, the decisions to advance to Syrian-controlled territory, the march to Beirut, and "cleansing" the western part of the city were presented and ratified individually during the first ten days of the war. Permission was sometimes requested only after the fact, as reliable sources stated, and as could later be inferred from the report of the Israeli committee that investigated the massacre in Sabra and Shatila. In addition, the American allies, the Israeli opposition, and possibly even the population would have raised objections immediately to the full war objectives.

These political obstacles led to a plan of attack that was risky and unsuitable for the real objectives of the invasion. If the war cabinet had had a free hand from the beginning, the troops would have advanced directly and on other roads to Beirut, and attacked PLO installations and Syrian positions in eastern Lebanon faster, more efficiently and more massively, and cut off their supplies. The slower procedure had left the defenders in Beirut and the Biqa Valley a lot of time to entrench themselves, reinforce the units, and provide supplies. All that had cost lives, of Israeli soldiers whose tank units had to fight in the impassable mountains with Syrian commandos and ambushes, and of Lebanese civilians who fell victim to the massive aerial bombardment of PLO positions in Beirut that became necessary later. The eventual failure of the political strategy behind the invasion, which turned out to have been naïve and shortsighted from the beginning, further undermined trust between the officer corps and the army leadership, between the population and the government.

In his tirade against the members of the lecturers' unit, the new general had chosen the coded attack, so it was only legitimate to answer him in code. What my colleagues thought about the war, I could only guess; but whatever their political views, these representatives of Israel's intellectual elite would not take a scolding from an uneducated infantry general, who didn't speak decent Hebrew, lying down. After a while, a familiar tone rose in the auditorium and everywhere heads began turning to locate the source of the disturbance. What was resounding behind me was not the rhythmic cracking, chewing, and spitting of sunflower seeds that formed the background noise of Israeli movie theaters, but rather the rustling of newspapers.

More and more colleagues had gradually pulled their newspapers out of their briefcases, spread them out fully, and started reading. The general turned red and broke off his litany. He twisted his face into a grimace of profound hatred and rage I will never forget. He started stammering, raised his arms, and clenched his fists. Apparently the right words eluded him. Never had he seen anything like that, and neither had we. Only after an interruption that went on much too long and whose length could augur nothing good either for us or for him, he pulled himself together and shouted into the auditorium: "Anybody who doesn't want to serve in this unit anymore can go!" I was sorry I had finished reading my newspaper and thrown it away.

It would have been easy to underestimate the significance of this protest. It was precisely the older lecturers, the core of the unit, who started it. They had to summon up all their courage to pull out the newspaper, unfold it in plain sight, and hide behind it. The protest arose from their loyalty to the army and their attachment to the unit and thus could not easily be dismissed. And cautious as the manifestation of dissent was, the place and time of the act made it explosive. The attack on Lebanon, it seemed to me, was not the target of the criticism. What the troops seemed to be responding to were the commander's reproaches that they were neglecting their duty: they, the leadership, had neglected their duty to us! The subject of the protest was really the same crisis of loyalty that had emerged in the Lebanese war between citizen and army, soldier and government. It resulted from the strategy of deceit and the gradual disclosure of hidden plans, and thus it did not fit the family-like intimacy of Jewish society, so typical for a community defined by nationalism, external enemies, and constant readiness for defense.

* 2 *

Ever since the second victory of Likud under Menachem Begin in June 1981, the army leadership and the Ministry of Defense now led by Ariel Sharon had been working on plans to remove the PLO militias in Lebanon. In the fall of 1981, the general staff presented three plans of operation—"Big Pine" and "Little Pine," of which there were two variations. All three plans started out by pushing the PLO back to a line forty kilometers north of the border, where Palestinian artillery and missile batteries no longer represented a threat. The maximum range of the artillery also formed the line of the political maximum if the government wanted to assure support of the U.S. and the Israeli opposition for its military action. "Little Pine" anticipated advancing forty kilometers into Lebanese territory and destroying PLO militias, their bases, and infrastructure there. In the smaller variant, the territory to be conquered stretched from the coastal town of Rosh Hanikra, the southernmost point of the Israeli-Lebanese border, to the Awali River in the north. The bigger variant of Operation Little Pine measured the maximum depth of the advance from the northernmost point of the border, the Israeli town of Metulla. From here, the cordon would reach to the Lebanese coastal city of Damur, only fifteen kilometers from the city limits of Beirut, and would stretch in the east to Syrian army bases in the Biqa Valley. According to this plan, the Israeli army would reach twenty-five kilometers from Damascus in the east. An invasion of the Lebanese capital was not anticipated. Expelling the PLO from West Beirut was to be done by the allied militias of the Christian Phalangists, and a confrontation with Syrian troops was to be avoided.

Operation Big Pine was much more ambitious. This was the plan finally presented by Prime Minister Begin and Defense Minister Sharon to the full cabinet for adoption in December 1981. The plan forecast an advance to Beirut, where Israeli troops were to join with those of the Phalangists. "Big Pine" aimed at expelling all PLO militias, including those in and around Beirut, and all Syrian troops, from Lebanon. "Purging" Beirut from PLO fighters in a street fight was reserved for the Phalangist units. The

Israeli army wanted to form a barrier south, east, and north of the city. The political ideas behind Operation Big Pine went further. The military campaign was finally to end Syrian influence on Lebanese policy and the interventions of Damascus on behalf of the Moslems and Druse. As Defense Minister Sharon saw it, the liberation of Lebanon from these radical, anti-Israeli influences had to lead to the birth of a new political order. In the new Lebanon, the Christian parties, allies of Jerusalem, would play the crucial role and grant Israel far-reaching influence. The plan meant substituting Israel for Syria as the protecting power and puppet master of Lebanese politics. However, the real objective of this very ambitious intervention was not Lebanon, but rather the pacification and annexation of the occupied West Bank. Only by completely annihilating the military potential of the PLO and inflicting radical political damage on the Palestinians and their allies could Israel have a free hand in the occupied territories.

According to reliable reports, a majority of the Israeli cabinet resolutely rejected this plan in December 1981. The cease-fire with the PLO forced by the U.S. that summer made an operation in Lebanon difficult in any case. Israel had to wait for an opportunity to offer the political pretext for an attack. The international press reported from Lebanon that, during this time, the Israeli army had positioned troops at the border four times and then withdrew. Then, the shooting of the Israeli ambassador in London by the Abu-Nidal group, which operated outside the PLO, offered the pretext. On the eve of the invasion, the cabinet in Jerusalem apparently agreed to an operation corresponding to the larger variant of Little Pine. Yet what was set in motion on that Sunday, June 6, 1982, at eleven o'clock in the morning was Operation Big Pine.

The following Thursday, the Knesset met in Jerusalem to discuss the attack on Lebanon. The news from the front was good. Israeli troops quickly reached the coast and the south. The east, where the Syrian positions were, had remained quiet. The Israeli population seemed to be in the throes of patriotic enthusiasm as in any other war. A no-confidence motion of the three Communist deputies was thrown out. In his declaration, the prime minister curbed his usually effusive rhetoric, speaking slowly and portentously, apparently distressed by the regrettable, unavoidable bloodshed. Israel did not want to annex a single "quarter millimeter" of Lebanese territory, he stated. Israeli troops would not attack Syrian troops as long as they could operate freely. Begin promised that the advance would come to a halt after securing the 40 kilometer buffer zone. "All we want is that our citizens in the north no longer have to languish in bunkers day and night," he stated. Up to this time, everything seemed to proceed according to the usual formula—a wise government had thought up a clever plan, the best of all armies successfully carried out the plan, and the people were united behind it. While the session was still in progress, a voice over the Knesset loudspeaker requested those present to give blood for the soldiers fighting in Lebanon. Blood donors were to register in an office on the fifth floor.

The next day, the fourth day of the war, Israeli airplanes and ground troops attacked Syrian air defense positions in the Biqa Valley. After the trauma of the successful Syrian Golan Heights offensive in October 1973, the prospect of a fight with Syria scared the Israeli population the most. The Syrian air force tried in vain to defend the positions situated along the Syrian-Lebanese border and, on this and the next day, lost 79 airplanes, while not one single Israeli jet was damaged. The Israeli press lauded this fight between a developing country armed with outmoded Soviet material and an industrial state provided with the most modern American technology, and called the unhindered shooting down of Syrian planes "the greatest air battle of all time." The advance against Syrian ground troops took somewhat more time and came to a halt on June 24, when the U.S. forced a cease-fire. The Israeli army was now in the suburbs of Beirut, controlled the roads from the Lebanese capital to Damascus, and the stretch of water before the Lebanese coast north of Beirut. This cut off all supply lines and possibilities of retreat for the remaining Syrian troops in Beirut and the PLO "army" in their bunkers in the capital and the refugee camps in the south.

The PLO combat units in the south, surrounded during the rapid advance, entrenched in densely settled refugee camps and in coastal towns, were now gradually attacked and destroyed, with great losses mainly among Palestinian civilians. In Beirut, the focus of world opinion, such a procedure didn't seem possible. Israeli intelligence assumed that the PLO had two or three thousand fighters and a lot of heavy weapons in the Moslem districts in the west and southwest of the capital. The Israeli government was inclined neither to sacrifice Israeli soldiers in street fighting nor to occupy the Arab capital, and expected the Phalangists to fulfill the agreements concerning the "purge" of Beirut. Israel's Christian allies, however, refused and thus confronted the government in Jerusalem with a difficult problem. The unannounced and politically risky advance to Beirut had to result in the complete expulsion of the PLO, their forces, civilian authorities, and chairman Yassir Arafat. Anything else was tantamount to a loss of prestige of the Israeli army, a disgrace for Israel, and an internal political disaster for the Begin government. Operation Big Pine demanded a total military victory to justify the political risk it entailed; a negotiated compromise wasn't good enough.

Despite the strong appeal to nationalistic sentiments and solidarity from the government, the parties, and the obedient media as at the beginning of every big military campaign, the situation in Lebanon posed a new challenge to Israeli society. The invasion of Lebanon was not, as announced, a preventive or retaliatory measure in a defensive war against the PLO, but an aggressive war with far-reaching geopolitical goals. Preventive and retaliatory operations were at the center of the Israeli military doctrine, the population had become accustomed to these two forms of aggression, and they were accepted by all political parties, except the Communists. The lack of strategic depth in little Israel, the small population, the scarce resources compared with the much bigger and more populated neighboring countries justified this aggressive "forward defense." Israel had to strike first and overwhelm the enemy in a fast, short war that depended on superior intelligence and technology. At the same time, the population expected their own losses to remain relatively low. Even the autonomy and aggressiveness of the retaliatory strikes were part of the doctrine. Unexpected operations or excessive responses were designed to demonstrate power and force, deter opponents, and provide evidence of the fighting spirit of both the army and the population, while their own losses could be kept to a minimum by choosing the time and place of the attack. The image of a modern Sparta, cultivated by Israel for decades, was both an expression and a part of this strategy. Fear and concern for their own losses were admitted only indirectly, and presented primarily as characteristics of the human superiority of the Jews vis-à-vis the Arabs.

The war in Lebanon endangered this consensus on several fronts. First, from the start, it seemed dubious whether the conditions for a defensive war really had been present and whether military action was necessary. Since the summer of 1981, the PLO had maintained a cease-fire, and the shelling just before the invasion had been triggered by an Israeli attack. The government in Jerusalem had argued that the shooting of the Israeli ambassador in London represented a violation of the accord, but the attackers, members of the Abu Nidal group, did not belong to the PLO. Going beyond the forty-kilometer limit, set by the government itself as the criterion for the legality and appropriateness of the action, meant crossing the line to an unprovoked war of aggression. The other danger to the consensus was in the imminent confrontation with the PLO militias in the middle of a big Arab city, involving heavy losses.

Right at the beginning of the public debate, opponents of the war steered the discussion out of the political and strategic realm to that of ethical principles. They propounded criteria to distinguish unequivocally between permissible and impermissible conduct of war by the state. The permissible use of force was defined by the term "war without alternative"—a democratic Israel was allowed to conduct a war forced from outside only in an emergency situation that could be remedied by no other means. Behind this was the tacit assumption that previous wars conducted by the current opposition fulfilled these criteria. The organizations leading the protest were Peace Now and *Yesh Gvul* (Enough, There's a Limit or Border), the newly formed organization of those who refused to serve in Lebanon. Peace Now, the first Israeli peace protest movement, had originated in a group of more than three hundred reservists, who, in March 1978, during peace negotiations with Egypt, had written an open letter to Prime Minister Begin demanding a renunciation of violence and the choice of political means in the Middle East conflict. "We will achieve real security only through a real peace," said one of the core sentences of the letter. The peace movement, consisting mainly of supporters of the Labor parties and kibbutzniks, regarded itself as an extra-parliamentary opposition to the first Begin government, and saw the Lebanese war as a deviation from the right path of Israeli history.

The situation unfolding now in Beirut was in fact brand new, for the population, the government, and not least, the army. The Phalangists' refusal to drive the PLO out of Beirut forced the army to develop plans for its own campaign. To postpone the use of ground troops as long as possible, Israel began a strategy of constantly stepping up pressure on the fighters and civilians in the

Moslem quarter of the city. On July 1, hardly a week after the cease-fire began, leaflets were dropped and fighter jets flew mock bombing raids over the western part of the city center. Israeli spokesmen alluded to an impending attack in the press. But the PLO was not to be moved to withdraw from Lebanon simply by psychological warfare. On July 3, Israeli troops advanced, occupied the access roads to the Green Line between the Christian eastern part and the Moslem western part of the city and began shooting at two refugee camps north of the international airport. The next day, cutting off electricity, water, and the food supply, the real siege began. A joke now made the rounds in the city and was quoted by the international press: "Visit Israel before Israel visits you."

The siege of the western part of the city lasted more than fifty days, until August 21, 1982. Along with the occasional advances of Israeli infantry units, which were quickly withdrawn because of strong counterdefenses and high losses, the pressure to force the PLO and its fighters to retreat came mainly from the gun barrels of the Israeli artillery, the cannons of the Israeli navy, and the missiles and bombs of the air force. Since PLO bunkers, guns, and other heavy weapons were placed in a densely settled urban environment, the Israeli government accepted a large number of civilian victims and the massive destruction of the Moslem quarter. Civilian casualties were weighed against the potential losses of the army in a ground offensive, and the Beirut population was the loser.

The weeks of merciless bombardments of Beirut by Israeli troops from water, land, and air, and high levels of civilian losses defined the image of the Lebanese campaign in world public opinion, together with the subsequent massacres in the refugee camps of Sabra and Shatila in September. Israel's image suffered irreparable damage in the West, and the previously broad European bias in favor of Israel disappeared. The climax of the air raids on August 12, when the city was bombed from six o'clock in the morning until five in the afternoon, also formed a domestic political turning point. The government revoked the defense minister's right to carry out military operations without a previous cabinet decision, and concluded an immediate cease-fire, which led to negotiations and eventually to the withdrawal of the PLO from Beirut. Among Israelis, the long siege led from initial agreement to skepticism and deepening concern.

Nevertheless, Israeli army operations in Lebanon did produce results. In the south, the bulwarks of the PLO were eliminated, the fighters were either killed or put to flight, and thousands were taken prisoner. The PLO was expelled from Beirut. Syrian troops were pushed back to the border and almost all of Syria's air defenses in Lebanese territory were destroyed. Annihilation of the Palestinian military potential strengthened Israel's Christian allies, at least temporarily. On July 30, Israeli Foreign Minister Yitzhak Shamir informed the Israeli press of the full objectives of the invasion: "The expulsion of the PLO from Beirut and all of Lebanon, the withdrawal of all foreign troops from Lebanon, the establishment of an independent and stable Lebanese government willing to conclude a peace treaty with Israel." On August 23, 1982, the Phalangist leader, Bashir Gemayel, was elected president of Lebanon in the shadow of Israeli tanks, and was to take office on September 23. Defense Minister Ariel Sharon raised the prospect of an impending peace treaty. The comforting phrase of the 1950s, that Lebanon would be the second Arab country to make peace with Israel, seemed to be coming true. In these few weeks of triumph, which ended abruptly with the assassination of Gemayel and the massacre in the refugee camps, the leader of the Likud basked in the radiance of a clearly successful geopolitical coup. The Israeli press sang psalms to the "surprising" and "brilliant" victory of the Israeli army. To hear other opinions, Israeli citizens had to resort to foreign newspapers or radio stations. Along with the usual military censorship, the government had banned broadcast commentaries by retired officers for fear of deviant analyses, and not to undermine the impression of a solid home front. So only abroad could you read about the costly errors of Israel's invasion, and the enormous imbalance of military forces, which left no doubt about the outcome of the fight from the beginning. Comparing the PLO with the Israeli army, wrote an American military expert, is comparing "the Wehrmacht with the Apaches."

Despite the success against the PLO, Jerusalem managed in short succession to mobilize all factions and parties of Lebanon against itself, including the Christian allies. The power structure of Lebanon was too complicated and unstable, and Israel was too inexperienced and too uncommitted. Thus, the many hasty measures of the occupation power led to a long-term aggravation of the situation in the area around Beirut and in the south. In any event, the price for achieving some of the Israeli war aims was high. In the siege of Beirut, 88 Israeli soldiers were killed and 750 wounded, about a third of all losses Israel had suffered in Lebanon so far. Of the two to three thousand Palestinian fighters in Beirut, about a thousand were killed. Most of the victims were civilians. According to the estimates of the various sides, the fighting in Beirut had cost the lives of between five thousand and eight thousand people. Along with the civilian casualties in the south, more than ten thousand Lebanese civilians were killed within the first three months of the war. When Israel finally withdrew to the buffer zone in the south three years later, over seventeen thousand Lebanese civilians had lost their lives. Solidarity with the Palestinians, partly voluntary and partly forced, cost Lebanese society dearly.

* 3 *

Israel's ambitious war aims soon led to complications. During August, in negotiations for the withdrawal of the PLO fighters and the stationing of an international peace-keeping force in Beirut, Israeli intelligence had learned of secret PLO plans. After the retreat of the militias, as the Israeli government later asserted to justify its invasion of the Moslem quarter of Beirut, two thousand fighters were to be allowed back into the city with concealed weapons and forged papers. If the return of such a troop to the capital should become a fact, control of Beirut and the arrangement pursued by the Israelis would be jeopardized. The army received orders to track down and eliminate the fighters. On September 1, the PLO concluded its withdrawal from Beirut, and the international troops, who protected the retreat of some eleven thousand Palestinian fighters, followed ten days later. On September 14, the future Lebanese president Bashir Gemayel was killed in a bomb attack in a Beirut suburb, affording Israel the pretext to break its promise to the U.S. and transfer troops to West Beirut as well. Within a few days, the Israeli army had occupied the whole city, encountering virtually no resistance. But at this stage, too, the Israeli government was not willing to use its own troops to "comb" through Sabra and Shatila, the Palestinian refugee camps in West Beirut. The camps were surrounded and Jerusalem asked the Lebanese army to take over the two camps. After the Lebanese prime minister refused the request, Israel's last hope were its auxiliary troops, the Christian Phalangists.

The Phalangist leaders were reminded of their promise by the Israeli chief-of-staff who had rushed in especially to give the "mobilization order," as the Israeli investigating committee of the massacre wrote in its report six months later. According to the testimony of the Israeli chief-of-staff, Raphael Eytan, the Christian leadership was informed that the Israeli army did not intend to enter the refugee camps and that "the necessary fighting was to be carried out by the Phalangists." The previous evening, Chief-of-Staff Eytan and Defense Minister Sharon had agreed on the Phalangist advance into the refugee camps of West Beirut.

The Israeli government, army, and secret service (the Mossad) were skeptical about the reliability and discipline of the Phalangists, but to various degrees. Under the protection of the advancing Israeli army, Christian fighters in the past two months had repeatedly taken revenge on Moslem and Druse civilians. Phalangist provocations in Druse villages of the Shuf Mountains outside Beirut had made the Israeli army exclude its Christian allies from any more battles. The secret service, which had maintained contacts with Christian groups since the 1970s, assumed that, when the Christians took power, this behavior would be a thing of the past, and raised no objection to using the Phalangists in the camps. Military intelligence warned that using them could lead to violations of civilians. The government, meanwhile, was concerned with internal politics. The cabinet estimated that, according to popular opinion, Israeli soldiers were pulling the irons out of the fire for the Christians, that the war served the interests of the Lebanese Christians rather than those of the Israelis. Thus, the government saw itself pressured by public opinion to involve the Phalangists in the fighting.

On Thursday, September 16, 1982, at six in the evening, Phalangist fighters advanced in two groups into the Shatila camp. As darkness fell, Israeli mortars launched flares at the request of the Phalangists. At seven p.m., an Israeli officer heard a radio conversation between the Phalangist fighters and their headquarters indicating targeted executions of women and children. About an hour later, an Israeli intelligence officer eavesdropped on a radio conversation about the killing of unarmed male prisoners. During the evening and into the night on Friday, Israeli officers, including both sector and division commanders, received more direct and indirect indications of a massacre. On Thursday evening, reports were discussed at a staff meeting, and the discussion was recorded by a member of the military history unit. More reports were written and passed onto the general staff. At eight o'clock

Friday morning, the military correspondent of the daily newspaper *Haaretz* received a call from his informant on the general staff and heard that a massacre was in progress in the camps. That morning, the journalist alerted the minister of information at a meeting, the minister of information called the foreign minister. At dawn on Friday, Israeli soldiers stationed at the edges of the camps had observed the death and abuse of civilians and had passed on their observations to their superiors.

Israel's political and military leadership did not react until Americans objected to Phalangist invasions of the camps later that morning. In the afternoon, Chief-of-Staff Eytan flew to Beirut to meet with Phalangist leaders, who reported to him that the campaign was progressing successfully and no "irregularities" had occurred. Eytan appeared satisfied and praised the Phalange for its smooth execution of the mission. He informed the leaders that the campaigns now had to be ended because of American pressure, and the Phalangist fighters would have to leave the camps at 5:00 the next morning, Saturday. The Phalange leadership then asked Eytan to make the bulldozers of the Israeli army available to the fighters to tear down "illegal construction" in the camps. Eytan later explained to the investigating committee that he had also heard of the problem of the illegal Palestinian dwellings. Thus he had greeted the Phalange plan as a positive sign of their political maturity and capacity to govern and had granted their request.

Meanwhile the massacre continued. On Saturday morning, Phalangists evacuated foreign physicians from the hospital in the Sabra camp. As soon as the physicians reached Israeli positions at the periphery of the camp, they reported dead civilians they had seen in the camp and the clearing that was in progress with the aid of Israeli bulldozers. That work apparently had not been finished, for the Phalangists did not follow the order to leave the camp at 5:00 in the morning. A few months later, Chief-of-Staff Eytan testified that he had received a call from Prime Minister Begin on

Saturday morning, the first day of the Jewish New Year holiday. Begin said that he had been called by the American ambassador who had heard that the Phalangists were massacring patients and staff in the Sabra hospital. Eytan replied that there was no hospital in the camp. At about the same time, the Israeli sector commander in Beirut issued an ultimatum to the Phalangist leadership to evacuate the camp immediately. At 8:00 the next morning, the Phalangists withdrew from the Sabra and Shatila refugee camps.

Right after the Phalangists withdrew, Red Cross workers and members of the international press entered the camps and found some four hundred corpses, mainly in Shatila. Everything indicated that the men, women, and children had not been killed in battle, but had been executed. During the following days, various organizations took charge of the dead, and four hundred sixty corpses were counted. According to the estimates of Israeli army research, seven to eight hundred people were killed in the camps, including as many civilians as suspected Palestinian fighters. During the afternoon, news of the massacre had also reached Israel. The holiday brought public life to a complete halt, and neither radio nor television broadcast current programs. Menachem Begin later reported that he learned of the events in Sabra and Shatila for the first time in the late afternoon, from the BBC World Service, which he and many other non-religious Israelis listened to on this holiday.

News of the massacre in Beirut triggered a wave of indignation and criticism in Israel, resulting in a massive protest a few days later at city hall in Tel Aviv. The mood in downtown Tel Aviv that warm Saturday evening was revolutionary. Hundreds of thousands of citizens from all over the country, all ages and classes of the population, a surging crowd that filled the big square and the side streets, saw itself unexpectedly transformed into a new force, the "other Israel." The massacre of Sabra and Shatila had turned widespread doubt about the invasion, the general uneasiness about the policy of the Likud government, and criticism within the opposition parties, into a new awareness. Here stood the Israel of the original, Ashkenazi settler society, the compromising Zionism of the Labor party, against the maximalist Zionism of the Revisionists and their Sephardi supporters. The text of the banners expressed the feelings in the "other Israel." Along with "Begin and Sharon step down" and "Bring our boys back from Lebanon," were also slogans like "I am ashamed to be a Jew." The protest was led in the name of a Jewish nationalism with a socialist bent that denounced the actions of the government as a deviation from the traditional Israeli ethos of the use of force. Shimon Peres, leader of the opposition, expressed it thus in a speech to the crowd: "There is another Israel that does not live only by the sword, but also by conscience."

The protest gathering demanded an independent investigating committee, and the opposition parties took up the cry the next day. Meanwhile, Menachem Begin referred to the accusations as a "blood libel" from abroad and declared the Christian countries unfit to reproach the Jews on moral grounds. With these counter-accusations, he withdrew to that line of defense erected at the start of the invasion by government spokespersons—criticism of Israeli actions was based on a "double standard," which, in an anti-Semitic way, condemned the actions of Jews more harshly than those of non-Jews. A few days later, however, Begin had to give in. The government assigned the Supreme Court to investigate Israel's responsibility for the events in the refugee camps. The correspondent of the *Financial Times* wrote of the mood in the country: "Some foreign journalists have made much of the current mood of moral doubt and self-questioning, in the belief either that it proves the superiority of Israeli values and Israeli society, or else that it will lead to a profound re-evaluation of the policies of Mr. Begin. But lurking behind the demand for an exculpatory enquiry is the knowledge that the state of Israel was not itself established by peaceful and democratic means."

In fact, neither the Israeli public nor the opposition was interested for very long in the causes of the massacre and the responsibility of the government. When the report of the investigating committee was published six months later, the focus was on internal political questions: Had the army leadership and the defense minister misled the rest of the cabinet and the head of the government about the goals of the war? Had the citizens been lied to by their government? Ariel Sharon had to resign as defense minister and a few army leaders were relieved of their command.

Only a few commentaries on the results of the investigation pointed to what may have been the most important background of the events, the dehumanization of the enemy and the rejection of Palestinians by Israeli society, which valued an Arab life cheaper than a Jewish one. When it became known that the massacre may not have been a spontaneous revenge campaign, but rather an atrocity planned by the Phalange in order to trigger a mass flight of Palestinians and thus to liberate all of Lebanon from the unpopular refugees, a few articles in the press pointed to parallels to the 1948 massacre of Deir Yassin carried out by Jewish militias. Then, too, Menachem Begin, head of the militia responsible for the massacre, declared that he had learned of the massacre only the next day on the BBC.

* 4 *

In the third week of the war, Peace Now had invited their Jerusalem members and supporters to a meeting. I, too, joined several hundred fellow citizens in the Khan theater in Jerusalem for the protest assembly that day. It was one of those warm evenings in late June that make Jerusalem so attractive and yet strange and alien. The evening sky over the Khan—a former inn across from the old railroad station dating from the Turkish time—had taken on that glimmering dark blue that shows the pink tint of the traditional sandstone of old Jerusalem. The dry season had begun and the few plants of the city were already covered with the thin layer of yellowish dust that would be washed away with the first rain in autumn. Around the theater on a small strip of land and in the clefts of the rock grew the big funny-looking cactus bushes called "prickly pears" in English. The native Israelis had been inspired by the fruit of these cactus plants to call themselves "Sabra": prickly outside, soft and sweet inside.

The Jerusalemites, who stood around smoking and drinking in the small courtyard and lobby of the former caravansary, formed an exception in this conservative city. Haifa and Tel Aviv were the centers of secular, European Zionist Israel; but Jerusalem had always been a city on the margin of Israeli society, shaped by the Arab culture of the Jewish, Moslem, and Christian groups and by the religious sites that had drawn a constantly growing number of Orthodox and ultra-Orthodox Jews to the city. The Oriental Jewish majority of the population also made the city the stronghold of the Revisionists. Ever since the early 1950s, the Herut party and its successor, the electoral alliance Likud, had emerged as the strongest force. The European middle-class that formed the demographic basis of the Zionist Labor parties and the political elite was a minority in Jerusalem. So it was exceptional that Peace Now could bring out a few hundred people to a protest gathering in this city.

The people who met here saw themselves as representatives of the "other Israel." This term described not only a specific criticism of the policy and ideology of the Begin government, as well as the leftist milieu that spawned this criticism, it also expressed a certain pride of ownership about the previous achievements of Israeli society. The "other Israel" did stand for the humanism of the original settler society and the search for a compromise between the interests of Arabs and Jews, but it was hardly pacifist nor did it give up Zionist goals. The "other Israel" claimed to be following the correct path of the history of Israel and Zionism, and regarded the Zionist right as deviant. But it too assumed Zionist premises, the primacy of Jewish claims to Palestine, the historical mission of the "ingathering of the exiles," and the inferiority of Arab rights. It was considered absolutely obvious that the Arab inhabitants of the country either had to adjust to this scheme or deal with the implacable hostility of the Jews. Pride of achievements expressly included the wars of conquest of 1948 and 1967 led by Labor party governments, and excluded the price the Arabs of Palestine had paid for these successes. I did not share this pride.

The speakers who now appeared one after another in the Khan sharply criticized the invasion of Lebanon. They mentioned misleading the public, the secret plans, the deception of the officers; they censured the war as a violation of the traditional ethos of the use of force. Above all, they lamented the sacrifice of Israeli soldiers for politically unrealistic goals. Only a defensive war, a war "without choice," was a just war. All other consequences of the invasion seemed so unimportant they were not even mentioned—the enormous losses among Lebanese civilians, the destruction of the civilian environment and infrastructure inherent in the logic of an anti-guerilla war, the breach of peace and international law. Those gathered suffered less from what had been committed against the Lebanese and Palestinian refugees in the name of the Israeli population than from what Israelis had done to each other. In the world of the "other Israel," too, the "beautiful" Israelis, as they were mockingly called by their opponents, only the Jews merited empathy and solidarity.

For me, the war was a very personal challenge. In the first weeks of the war, I was torn between solidarity with the country and the people and loathing for the nationalism and militarism of

Israeli society. This was followed by months of uneasiness and melancholy when internal conflicts were vented in other ways. Along with the political and moral problems it raised for everybody, for me the war in Lebanon increasingly became a personal matter. All questions about my immigration and life in Israel suddenly seemed more urgent and sharper than usual. The Jewish community of Israel I had joined so spontaneously and a little thoughtlessly was in an emergency and demanded solidarity and sacrifice from its members. Was I in a position to do that? Unlike most people around me, I felt more empathy with the victims of Israel than with the dead and wounded soldiers on our own side. After all, the "others" had been the target of a brutal and unprovoked attack and I felt solidarity with them. I no longer wanted to follow the dictate of ethnic solidarity, nor the arguments of the protest movement that the Israeli army in Lebanon was itself a victim of the wheeling and dealing of an unscrupulous government under Menachem Begin and Ariel Sharon.

Meanwhile, the government had launched an exceptionally polemical counterattack on critics abroad. At a press conference in late September, shortly after the massacre, the spokesman of the Foreign Ministry posed the rhetorical question: "What did the West do to end the civil war in Lebanon in which 70,000 people lost their lives in the last seven years? When did you"—that is, the reporters present—"criticize the massacre of the Syrians in Hama, when over 20,000 people were killed? Why are we measured by a double standard?" When the massacre of Sabra and Shatila came to light and outrage spread everywhere, Prime Minister Begin expressed his private opinion about the outrage through his press spokesman: "Goyim kill Goyim, and they come running immediately to hang the Jews." Primitive as these arguments were, guilt-ridden non-Jews in the West were still impressed by them. And among Diaspora Jews, the rallying cry of the danger of anti-Semitism had not yet lost its effect either. After all, they were the people who Israel considered part of the nation, at least rhetorically, and who were thus implicated in Lebanon as well. According to one of the most telling phrases in the political culture of Israel, it was the "people of Israel," that is, all Jews, that had defended itself in Lebanon against Palestinian aggression, and thus was hated by the Goyish world.

How strongly the war touched on my identity problem was shown in the following episode. In those days, I maintained an intense correspondence with friends in Germany, and in this correspondence I complained not only about the war and the attitude of my Israeli compatriots. I complained just as decisively and verbosely about the alleged anti-Semitic subtext in reporting on the Lebanese war and the statements of politicians and intellectuals in Germany. My friends replied angrily that they sensed no anti-Semitism. I wrote my letters by hand and by typewriter and, recently convinced of the importance of preserving private correspondence, I made copies of my typed letters. Thus, I could later reconstruct that remarkable convergence of arguments and moods that determined my thoughts at that time. The historical truths an author can discover in his old letters are not always welcome in the present, and that also applied to me when I picked up the letters again two decades later. I had swallowed lock, stock, and barrel the government argument accusing critics of the invasion of anti-Jewish motives, and accused my non-Jewish friends of having no feeling for the special situation of the Jews. At this moment, when my ethnic identification with Jews and Israel began to collapse completely, I could not bear the alleged rejection of my Jewish identity.

I was especially upset about one appeal placed by several German politicians and scholars in German and Israeli newspapers during the first month of the war, criticizing Israel's action in Lebanon in a general and harmless language and requesting the Israeli army to withdraw. Not even with the best will were anti-Semitic undertones to be discovered. But the assumptions behind it infuriated me and other citizens of West Germany living in Israel so much that we decided to undertake a concerted counteraction. Along with a few Jerusalem friends, I wrote letters to the editor of the newspapers where the appeal had appeared. Anyone who had been silent about injustice to others in the past but now makes an exception of Israel, we wrote, could only be acting out of wrong motives. At any rate, the non-Jewish world lacked moral sensitivity regarding a state like Israel, which had risen from the ashes of the Holocaust and deserved special consideration. Our reasoning thus followed the obscure logic of what has become the now classical defensive allegation of anti-Semitism. On the one hand, we complained of the double standard that allegedly condemned Israel's behavior, and on the other hand we demanded that the behavior of the State be measured only by the special standard of the Holocaust. The fairness we demanded for judging Israel was justice à la carte.

What had provoked us so much? Apparently it was only the idea that non-Jews had dared criticize Jews with moral arguments, thus questioning that position of indisputable moral superiority allocated by Jewish nationalism to the Jews as perpetual victims of the Christian world. But my own excitement at that moment of crisis about the alleged anti-Semitism in the country of my childhood had its own logic. Nothing else could any longer make me a Jew with an ethnically unambiguous identity. Only the notion of a comprehensive hostility toward Jews that still threatened the cultural and physical survival of Jews outside Israel could still have kept me from admitting that a nationalistic "Judaism without the Goyim" was alien to me. For a few weeks I went back and forth, upset about Israel's action in Lebanon and about the alleged outburst of anti-Semitic opinions in Germany. Then this crisis also died away and I could let go of the scapegoat of anti-Semitism.

If I had to cite a single day when my conversion to an opponent of Zionism was complete, it was August 12, 1982, a Thursday. That was the day of the almost uninterrupted artillery attacks and air raids on West Beirut, which was to set the stalled negotiations about the PLO withdrawal back in motion. Other days of almost uninterrupted bombardments had preceded this horrible day. The attacks had made the midsummer sky above the Cornice of Beirut so dark with the smoke of explosions and fires that the Israeli air force had to use flares during the day to find its targets. I followed the incredible events on the radio, usually on BBC, whose reports came directly from Beirut. That morning I left the house with my transistor radio, ran around with it all day, and kept it plugged into my ear even on the way home from work. In the evening, I sat down at my desk and wrote letters. The entries of the sent mail in my journal that day indicate five recipients, close friends in Germany, France, and the U.S. Judging from the preserved copies, I wrote almost a hundred pages that night. I wrote and wrote and wrote myself out of the confusion the Lebanese war had thrown me into.

* 5 *

The "lessons from Jewish history" to be drawn for the Lebanese war had increasingly become the subject of my lectures as a reservist in the lecturers' unit. In the twelve months after the beginning of the invasion, I received half a dozen invitations from the most varied units to talk about the current situation from the perspective of Jewish history, anti-Semitism, and the Holocaust. I had to mobilize all my skill and inventiveness to steer these absurd demands into suitable channels and find transitions to my subjects that did not refer as directly as desired to the present. Most commanders and officers I encountered had almost a naïve belief in the power of these interpolations and apparently expected a marked positive effect for executing their current orders. Apparently, doubts about the war in Lebanon came to the fore in this intensified need to be assured of fundamental beliefs. The troops themselves reacted with that traditional blend of skepticism and opportunism probably found in all armies. To them, my presentations brought a welcome break from routine, provided the opportunity for a few hours of leisure, or offered the chance for a snack and even a little nap.

Meanwhile, the situation in Lebanon didn't improve. After the failure of a political solution, the so-called "peace treaty" with the Lebanese government, and because of the constant increase of its own losses, in the summer of 1983, more than a year after the war broke out, the government in Jerusalem was forced to a partial withdrawal. Since most of the incidents took place in the Shuf Mountains, along the Beirut Damascus road, and around Beirut, the new defense line was drawn along the Awali River, some 40 kilometers north of the Israeli border. During August, the army reinforced the new lines in great style—bunkers, artillery ramps, control posts, and helicopter pads were built, supply and travel roads were drawn and paved. Thus the second phase of the Lebanon adventure began.

The division of Lebanon and the suspension of traffic between the south and the rest of the country soon produced problems with the population. The turning point came on October 16, 1983, when a convoy of Israeli vehicles wanted to make its way through a religious procession in the marketplace of Nabatiya, barely 20 kilometers north of the Israeli border town of Metulla. On that day, more than five thousand worshipers were celebrating the Ashura holiday, a day of thanksgiving for Hussein ibn Ali, grandson of the Prophet and martyr of the Shi'a, who had been killed in October 680 in the Iraqi town of Kerbala. As the crowd of black-clad men whipped themselves in the traditional ritual, the unwitting Israeli drivers tried to get respect by beeping their horns and waving their rifles. When the crowd engulfed the vehicles, panic broke out among the Israelis, and the soldiers began taking aim, killing and wounding many civilians. Two weeks later, a Shi'a suicide bomber drove a truck full of explosives into Israeli army headquarters in the port city of Tyre. Sixty people were killed. Israel reacted with air raids and by further restricting movement in the south. The Shi'a militias—Islamic Jihad, Hezbollah, and even the moderate Amal, which had long cooperated with Israel—retaliated by attacking Israeli soldiers everywhere with all means at hand. Within a few months, the struggle between Israel and the PLO had turned into a war with the Shi'as.

The constant attacks of the militias and the friction with the civilian population was soon expressed in a decline of army "morale," in the growing number of dropouts for health reasons and in other signs of increasing combat stress. Willingness to serve and motivation were endangered in all units stationed in Lebanon. The army leadership believed they had a countermeasure available for that by reinforcing the indoctrination of the troops with Zionist values, and they prepared to use the lecturers' unit in Lebanon. In November 1983, when we met with the new commander of the Education Corps in the cinema in Tel Aviv, the Israeli press had just published the results of an opinion poll showing that almost 40 percent of all Jewish Israelis were for an immediate, unconditional withdrawal from Lebanon. The war and the occupation were extremely unpopular. Every day that brought new Israeli losses made it harder for the Israeli government to find support among the population. The situation of the army was not any easier. Hundreds of citizens had signed open letters announcing that they would not obey orders to serve in Lebanon as reservists. A few dozen officers and soldiers on active duty had also refused to serve in Lebanon and were convicted and imprisoned. An Israeli colonel, commander of a tank unit, had even given up his command in the field not to have to lead his troops to Beirut. The "battle morale" of the troops had sunk dangerously low.

Given this context, the protest of the lecturers in the Tel Aviv cinema seemed like the faint echo of a stronger criticism on the outside. The act itself had lasted only a few minutes. Afterward, most of those present folded their newspapers and put them away. The commanding general, who had roared at us briefly, also calmed down and resumed his lecture. A while later, it seemed as if the whole episode had never taken place, and that's where it stayed. In my remaining time as a reservist of the Education Corps, I never heard anything about it again, either privately or in service.

The meeting had been called to discuss our assignments in the framework of the Lebanese war, and after the unexpected interruption the general started explaining the measures the Education Corps planned to take to raise "morale." Not only in lectures, but also in personal conversations in small groups, members of the lecturers' unit were to contribute to combating defeatism and to improving motivation. We were to talk with young soldiers as fatherly friends, in frank conversations about the stress, the uneasiness, and the fears involved in serving in Lebanon, and were to offer consolation. These psychological measures were to be augmented by "ideological encouragement." It would be our task to indicate the great historical significance of the campaign in Lebanon, where Israeli soldiers were defending the future of the Jewish people. The war against the PLO and the Shi'a militias was nothing less than preventing a new Holocaust. This new front line against the enemies of the Jews had to be held at any cost.

I listened to the explanations in amazement, but didn't assume that I would also be sent to such conversations in Lebanon. I didn't seem old enough or paternal enough. Meanwhile, I had also discovered a simple means, evidently used by many colleagues as well to influence and direct the timing and place of reserve duty—the strategically placed trip abroad. According to the rules of the army, a professional obligation abroad took priority over other obligations, as long as it had been registered before the new duty roster was compiled. Ever since my discharge from the regular army in 1981, I had used this system and had learned to refine it. My work at the institute, where I had now taken over many administrative duties as deputy director, gave me frequent opportunities to travel abroad for a few days of meetings. That was usually enough to block my duty roster in the army so that, ultimately, it was up to me to accept a date for a lecture or not. Thus, I was even more amazed in early December, shortly after the meeting in the Tel Aviv cinema, when I got an order to report not for the usual one or two days of service I was usually assigned, but for two weeks. Only now did I start worrying.

The assignment was planned for the end of February at the headquarters of the Education Corps, which had moved from downtown Tel Aviv to that big base on the edge of the city, with the big army hospital and many other administrative departments. What I felt as a real stroke of fate was the fact that at this time, of all times, there were no trips abroad registered or planned. What could I do? I called headquarters to find out details, but encountered an unusual reserve. The officer I talked to dodged my questions and all I had left was a tactical maneuver. I asked how many overnight stays I should pack for. His answer, as it later turned out, contained the ambiguity of an oracle. He told me that I didn't have to take any bags at all. This led me to conclude that the assignment would take place at the base itself and I would be allowed to return home to Jerusalem every night.

* 6 *

According to entries in my journal, a period of hectic activity followed in subsequent weeks. I prepared a book project, the latest edition of the quarterly journal I edited for the institute had to be completed, and the typesetting had to be supervised. At the same time, along with two Jerusalem friends, I was trying to purchase a German-Jewish publishing house rich in tradition that had been established in Berlin in 1902 by several German-Jewish intellectuals and had since the war led a wallflower existence as part of a big publishing group. The publishing house harbored treasures of prewar German-Jewish intellectual life we wanted to republish for a German-speaking audience. In December and January, negotiations about purchasing the publishing house took me on brief trips abroad, and perhaps it was because of these exciting discussions and the even more exciting prospect of acquiring the publishing house that I gave no thought to my impending reserve duty.

The prospect of spending two weeks under military rule and in uniform again made me uneasy, but the hardship seemed limited, and I lulled myself with the certainty of being able to return to private life and my own bed at night. Whatever duties were in store for me during the coming service, I didn't doubt that I could master the situation. What remained were practical preparations. Appointments had to be shifted and substitutes found for my work at the institute and the university. My uniform, boots, and the sparse remnants of that comprehensive dowry all recruits receive on entering the military had lain in the back of the closet since my brief mobilization at the beginning of the war in June 1982, and had to be inspected. At least to keep my external appearance from giving offense, I washed and ironed the uniform. That was the only defensive measure I took for the impending duty.

The first morning of reserve duty began with the obligatory discussion of assignment in the rooms of the lecturers' unit. I had little connection with the staff of this division. I knew the people only in passing from telephone conversations about information of lecture dates, the only necessary contact between the unit and its pool of reservists. The less personal atmosphere also seemed to be a result of the just completed conversion of the education branch into a separate corps and a consequence of the move out of the charming makeshift green barracks on the grounds of army headquarters to the permanent gloom of the new building that had the feel of a provincial hospital. These meager and formal contacts with the leadership of the department soon proved to be a big disadvantage. Still, I didn't yet sense any great tension. My calm was probably a product of repression, my need to deny the whole matter as far as possible. Aside from me, there were a dozen lecturers, only a few of whom I knew so superficially I didn't even know their names. The discussions were led by the chief of the lecturers' department, Major Krauthammer, flanked by her two deputies, whom I had met here and there in the office of the unit.

Major Krauthammer explained our orders in a few words. We had to be in the border town of Metulla at eight o'clock the next morning and register with a transport battalion. The battalion was lodged in a grammar school that was easy to get to from the bus station. We were urged to leave our cars at home and use public transportation, which was free for soldiers and reservists in uniform. At the time, Metulla was the most important launch base for Lebanon and there was a big mess in the small town. The transport battalion would provide us with one jeep for every four persons, weapons and bulletproof vests; maps and a description of the road would be distributed to us. We would then be on our own. From Metulla we were to cross the border after dark and in the next two weeks were to wander around Lebanon in independent teams of four lecturers, visit units in the fields, and conduct motivating conversations with the soldiers in bivouacs, bunkers, and dugouts. There would be no room for baggage, added Major Krauthammer, and even the usual kitbag was too big for the two-week tour in the jeep. This time we had to get by with knapsacks, sleeping bags, and blankets.

Following tradition, Krauthammer made only the most general remarks about the nature and subjects of the conversations. We were to talk about the great significance of the campaign in Lebanon, about the mission produced by anti-Semitism and the Holocaust, and the duty to be shouldered by the current generation in the struggle of the Jews to survive. Ideological indoctrination was the core task of the unit, and more precise instructions were superfluous, as always. The leadership of the corps probably assumed that just sending a group of lecturers to Lebanon would already be considered a sign of concern and have a calming and encouraging effect on the soldiers.

Right after the major's first words, I realized with a jolt that I had come to a turning point in my army career. The latitude I had always used so far had disappeared all at once. The reasons for that were banal and lay in my thoughtlessness. Only a few weeks earlier, I would still have been able to avoid duty with ease. Even yesterday, a clumsy excuse could still have saved me from what had now become an impasse. As the civilian I had been until this morning, I still had possibilities I no longer had as a reservist on active duty. I now fell under other rules, other laws. Now refusing an order was a serious crime punishable by prison.

I was determined not to take part in the operation in Lebanon. But how to approach the matter? I knew nothing of the political convictions or sympathies of the head of our unit. Would she offer me a way out or treat me like a criminal? Nor did I know if other lecturers had refused the order and been tried for it. News about refusing duty became public only when it was launched by the refuseniks themselves. In these matters, the army avoided all publicity and reacted only when the publicity of others forced its hand. Should I pin my hopes on Krauthammer's sympathies, her sense of fairness, or on the natural tendency of an administrator not to create any new problems? Should I justify my refusal on political and moral grounds or present a practical reason? I had to consider that a complex political argumentation could provoke even more resistance. The less said, the more latitude for the department. I assumed that the lecturers' unit should have no interest in a refusal in its own ranks. I decided to present my refusal to take part in the campaign in Lebanon as a fait accompli and not to justify it. The resulting problem concerned the department as much as me and I wanted to ask Major Krauthammer to try to seek a solution with me that would serve the interests of both sides.

But for the time being, I had to be patient. I wanted to wait for a favorable moment to deal with the delicate subject privately. In the meantime, my fellow lecturers posed questions that seemed absurd to me under the circumstances and made me question their intelligence. One of them wanted to know what happened to the dirty laundry if we really spent every night in a different place. In general, practical arrangements for a stay in the field seemed the most urgent problem. Nobody dealt with the circumstances and objective of the operation. I grew angrier by the minute. A group of badly equipped, badly trained, and practically unprotected reservists were to be sent unprepared, in open jeeps, into a battle zone where deadly attacks on Israeli troops took place every day. The regular combat units had heavy weapons, armored vehicles, and especially a tactic, often trained, that gave them a chance of survival in attacks or in an ambush. Besides, it was extremely dubious whether the planned conversations would have any influence at all on fighting morale. Only one thing was certain—the danger to which the group was to be exposed had no relation to the possible results. I was sure that everyone present was worried about that, but talking about this fear violated military etiquette. Finally, one of the lecturers asked what to do in case of danger. Major Krauthammer referred to the radio available in the jeeps. We should call for help. It seemed to me that refusing this ludicrous and dangerous operation had become less a question of political principles and more of just plain sanity.

The gathering broke up at noon and the lecturers went off depressed. I followed Major Krauthammer to the canteen and stood behind her in line. I still hesitated about talking to her, knowing full well that my future weal and woe would be decided in the next few minutes. Waiting for the food to be distributed offered me one last respite; I reviewed my arguments and practiced the pitch. Then I spoke to her and we sat down with our trays at an empty table. After a little small talk, I put the problem to her.

Krauthammer reacted calmly. She had often encountered these things, apparently. She approached the matter like any other organizational question and immediately suggested seeking a practical solution, as if this weren't a refusal but a sudden illness. I had not given any reason for my refusal and she didn't ask for any, but her next question showed that she had apparently grasped my meaning. She asked me if I was willing to accept an assignment in the Golan Heights instead of Lebanon. Along the border with Lebanon were several Israeli positions that also had to be visited by lecturers. Lebanon had long had priority, but now that a lecturer was available she could assign me there for the next two weeks. My orders would be the same as in Lebanon, but I would have to do the tour of duty by myself. The Golan Heights was occupied territory and in other circumstances, I would have tried to avoid this assignment as well. But now I was so relieved that I agreed immediately. Obviously it was also in the interest of the unit to avoid a confrontation and the consequences of an open and explicit refusal to obey an order. I was so grateful for this gift horse that I didn't look it in the mouth. Major Krauthammer promised to arrange for me to go to the Golan that very day. The transport battalion in the border town of Metulla was the logistical base for this assignment, too, and I was to appear there the next morning. She would make sure I got more precise instructions there. With that I was dismissed.

* 7 *

Until my departure the next morning, I was extremely uneasy. I tried to imagine what was in store for me in the Golan Heights. Just the idea of wandering around alone for two weeks in an area and among people I knew nothing about made me nervous. I tried to console myself with the idea that this uncertainty and the prospect of an unpleasant time were preferable to a court martial and prison. But my very pronounced need for privacy also stood in the way of this simple consolation. Weren't the calm and seclusion of prison preferable? I didn't know much about conditions in military prisons, but I knew more about that than about my impending assignment.

I had visited the Golan Heights as a civilian several times since the conquest in 1967. In 1968, I had been in Kuneitra, the biggest town in the Israeli occupied part of the Heights, and had found an almost perfect ghost town. The sight of the empty streets and abandoned buildings had impressed me more deeply and revealed more to me about the war between Israel and Syria than the Syrian trenches and bunkers, from where the Jewish settlements around the Kinnereth had been shelled and which all Israeli visitors had been shown after 1967 as a symbol of the aggression and hostility of the regime in Damascus. A few years later, after the 1973 war and the disengagement agreement of 1974, under which Israel had to give a small strip of land back to Syria, I was once again in Kuneitra. This time the town was a few kilometers east of the cease-fire line secured by U.N. troops. From the border fence, you could see clearly what had happened in the meantime. The Israeli army had completely destroyed the city before it withdrew.

Israel had started putting settlements on the Heights back in 1967. The Labor party government of that time had allowed kibbutzim and other cooperative settlements to be built in this part of Syria and seemed to be bothered neither about the long-term consequences in relations with this neighboring country nor about the most important principle in international law, which categorically excluded appropriation of territories by war, even a defensive war. Under the Likud government of Menachem Begin, in 1981 the Golan Heights was finally annexed formally. Meanwhile, there were just as many Jewish settlers on the Heights as Syrians, mostly Druse, the only native population left in the territory. Several dozen Jewish settlements used the abundance of water and the temperate climate of the Heights to conduct an extremely profitable agriculture and export the local wine all over the world.

The Israeli-Jewish border town of Metulla, my destination that morning, was a little more than ten kilometers from the foot of the Golan Heights, right on the border of Lebanon. From there, I was to start my involuntary adventure. I had followed Major Krauthammer's advice, had left the car in Jerusalem, and had to start the long bus trip long before dawn to get to Metulla by eight. The shortest bus route went from Jerusalem to the occupied territories, down into the Jordan Valley, and then directly north. The seemingly endless road snaked along the Jordan, from Jericho toward the Kinnereth at the foot of the Judean Mountains, and was bordered right and left by the fields of the kibbutzim and moshavim. The Jordan Basin, until 1967 the Jordanian-held heartland of Palestinian agriculture, now seemed to have been changed into the heart of the Israeli agrarian industry. In Zionist mythology neither the Golan nor this basin was considered a stronghold of Jewish life in antiquity. Nevertheless, since 1967 Jewish settlements had risen everywhere here. The cafes and gas stations of these settlements formed the only stops where the bus released the impatient passengers for a brief rest. The poor Arab villages along the road, on the other hand, whose clay-colored houses hardly stood out from the surroundings, seemed to belong to nature, along with the herds of roaming camels that offered a meager livelihood.

On this gray February morning, the inhabitants of Metulla still lay well-protected in bed. There was hardly a trace of the army supplying the troops in Lebanon through a gate in the border fence. Only in the square at the bus station where I arrived did a crowd of young soldiers laden with colorful bags and shiny weapons push out of civilian buses into the waiting army trucks. I didn't know what I could expect, so I didn't rush and decided to walk down the road to the edge of the city and the school that was to be my base. The dawn and the rapid walk put me in a better mood. I remembered the visit to a Druse village on the Golan Heights and the memorable lunch in a small pub, and these memories made me feel even better.

The pub and the whole Druse village had shown those traces of the hasty emergence into the world of the twentieth century that had taken place twenty or thirty years earlier and hadn't advanced any more since. Half-completed facades and concrete skeletons of abandoned constructions were everywhere. The pub where I had eaten with friends was decorated with the owner's many reminiscences of Europe. Green plastic ivy climbed next to chains of Christmas tree lights, enormous photos of Swiss Alpine valleys looked down on miniature Eiffel Towers and a flamenco dancer. Colored prints of Sacré Coeur in Paris hung next to portraits of sad Gypsy children. After his travels, the owner had apparently posed the hard question of where in the world he had left his heart, a feeling I, an eternal wanderer, understood only too well. The prospect of visiting this pub in the coming weeks certainly improved my mood.

The grammar school where the transport battalion was bivouacked seemed abandoned. Only in the small room apparently used as a janitor's closet in peacetime did I find a man in uniform, the officer on duty. I immediately inundated him with questions, impatient to find out something about my assignment. He knew nothing. His instructions were to provide twelve reservists from the lecturers' unit with arms and jeeps and send them to Lebanon that evening. He hadn't heard about any special instructions for me. This could certainly be the sloppiness of the regular army and so he put me off until his superior, on duty at night and now sleeping, showed up. Maybe he had the new orders. At this moment, I wasn't yet worried that yesterday's compromise could have failed. I asked the officer to contact my headquarters in Tel Aviv to prevent an unnecessary delay in my departure. Then I looked for my colleagues who had appeared in the meantime and had parked themselves in an empty classroom. On the way to Metulla I had entertained the question of whether I should tell them about the change of plans and my dispatch to the Golan. In any event, they would soon find out that I wasn't accompanying them to Lebanon. I hesitated, not because I wanted to avoid the inevitable quarrel about politics, civic duties, and loyalties, but because I didn't know if silencing the real reasons was part of the agreement with Major Krauthammer. I didn't want to make trouble for her.

My colleagues were even more taciturn than yesterday. Whatever advantages a two-week reserve duty could usually bring to the professional and married life of a citizen, a tour in Lebanon in an Israeli uniform at that time didn't promise to be much fun. So, discussing the circumstances and objectives of the impending operation, I didn't have to exercise restraint. The subject wasn't touched on, nor was there even much general conversation. What my colleagues thought about the operation I didn't know, but I had some assumptions. They also must have considered the assignment absurd or at least dangerous. This was a unit of middle-aged men, who for decades had not been expected to do anything worse than temporarily leaving the comforts of home and producing not always respectable intellectual feats. The only disobedience they indulged in, as indicated by the bags strewn on all chairs and tables of the classroom, was taking excess baggage.

This scene also confirmed the rule of thumb that 90 percent of a soldier's activity consists of inactivity. All of us waited for the distribution of weapons, clothing, and ammunition, and I for my orders. Meanwhile, I had covered the route between our classroom and the makeshift headquarters on the ground floor countless times. Major Krauthammer could not be reached by phone, neither on the internal nor the external line, and none of the other staff of the unit at headquarters had heard anything of special plans for me. Even now, I still believed firmly that it was a momentary and accidental lapse in the organization that was to be rectified very soon. Major Krauthammer had to be found. Meanwhile, after the morning break, the transport unit had opened for business and even a makeshift canteen had opened its doors. This institution, called "Shekem," was to be found on all bases and held a special position in the firmament of Zionist institutions. Surrounded by the egalitarian flair of cooperative consumerism, the soldier could get cookies or chocolate here, buy shoelaces or razor blades, and indulge in the traditional delicacies of Israeli coffee culture, "Nes" or "Botz." The first was Nescafé or a solvent Israeli variant, the second was Turkish coffee that wasn't soluble and on contact with water turned into "Botz," that is, mud. Shekem and the peculiar aroma of Nes and Botz were as integral to the army as the Uzi, the M-16 assault rifle, and the Arab enemy. Thus, the army had set its seal on this grammar school, too. A table was put across a doorway, setting up a temporary Shekem. Here the soldier could relax, dream of his girlfriend, and calmly smoke his "Nelson Filter" cigarette.

Meanwhile, the attempt to find Major Krauthammer or to get a confirmation for the changed assignment had now reached a critical stage. I began to suspect that she hadn't really intended to keep the agreement and that our conversation had been a maneuver to get rid of me and pass the buck. As I doubled my desperate and now almost hopeless attempts, the increasing displeasure, even disbelief, of the officers in the transport battalion could hardly be ignored. I mentioned calling a Jerusalem attorney I had consulted before I went into the regular army in the 1970s about the legal possibilities of refusing service. He had specialized in refusals and conflicts with the army and I always carried his phone number on a small slip of paper whenever I wound up in the claws of the military. Mentioning the lawyer exhausted the last drops of good will the commander of the transport battalion had shown me. If this was about refusing an order, politics, and related complications he had to withdraw his protecting hand from me. He recommended that I join my colleagues on the trip that evening and resume my efforts at the next stop in Lebanon. Since I wasn't connected with his unit and he couldn't give me any orders in any event, the decision was up to me. If I left the troop without permission, he wouldn't restrain me. In that case, however, he would be forced to notify my superiors in writing about the incident.

Thus, it was clear what my possibilities were. I could hope for a miracle, join the convoy to Lebanon, or leave the temporary base in the grammar school and thus unambiguously and officially refuse the assignment. Meanwhile, I was so nervous that my knees trembled and I felt sick. I decided to talk with the only one of the eleven lecturers I knew a little better. He was a political scientist at a university in the south and our acquaintance went back to a seemingly endless drive together to a meeting in a remote conference center, when we had long and comprehensive discussions about personal things. I sought neither advice nor understanding from him, but urgently needed to talk to somebody about the situation. I hoped a conversation would relax me and calm me down enough to take the next step with a clear head.

I found him in another classroom where the lecturers had just been sent to receive weapons and equipment. Everybody had noticed my nervousness and persistent absence in the last hours. As soon as I spoke to my acquaintance, the colleagues still in the classroom surrounded us and immediately asked what had happened. I had no choice. I revealed to them that I didn't want to take part in the campaign in Lebanon and had tried so far in vain to find an alternative. I didn't mention my agreement with Krauthammer, but had to admit to everything else. I explained to them that I had to be true to my criticism and rejection of the Lebanese invasion, but also that I considered the planned campaign to boost morale in Lebanon so absurd and dangerous that I would have refused it no matter what. My colleagues reacted with a long silence I couldn't interpret. After a while, one of them said: "It's true that our assignment is dangerous. I don't want to participate in it either. But it's not up to me to decide which order is correct and which isn't." If such decisions were left up to the individual, the army couldn't function. Therefore, he had to carry out orders even if they seemed absurd to him. My acquaintance didn't even try to present counterarguments, he appealed to my common sense. I should keep in mind that the guards in the military prison weren't choirboys and certainly wouldn't treat me with kid gloves. Two weeks in Lebanon would pass quickly and I could then express my political opinions any time outside the army.

The statements were well-meant and surprised me. I had counted on an immediate, symbolic exclusion from the group, a withdrawal of sympathy and solidarity. The other lecturers following the conversation were obviously less friendly to me. They contributed nothing to the conversation, but stared at me with an expression of surprise, shame, and disgust that spoke volumes. Then they left the room without another look. As they went out, one hissed to the two colleagues who had gotten into a discussion with me: "Leave him alone. Let him do what he wants to." But I still hesitated to pack my things and go. There were still a few more hours until dark and there was still hope that the agreement with Krauthammer would materialize and spare me a court martial. To gain time, after a while I followed my colleagues to the ground floor to get weapons and equipment.

Even under the most unpleasant circumstances, this procedure reminded me of a slapstick comedy from the silent movie era. Every individual item of equipment had to be chosen passing by the corresponding distribution table, searched for defects, and listed on a receipt. Then the serial number of the gun was deciphered, recorded, and countersigned, everything under the constant shouting of the seven-digit personnel number every soldier received when he entered the armed forces and had to learn by heart immediately. All parts of the equipment were entered in handwritten lists and provided with sloppily smeared name, number, and date. It was apparently part of the venerable tradition of the army that these lists be done so that right after they were made, they could no longer be deciphered by anybody. It was February and there was snow in the mountains of Lebanon and on Mount Hermon, visible from Metulla, and along with warm underwear we also got a fur-lined parka and sleeping bag. I knew that I would give back all items in the next hours and go through the same procedure in reverse, but first we had to reach the real climax of the distribution of equipment—trying on uniforms.

All parts of the working uniform distributed at the beginning of duty, and afterward in the laundry exchange once a week, were traditionally placed in big piles or in disorder on shelves, where they had been heaped up helter-skelter from the laundry. In regular bases, the sergeant responsible glanced professionally at the soldier before him, reached deliberately into the piles, pulled out a jacket or trousers that, according to his expert judgment, had to fit, and roared curtly: "Try this on." In less orderly circumstances, it was up to the soldiers to distribute the loot among themselves. Here, too. In the makeshift storehouse of the classroom, the disorderly heaps had turned into a green uniform carpet on which my colleagues ran back and forth helplessly. Hardly anybody had the good luck to find a jacket or trousers that was neither much too big nor much too small. My colleagues tried on and tried on and meanwhile hoped only for a part of a uniform that didn't make them look too ridiculous. The soldiers of the transport battalion had obviously taken all the standard sizes for themselves in the last laundry exchange, and so the lecturers were condemned to appear in the country of the northern neighbors in an outfit that could hardly enhance their authority.

After the equipment was distributed, I went back to my acquaintance. We decided to go to the canteen. There we tried to start a conversation, but no matter what subject we broached, we couldn't. He stared at my boots and I at his, while, leaning against the wall, we slurped the hot, hardly enjoyable coffee from plastic cups. The time had come for me to part from the unit and my colleagues. Despite my external reserve, I felt uncertain and miserable. This last step to refusal was final and thus the hardest. I went to the battalion commander in his room. Half for form, I inquired one last time if there was news from Major Krauthammer, and he asked if I didn't want to give up my plan. He warned me again that he had to report the unauthorized departure from the troop and the issue would have inevitable consequences. Then he didn't look at me anymore, as if he wanted to spare himself and me the shame of the moment, and turned away.

* 8 *

In the following days, I suffered from the obsession that my arrest was imminent. I was plagued by compulsive fantasies about the arrival of the military police, the exchange of words, the drive to Tel Aviv. I concluded that I had about twenty-four hours of freedom after my return from Metulla. I remained petrified in my flat and didn't venture out. I left my bag packed to be ready at any time and slept in my underwear and bathrobe. However, it took the military police a long time to come.

I promised myself not to resist in any way and not to blurt out anything. I didn't want to give anyone a pretext to beat me or abuse me. It seemed best to say as little as possible about my motives. My refusal to take part in the campaign in Lebanon, even in a marginal function, could not be seen as a demonstration, a rallying cry aimed at recruiting like-minded people. I didn't want to seem arrogant. I wanted to avoid the impression that I thought I was superior or despised others who had made another decision. I told myself all that out of fear and worry of being the target of fury and outrage, social and political resentment. I felt guilty and shuddered at the thought of how I must look in the eyes of others —like a coward and a traitor.

I remembered the expression in the eyes of the man who had tried to run over me in the first summer of the war when I was marching through downtown Jerusalem in a protest march. The demonstration offered a typical political scene for the capital. There were the few well-known peace activists, members of the Labor party or the small civil rights movement, the handful of lecturers of the Hebrew University who were openly committed, and the usual spectators. We were barely a hundred demonstrators, surrounded by a hostile mob that was several times bigger. The procession started from the square near the prime minister's residence, where the police had expelled us, to the pedestrian mall downtown. Instead of blocking traffic and leaving the streets to the demonstrators, the police had pushed us onto the narrow sidewalk. The organizers of the procession protested and indicated the danger from passing cars to the participants of this authorized protest.

At the height of the Chief Rabbinate, what we had feared happened. A driver broke ranks, ran over the curb, sped toward us and turned the steering wheel only at the last moment. Three or four demonstrators, including me, jumped aside. I had seen the man's face as he drove toward us and noted that his expression didn't fit what I had instinctively expected—that the driver had lost control of the steering wheel and was now trying to save the situation. I expected signs of shock and panic, but what I saw in the man's face was concentration and calm. He knew what he was doing and what possible consequences he had accepted. His act was intended as a threat of murder and intimidation and it made its effect. All at once I realized how much hatred and confusion dissent provoked in this ideologically and politically intolerant society and what a risk we were incurring. We were traitors to the nation and the fatherland.

The hatred was not by chance. The government missed no opportunity to demonize the opponents of the war and brand them as stooges of the enemies of the "Jewish people." One member of the government had even accused the peace movement of being financed by Saudi Arabia. While we laughed heartily at this stroke of propaganda, others took it seriously. In February 1983, a resident of a Jewish settlement in the occupied territories converted the threat of death to death. On February 8, the committee investigating the massacre in Sabra and Shatila, published its results, including a recommendation for the resignation of Defense Minister Ariel Sharon. Two days later, Peace Now held a protest march demanding the implementation of the recommendation. This time, too, the participants went through downtown Jerusalem, surrounded by a furious mob. After the demonstration ended, a handful of activists remained at the square outside the prime minister's residence to roll up banners and clean up. This was the moment the settler had waited for. He threw a hand grenade into the group and killed one of the demonstrators, an assistant at the Hebrew University.

My fears, speculations, and fantasies about what was coming kept me petrified for days. At the same time, I was ashamed, felt that my refusal was exaggerated and unreasonable. None of my colleagues and friends, I told myself, would have been foolish enough to do that, and only I had been so dumb. I began worrying what consequences my refusal could have for my work, my social position, my life in Israel. I still faced more than fifteen years of annual reserve duty. How would my refusal affect that? It also began to dawn on me that this step had to complicate further my difficult relationship to this country and destroy the precarious balance between professional satisfaction and my dissatisfaction with everything else. Only one thing was clear: for the time being, I didn't want to talk about it with anybody. My friends and colleagues imagined that I was on assignment in the Golan and nobody missed me. I stayed at home and used up canned goods and my stocks of frozen food so I wouldn't meet anybody in the street.

After a few days, I tried to calm down and control my fears. So far, I hadn't heard anything from the army, and I judged that as a good sign. Had my expectations been too dramatic? I began to grasp the possibility that the affair could just fizzle out. To date, I had had only one run-in, during basic training, with the military justice system and this experience seemed more like farce than tragedy. Back then, I had torn much too fast over the road in a jeep in a remote stretch of the south on the way to the next kiosk to get some refreshments during a break. Speed was necessary because my absence was neither requested nor approved. On the way, I came upon a military police patrol. I expected a reprimand for not having a pass or for speeding, but to my great relief they criticized only my eyeglasses. If you drive a jeep you have to wear a helmet and big, heavy goggles that made you look like an alien, which alone would have deterred every enemy of the Jewish people from hostile acts. Instead of this monstrosity, I had put on my own sunglasses, which were conspicuous from far away because they were red, and I had also gone off without a helmet.

I was reported and long after the exercise was over and I had returned to civilian life, I received a summons to be sentenced for acting contrary to regulations. I had to appear at the headquarters of the unit, a former British police station in the south, which had undergone the usual change of occupiers, in this case from the British to the Egyptians to the Israelis. I appeared before a battalion commander who discussed this important incident with me with a serious expression and a curt tone. Since I could not point to any mitigating circumstances, I was fined a sum much less than the cost of the gas I had used that day between Jerusalem and the desert fort.

After a week of waiting, I began to get bored at home and decided to resume my normal life. I went back to work. When asked why I had been released from the army sooner than expected, I answered evasively. I spoke with very few people about the incident at the border, reported on it broadly and without a detailed explanation of my motives. I felt that my behavior was clumsy and exaggerated and I accused myself of acting thoughtlessly in a situation that left me only one escape route. I presented the incident as a chain of unfortunate circumstances beginning with my lack of foresight and ending with the failure of my agreement with Krauthammer. This way, I managed to convince myself that circumstances had forced me to take a step I would normally have avoided. Where the truth lay, I no longer knew. At the end of the second week, I finally heard from my unit.

A non-commissioned officer of the lecturers' unit had called the Institute and left a message. I went home to be able to answer the call undisturbed. The measure turned out to be unnecessary. I was simply informed that I had to appear the next morning, the last day of my original reserve duty, at the headquarters of the Education Corps for a discussion with my colonel. The staff sergeant gave the man's name and function, but neither was familiar to me. I immediately called the lawyer whose number I carried with me in case of emergency, told him everything, and showered him with questions. Did I have to count on imprisonment? How should I argue? Should I appear for the discussion at all? He indicated that it was within the unit's discretion either to sweep the incident under the rug or to try me. He advised me to wait for the discussion and not to be intimidated. He didn't respond to my request to speculate with me about possible developments and appropriate countermeasures. I was to calm down and, if necessary, to call him from the base. This phone conversation didn't give me any clue to what was in store for me the next day. At that moment, I could hardly imagine anything worse than going into such a consequential discussion so unprepared. I was flustered and pessimistic, but also felt relief. The discussion had to end the tormenting uncertainty and the vacillating feelings I had lived with for the last two weeks.

Years later, what remains most clearly in my memory from the meeting the next morning were the seemingly endless walk through the corridors and the equally long way back. Of the scene in-between, there wasn't much to remember. There was the arrangement of the table and the chairs, the position and the expression in the faces of those present, the pale blue walls. I had registered in the anteroom and was immediately sent into the commander's office. The door of his office was open. I turned the corner and stood still. At a table next to the colonel sat Major Krauthammer and her deputy. In front of the table was a chair. Nobody greeted me, nobody asked me to sit down. I stood still. The colonel said: "We have no place for someone like you. You will be dismissed from the Education Corps." I looked from one to the other. Major Krauthammer returned my look, as if I were a complete stranger, the others stared back stonily. Then she said: "You can go now." I went.

That was the last time I dealt with the Education Corps. I never heard anything again about the incident at the border. It was as if it hadn't taken place. I was transferred back to the personnel department of the army and they took more than a year to find a new unit where I was to fill my reserve duty from now on. I wound up in the air force attached to a battalion responsible for the security of air force bases. In subsequent years, I kept quiet about the incident at the Lebanese border and began talking about it freely only years later, long after I had left Israel and was no longer ashamed of the past.

Only once did I get mail from my old department. After the official conclusion of the war in May 1985, when the Israeli army had withdrawn to a new security zone in the south of Lebanon, I received a certificate and a medal, a campaign ribbon I could attach to my uniform. The brief text was framed by the emblem of the Israel Defense Forces, the sword in the Star of David surrounded by an olive branch, and the insignia of the Education Corps, an open book under a sword and an olive branch. The certificate was signed by the commander of the Education Corps. The text read: "For Daniel Brecher, with our respect for his educational contribution to the war 'Peace for Galilee.' J. Eldar, Brigadier General."

* EPILOGUE *

* 1 *

The history of the Middle East conflict described in this book ends in 1984. Since then, Israel and the region have changed a great deal. In the twenty years following the invasion of Lebanon, Israel and Jordan have signed a peace agreement, Israel withdrew from the Gaza Strip and parts of the West Bank, the PLO leadership returned home to Palestine, and for the first time Israelis and Palestinians began to negotiate a settlement of their conflict. At the same time, the south Lebanese militias fought a guerilla war against Israel, which still occupied their country, and the Palestinians began a guerilla war against the prolonged occupation of the territories conquered in 1967. The region was gripped by hope and stricken with despair.

The campaign in Lebanon was declared officially over in 1985. This was followed by another fifteen years of almost daily clashes with the fighters of the Shi'a Hisbollah militia, military campaigns in the Israeli-occupied part of southern Lebanon, and violent political quarrels within Israeli society, until the last Israeli soldiers were withdrawn from Lebanon in May 2000. For Lebanon and the Palestinians, the war had brought death and destruction—more than twenty thousand people had fallen victim to it. For Israel, it is more difficult to assess the result. The military potential of the Palestinians in Lebanon was destroyed, Arafat and the PLO leadership were driven out of Beirut, and "Peace for the Galilee" was restored, but the price in human life was also high for Israel. The far-reaching calculation of the 1982 invasion—a peace agreement with Lebanon and the removal of the PLO under Yassir Arafat as a political factor in the Middle East—was not realized. The headquarters of the Palestinian Liberation Organization and the Palestinian National Council did move from Beirut to Tunis, but the expulsion of the political leadership of the Palestinians out of the region—along with other developments in the region and in international politics—led to unexpected results. Barely ten years later, Yassir Arafat once again entered Palestinian ground, was hailed by the population as a hero and liberator, and, at the invitation of an Israeli government, settled in the West Bank city of Ramallah, fifteen minutes from the prime minister's residence and the Knesset in Jerusalem.

This amazing development, climax of the Oslo peace process begun in 1993 and suspended in 2000, was due to a combination of factors that created a unique chance for peace in the 1980s. After the collapse of the Soviet Union, the Arab "Rejection Front," including the PLO and Syria, was weakened. For the first time since 1948, the end of the Cold War offered a prospect for the success of the "Western" model of solution to the Middle East conflict, the establishment of two states. At the same time, the Islamic revolution in Iran and the first Gulf War beginning in 1980 threatened the stability of the region so much that a rapid settlement of the Israeli-Arab conflict seemed to offer all participants, including the PLO and the Likud government in Israel, more advantages than disadvantages. When the U.S. governments under

Ronald Reagan and George Bush offered the PLO a political dialogue on condition that the Palestinian leadership renounce "armed struggle" and recognize Israel in the borders of 1967, the PLO accepted. In the "Cairo Declaration" of 1983 and the so-called Declaration of Independence of 1988, adopted by the Palestinian National Council in Algeria, the Palestinians fulfilled these obligations. That step signified not only recognition of the 1947 U.N. Partition Plan, considered until recently a colonial arrogation, but also the acceptance of the territorial expansion of the Israeli state in the war of 1948–1949, which split the possible Palestinian state into two unconnected parts and reduced the territory foreseen in 1947 even more. This unparalleled concession stirred protest among independent Palestinian intellectuals and strengthened Hamas, an Islamic movement that emerged in the occupied territories during the first Intifada in 1988.

The Iraqi occupation of Kuwait in 1990 and the second Gulf War in 1991 opened an even more unusual perspective—the convergence of the interests of Israel, Saudi Arabia, and the smaller Gulf states. The U.S. administration under George Bush again seized the initiative and called a peace conference of Israel, Lebanon, Syria, Jordan, and the Palestinians, which met in Madrid in October 1991. This "Madrid Process" led to a peace treaty between Israel and Jordan, but fizzled out when it came to negotiations between Israel and the Palestinians. The Likud government led by Yitzhak Shamir was interested in a peace with the neighboring countries, but not in a peace with the Palestinians because negotiations could have only one subject—a partial or complete withdrawal from the territories occupied in 1967, a concept the Likud opposed at that time. The election victory of the Labor party under Yitzhak Rabin in 1992 and the formation of a coalition with the newly established Meretz party, a merger of the socialist Mapam, the civil rights movement Ratz, and the left-liberal Shinui, made the situation finally ripe for an Israeli-Palestinian peace. For the first time in fifteen years, a government was back in power in Israel that represented the leftist-Zionist legacy of reconciliation with the Palestinians and the division of Palestine into two states.

Meanwhile, the situation in the occupied territories had deteriorated. Ever since Menachem Begin's victory in 1977, Likud governments had proceeded in the occupied territories according to their political conviction that the Jewish state was entitled to the entire historical territory of Palestine and there was no place for another, Arab state between the Mediterranean and the Jordan. The first Begin government intended to offer those non-Jewish inhabitants of the occupied territories who insisted on remaining communal autonomy limited to their residential areas, but not citizenship. For the time being, however, even the hands of a Likud government were tied by international obligations, and only the tried and true strategy of creating "facts" was feasible: expanding the Jewish population at the expense of the Arabs, by displacement through worsening living conditions and by preventing all economic and political progress. An Israeli attempt to create a new leadership class of Arab politicians in the occupied territories to function in the future as the representatives of the community autonomy and as an alternative to the PLO, failed. This group was the first victims of the Intifada, which erupted in late 1987 as a reaction to the deteriorating conditions of life and the harsh occupation regime.

This first Intifada, which subsided only in the early 1990s, demonstrated to Israeli society the limits of its own visions of the future. Throughout the political spectrum of Zionist parties, the conviction grew that ruling this big and recalcitrant Arab population could not be managed in the long run. The Right and the Left developed different solutions to this problem. The election victory of the Labor party in 1992 gave the Zionist Left a chance to put their ideas into practice first. In the winter of 1992, the government of Yitzhak Rabin, in secret talks mediated by the

Norwegian government, offered the PLO self-government in the occupied territories, except for Jerusalem, a rapid evacuation of Gaza, and after a period of transition, negotiations about the final shape of borders and sovereignty. The Rabin government was aiming at a final situation in which the Palestinians were to receive neither full independence nor more than half of the territory conquered in 1967. The formulation of "land for peace" launched by the Rabin and Clinton administrations really meant "some land for peace."

The Palestinian leadership entered the talks in 1992 because in the Arab camp as well, the visions of the future were rapidly changing. The first Intifada had produced a new young class of leaders, who did accept the authority of the PLO but found itself in Palestine, not in Tunis. The Intifada and the deadlocked situation in the territories had also given legitimacy and a claim to a share of power to the adversaries of the PLO, Hamas and Islamic Jihad. Moreover, the PLO had allied itself with the regime in Iraq during the second Gulf War and immediately embarrassed its new partner, the U.S. The willingness of the Western-oriented Arab states to come to an arrangement with Israel must also have seemed threatening. The leadership claim of the old guard in the PLO, based on a now completely irrelevant influence in Moscow, Baghdad, and Damascus, and their support in the Arab population of the occupied territories, was no longer unchallenged. Finally, the massive settlement of Jews in the remaining areas of Palestine—in the fifteen years of official construction, a hundred thousand Jews had moved into the occupied territories and some hundred and fifty thousand into annexed parts of Jerusalem—raised another essential question: What would remain for a future Arab state in Palestine?

In the Oslo talks, Israel and the PLO agreed on an interim solution that brought short-term advantages for both sides, but avoided all problems of a final peace settlement. The Oslo

Agreement signed in Washington in September 1993 provided for Israel's gradual withdrawal and the temporary establishment of autonomous areas, nine enclaves within the sphere of Israeli control, and created a framework for negotiations that were to lead to a final solution within six years. The negotiations placed the easier problems at the beginning and all basic questions of the conflict—the international legal status of the territories, the borders, the fate of the refugees, and the future of Jerusalem—at the end. The agreement allowed the PLO leadership to return to Palestine, exercise direct control, and guide the fate of the population for the first time, even if in an extremely limited scope.

The Israeli side profited far more from the planned transition phase and, from the beginning, had good reasons to make it permanent. Israel could withdraw from Gaza and the most densely populated parts of the West Bank without giving up a single settlement or control over the entire area, and save costs. Through tax revenues—Israel had levied sales taxes, duties, and customs in the territories—and the economic advantages of a "captive" market for Israeli products and a reservoir of cheap labor, the net costs of the occupation had remained low for the first twenty years. The first Intifada, which had necessitated a massive use of the army and had led to local boycotts of Israeli products and to closing the borders for commuters and day laborers, had put an end to this occupation deluxe. The economic decline and collapse of the infrastructure in the occupied territories also meant that the costs of the occupation would rise enormously in the future.

The "interim solution" of Oslo that divided the occupied territory into areas with different legal status and released the occupiers from responsibility for most of the population closely resembled the leftist Zionist vision of a final solution. The territory of the state had been expanded to those parts considered important for defense, and the growth of the economy and population, from the beginning, to optimal borders already suggested in 1970 by the former foreign minister and strategist of the Labor party, Yigal Allon. In a small part of the West Bank—some 30 percent—lived 90 percent of the Arab population under self-administration. Israel still controlled the borders and maintained full sovereignty over the entire area, without having to take care of the impoverished and undesired population. That was the old vision of "a land without a people for a people without a land."

Despite the joint peace plan, the future perspectives of both sides still remained incompatible. It was on this extremely unstable basis that the return of the Palestinian leadership took place, with corresponding results. In 1994, Yassir Arafat and his close associates landed in Gaza, then moved to Jericho and finally to Ramallah, which was to serve the Palestinians as a temporary capital until a return to Jerusalem. Elections were held in January 1996. A Palestinian parliament and a government were soon constituted, which took power in the enclaves evacuated by Israeli troops, in Gaza, Jericho, Jenin, Kalkiliya, Tulkarem, Nablus, Ramallah, Bethlehem, and parts of Hebron. This hasty development increased the expectations of the Palestinian populations and greatly intensified the tensions inherent in the peace process from the beginning.

Initially, the peace process created optimism and a new dynamism in the Middle East. In a very short time, the barriers of the official Arab boycott began to fall, together with political reservations that had severely limited trade and restrained investments since the establishment of the State. Markets opened for Israel, from its Arab neighbor Jordan to the Asian power of India and the world power of China. In the West Bank, too, Israel behaved as if peace had already been achieved and all "painful sacrifices" had been made. Following the Allon Plan, in the four years of the center-left government under Prime Minister Rabin, assassinated in 1995, the Jewish population of the areas increased almost 40 percent to 145,000. And at the edges of Jerusalem, on both sides of the city limits established unilaterally by Israel, construction proceeded on a grand scale. The rapid growth of the Jewish parts of the city and suburbs and of the roads connecting them was a clear sign that the parts that did not come under Palestinian autonomy were already de facto incorporated into the official territory of Israel. Nevertheless, the fiction was maintained that in future negotiations about a final status, all possibilities remained open. The representatives of the Israeli government spoke one language, the "facts" spoke another.

In other respects, too, the peace process did not offer the Palestinian population a rosy future. After twenty years of occupation, the Arab population was now under the rule of an autonomy authority that showed no respect for human rights, disregarded the independence of the courts, and did not observe democratic rules. Moreover, the Palestinian administration had assumed the ungrateful task of disarming the opponents of the peace agreement and neutralizing their political influence. What Israel expected from its Palestinian peace partner was calm and order in the autonomous areas, not democracy and free speech. Great as the potential for a development of civil rights and democracy was, under these conditions it could not develop. Despite investments and massive aid from abroad, economic life did not take off either. The gross national product per capita fell about 15 percent from 1993 to 1995. With Israel's withdrawal, the occupation power began to cut the economic umbilical cord, a loss the Palestinian economy could not make up by internal growth. But what was mainly lacking were hopes for a peaceful future and a stable development, especially an unambiguous goal. Israel neither could nor would offer its Palestinian neighbors a clear perspective, a development toward independence or a federation with Israel or Jordan, for reasons inherent in Israel's internal politics and its national ideology, and not in the behavior of the Palestinians.

In protest against the Oslo concept of peace, the internal Palestinian opposition, which considered the rapprochement of Israel and the PLO as a betrayal and sell-out of Palestinian interests, took up a strategy only recently renounced by the PLO leadership—terror. By the end of 1992, attacks on Jewish civilians within the Green Line and the occupied territories had increased dramatically culminating in a wave of suicide attacks in February–March 1996, shortly before the Knesset elections. The opposition led by Likud politician Benjamin Netanyahu could point out to the public that in the two and a half years since the signing of the Oslo Agreement, more Israelis had fallen victim to Palestinian attacks than throughout the previous decade. Likud accused the government of establishing the PLO in the occupied territories and thus putting the protection of the Jewish population in the hands of Israel's enemies and demanded that further progress in the peace process be dependent on the good behavior of the Palestinians. "If they give, they'll get. If they don't give, they won't get," became Netanyahu's negotiation motto. This position successfully propagated by Likud in the 1996 election campaign was taken over in subsequent years by all Zionist parties. This argument suggested that—after concluding peace treaties with Jordan and Egypt, and after recognition by the Palestinian parliament—it was not the responsibility of Israel to evacuate the territories conquered in 1967 without delay or preconditions, but was up to the occupied to earn their freedom, by showing good behavior vis-à-vis the occupier. This notion corresponded to the basic tendency in Israel's Jewish society to reverse cause and effect in the Middle East conflict.

Likud's victory in May 1996 brought further progress in the peace negotiations to a standstill. Even the current obligations Israel had accepted in the treaty of 1993 and in the detailed implementation agreements signed in 1995 and 1997—a further withdrawal from the West Bank and an expansion of the autonomous area—were honored only in part by Netanyahu's government. His coalition had brought all adversaries of the two-state solution and the Oslo Peace Agreement under one roof for the first time—the Likud, the religious parties, and the settlers, all those who saw the withdrawal of the troops as a strategic disaster, and the return of land and the dissolution of settlements as a breach of religious and national maxims, even a violation of the will of God.

The short-lived détente in the language of the Israeli parties and media was now followed by a re-demonization of the Palestinian people and the Palestinian leadership. Politicians, even government ministers, were now allowed publicly to demand the expansion of Israel into all of Palestine and the "transfer" of the Arab population to other countries. On the other hand, a Palestinian politician who insisted on the return of refugees to Israel itself, expatiated on the injustice of the peace solution of Oslo, or who considered a re-Arabization of Palestine possible within a few generations based on the demographic development, was labeled an "enemy of the Jewish people" and a potential perpetrator of genocide, whose ideas were only another proof of the devilish intentions or anti-Semitic tendencies of the Palestinians, and who had to be resisted with all means. The Zionist Left, creators of the peace process, were labeled "Oslo Criminals," who had opened the gates to terror and the enemies of the Jews. The New Right, whose ranks spawned Rabin's murderer, demanded an uncompromising continuation of the settlement of all parts of Palestine and characterized itself as the redeemer from the yoke of "Goyish" thinking, which demanded respect for international norms and human rights in relation to the Arabs.

After three years, in 1999, Netanyahu's government fell because of internal dissensions. The last chapter in the Oslo Peace Process was written again by a Labor party politician, former Chief-of-Staff Ehud Barak, who functioned as prime minister of a short-lived coalition of left and religious parties. In the preamble to the coalition agreement, the new government no longer declared "peace" as the supreme goal, but rather the "security of the nation and the individual through a resolute struggle against terrorism." Thus, a decisive turn had come about. While the creators of Oslo still saw the peace efforts as the only way to end violence in the Middle East and to achieve "security," it was now "peace" that endangered security. In the six years since the signing of the Oslo Agreement, in the internal Israeli discussion the meaning of "peace" had changed from reconciliation with the neighbors by withdrawing from the territories into a defense against terror by holding onto the territories.

In Palestinian society, too, the six years had strengthened the opponents of Oslo. The clearer the limits of Israeli concessions emerged, the more the frustration and disappointment grew among the Palestinians. Anyone who expected a partial revision of the injustice of 1948—the return of the refugees to their homes in Israel, the complete evacuation from the occupied territories, and the division of Jerusalem into an Arab and a Jewish city—had to feel betrayed. The "legitimate rights" of the Palestinians, discussed for generations—the right to self-determination, to return home, to compensation for confiscated property—appeared worthless given the real balance of power. "Oslo," as many thought, was not a peace treaty, but a treaty of surrender, dictated by the victor. The violence of the last three years, the attacks in Israel and the countermeasures of the Israeli army in the occupied territories, had undermined trust and had polarized opinions in both societies. Not only in Israel, but also among the Palestinians, the opponents of "Oslo" gained the upper hand. In both societies, that power bloc in the center of the spectrum of public opinion, the only force to move the peace process forward, dissolved. Those were the circumstances under which the final negotiations of the Oslo Agreement took place in the spring and summer of 2000.

With the help of Egypt and the U.S., talks about the final status resumed quickly after Barak took power in June 1999. In early November, the delegations met for the first time, but by early December negotiations were interrupted again, accompanied by mutual recriminations about negligence and lack of seriousness. Since Barak could count on very little support in his own coalition and in Israeli society, he decided now on a dramatic and extremely risky step—to pose an ultimatum on the negotiations, to make all necessary concessions in a summit meeting and force those of the other side, and then present the result of the negotiations with all advantages and disadvantages as a total package to the Israeli public—hoping that a favorable outcome would justify his step after the fact. Barak assumed that he could force a successful conclusion of the negotiations within the time frame he set. When the negotiations culminating in the summit meeting at Camp David in July 2000 showed no final result, Barak had to draw the consequences from his strategy. He declared the talks a failure and blamed Yassir Arafat. After the second Intifada erupted in September, which claimed 370 dead and 10,000 wounded on both sides by the end of the year, there was no longer a way back. Barak's dwindling government coalition collapsed and Ariel Sharon became prime minister of a transition government formed by the big parties.

Despite all political legends, in the final Oslo negotiations the two sides had very quickly come very close, especially in questions of territory. In exchange for its own territory in the south, Israel was to annex three blocks of settlements in Judea, Samaria, and around Jerusalem, and could maintain military bases at strategically important places for a decade. Sovereignty over Jerusalem was to be divided, but the city was to remain united. Even in the ticklish question of the return of refugees to Israel, an understanding was on the horizon. According to statements of the participants, Israel and the Palestinian leadership could have agreed within a few months. But external circumstances, the outbreak of violence and the challenge to Barak by the opposition, which wanted to prevent a success of Oslo, allowed no further concessions. In unofficial talks after the failure of the Camp David summit, which lasted until January 2001, the still outstanding questions were almost completely cleared up. However, the compromises achieved could no longer be implemented. In subsequent years, the political developments in Israel kept these advances politically ineffective.

The Knesset elections of February 2003 led to an extraordinary strengthening of the rightist parties. Ariel Sharon, the leader of the Likud, now re-profiled as the party of the religious-nationalist settlers, brought together in his new government all opponents of Oslo and the two-state solution, and made the fight against Palestinian terror the main mission. Meanwhile, the Intifada had broadened to a guerilla war, conducted by a growing number of Palestinian groups against the occupation troops and civilians in the occupied territories and in Israel itself. The Israeli army also changed its tactics. The police actions of the past changed into military operations involving infantry, tanks, and even the use of the air force in residential areas. This confrontation marginalized the peace forces in both camps. The suicide attacks on targets in Israel, on full restaurants and buses, especially contributed in Israel's Jewish society to reinforcing the idea that the concept of "land for peace" was outmoded, and "peace" had to be the precondition for a withdrawal from the occupied territories and not the result.

In the West Bank and the Gaza Strip, a territorial and political status quo had emerged by 1995 with the establishment of autonomous enclaves that, aside from the acts of violence, was not much different from the situation the majority of Israeli voters and the big parties favored as a final solution. The great majority of the Palestinians lived under self-rule within boundaries that, from the Israeli point of view, represented an optimal compromise of adding territory to the Jewish State while separating as much as possible from an undesired population. All strategically important points of the country—the external borders, the ridges of the Judean Mountains, the Jordan Basin, and the edges of the Jerusalem corridor—were in Jewish hands. And the economically extremely important territorial growth reserves of the cities of Jerusalem and Tel Aviv, severely limited before 1967 by international borders and geographical factors, were secured for the Jewish state. The same was true for the vital water resources.

Achieving a final status in the occupied territories acceptable to the majority of Israeli voters also forms the background for the construction of the security fence begun in 2003 and the withdrawal from the settlements in the Gaza Strip in 2005. The fence was initially considered as protection of the Israeli population against Arab attacks, which killed some thousand Israeli civilians and soldiers and wounded more than five thousand in the first four years of the second Intifada. But the fence also served political functions. The anticipated more effective protection of the population against attacks from the Arab enclaves was to allow Israel to hold onto the territory without a negotiated solution to the conflict and to resist the violent attempts of the Palestinians to shake off the occupation. The withdrawal from Gaza had the same goal—to abandon some territory, the enclave with the largest and most militant Arab population, with the hope of securing the rest. As a temporary security measure, the construction of the fence won wide approval in Israel, even among those on the right, who saw in it the danger of a permanent withdrawal to smaller boundaries. In fact, in this very comprehensive and costly construction, the potential for a permanent marking of boundaries was set. The course planned in 2005 encompassed 60 Jewish settlements with 355,000 inhabitants, including the annexed parts of Jerusalem and 12 percent of the land of the West Bank. Sixty-nine

Jewish settlements with 52,000 inhabitants fell outside the planned route. To bring the majority of settlers and their land under Israeli sovereignty, 42 Palestinian towns with 246,000 inhabitants were to be included on the Israeli side of the barrier, and an additional 50 Arab communities with 244,000 people were to be surrounded on at least three sides.

In March 2006, the prime minister and leader of the newly formed center party Kadima, Ehud Olmert, confirmed his government's intention to impose these boundaries unilaterally on the Palestinian population as the final border of Israel, with minor corrections. But the fence was seen by all concerned as not only a potential borderline, but also a barrier in a more comprehensive sense—as a permanent demographic boundary between Jews and Arabs and between East and West, between an industrial state and a developing nation. With an income disparity between Israel and the occupied territories four times bigger than that between Mexico and the U.S., Israel had to count on an illegal immigration of Arabs or other non-Jews, motivated primarily by economics, which in the long run endangered the dominance of the Jewish population and the Zionist dimension of Israel even more than the present Arab population of Palestine.

Ever since the outbreak of the second Intifada, growing poverty and chaos prevailed in the occupied territories. In the first four years, the Israeli army killed some three thousand inhabitants of the territory and wounded more than 25,000. The survival of autonomy in the enclaves led to a military tactic, which Israel had used before 1967 in border areas of Jordan and Egypt—short, massive incursions of relatively big armored units that imposed curfews, searched villages and neighborhoods for fighters, and used heavy weapons in clashes. The results were high losses among civilians and damages to the civilian infrastructure. Israel treated the autonomous areas as a hostile country and thus violated the regulations of the Fourth Geneva Convention, which made the occupation power responsible for the protection and equal treatment of the civilian population. Other measures for suppressing the uprising also had far-reaching consequences for daily life—arbitrary arrests, the destruction of houses as punishment, and the creation of sight zones and firing zones in front of control posts and around Jewish settlements. The most extensive disruption of life, however, was caused by the radical limitation of the freedom of movement by encapsulating the enclaves with blockades and road closings.

In the first four years of the Intifada, the conditions of life of the Palestinian population grew drastically worse. In 2003, 60 percent of the people were strongly hindered in the practice of their professional or economic activity and in access to doctors, hospitals, and schools. In 2004, after fifteen years of uninterrupted growth, the Gross National Product fell back to the level of 1986. In 2003, at the height of the Intifada, two million Palestinians, 63 percent of the population, lived under the poverty line of $2.16 per person per day. In April 2006, more than a year after the second Intifada had fizzled out, this rate was still at 56 percent.

The great progress in the peace attempts and the gigantic step back, bringing failures for both populations, raises an obvious question: Why was it so hard for Israel and the Palestinians to find a solution to their problems in these ten years? The direct causes for the failure of the first attempt to settle the century-long conflict are easily summarized. The Oslo concept of peace had too little support and too many opponents—the Jewish rejection front led by Likud and the maximalists within the Palestinian camp, for whom a territorial compromise and divided sovereignty of Palestine are a betrayal of their principles. The terrorist attacks by the Arabs and the incitement by the Jews undermined the process and shortened what was anyway a tiny stretch of time available for reaching an understanding and a solution of the extremely complex and extraordinary questions.

But an understanding also encountered hurdles inherent in the situation from the beginning. Both groups entertained completely incompatible notions of the causes and results of the conflict. The Jews of Israel regarded their presence in the Middle East as a return to the old homeland, while the Arabs of Palestine saw it as an act of European colonization. For Jews, expanding and securing the territory is an act of nation building, for Arabs it is robbery and a crime against humanity. While the Arabs had fought for generations against the Jewish conquerors and looters of their towns and villages, the Jews defended themselves against unjustified aggression and terror. For most Israelis, settling the conflict means the recognition of Israel in its Zionist dimension, as a state for Jews in borders that take into consideration both military and demographic factors. For most Palestinians, peace means an end to the occupation and a rectification of the injustice from 1948 to 1967, thus a withdrawal of the colonial state to the borders of 1967, the return of East Jerusalem, the re-admission of refugees, and the payment of reparations.

Mixing Jewish and Arab populations in Palestine forms the biggest obstacle to a conventional solution of the conflict. That two hostile populations live next to one another almost inseparably is the result of the Zionist strategy of conquering Arab space by settlement, between 1920 and 1948 and after 1967. Disentangling the populations was blocked for a long time by the logic of Zionism that immediately makes every newly conquered area within the historical homeland a legitimate part of the state. This process was aided by the notion that territory was "won" involuntarily, as the result of wars Israel was forced to wage.

It is hard for both sides to give up their view of things. For both, nothing less than their national identity is at stake, which was established only in the conflict itself. This fact made a rapprochement through mutual understanding and reconciliation in the short time of the peace process practially impossible. Nevertheless, a solution of the conflict still remains urgent and advantageous for both sides. The advances of the post-Oslo negotiations made in January 2001 in the resort city of Taba on the Red Sea retained its potential as a starting point for a new peace process, even after the outbreak of the second Intifada. Measured by the national myths and reservations of both sides, these final negotiations made enormous progress, and several initiatives by Arab and Jewish politicians used this breakthrough to formulate new peace plans.

The starting point of Oslo—the division of Palestine according to the demographic and political conditions of 1993—remains, however, linked to its time. Israel, as the regional superpower, continues to change these conditions to the disadvantage of the Palestinians. This makes a future solution on the basis of dividing Palestine into two nation states ever more difficult to achieve. The region is heading for a situation in which a just and rational solution is possible only in a binational or federative state, an idea rejected by most Israelis because it threatens to make the Jews a minority in Palestine and would mean the end of Zionism. Thus, the Zionist goal of a nation state for Jews is undermined by the action of Israel itself.

* 2 *

For a long time, I kept quiet about my experiences on the Lebanese border in February 1984. I wasn't proud of refusing to perform my duty and was afraid of being rejected by my surroundings. Nevertheless, I felt liberated—from the burden of wanting to belong to the politically conformist Israeli society, of having to adjust to the views of Zionism and Jewish nationalism. I went back to my old views and, as I think, to myself. What remained much longer was the shame. In February 1984, just eight years after I came back to Israel, I started thinking about emigration.

It wasn't my political convictions that forced me to weigh this step. In the Israeli political spectrum, there is a small but not insignificant group of anti-Zionists. In opinion polls, some 5 percent of the Jewish, non-religious voters regularly identified with anti-Zionist positions. In elections for the 120-member Knesset, non-Zionist, Arab-Jewish, and Arab slates usually won between four and nine seats. Yet it was not freedom of opinion that characterized life in Israel, but rather the nationalism and conformism of the overwhelming majority. Zionism was the national ideology voluntarily supported by over 95 percent of the secular Jewish population, not through any censorship or repression. That made opponents of Zionism into dissidents. Living as a dissident within Israel's Jewish society was certainly possible, but the prospect didn't excite me. The aggressive nationalism, the role assigned me as a Jew in this colonial society, confrontations between majority and minority—all that struck a sore point with me. For the second time, I longed for a country where I wouldn't be monopolized by nationalism from the start.

What kept me in Israel for the time being were practical issues and the feeling that my emigration had to be an admission of my failure. It took more than two years to find a solution for the practical aspects. The sense of shame continued to pursue me. In Israeli society, immigration to Israel is considered an "ascent," emigration is thus a "descent" and a "betrayal," and even before they leave, future descenders are marginalized. The first time I discussed my plans with colleagues, I met with an unexpectedly abrupt rejection. The reaction I encountered most, however, was that of ostentatious disregard. The announcement of my plans was accepted without comment, as if it wasn't emigration but plans for next weekend. But friendships cooled, professional contacts became more formal, and invitations were withheld. Only once did my announcement lead to an outburst of feelings. During a reception at the university, I was talking with a prominent scholar, who occupied a university chair abroad and spent only a small part of the year in Israel. When I mentioned my emigration plans, he reacted with a true battery of curses. He accused me of lacking idealism and reproached me for not being up to the difficult life of sacrifice in Israel. I was shirking my duty to this most significant of all Jewish projects, and my motives could only be base. Clearly I wanted to turn my back on my brothers to indulge in a hedonistic life style abroad. After he had given me this tongue-lashing and trampled me in the dust, he left me alone.

In the fall of 1986, I emptied my Jerusalem apartment and filled an imposing shipping container with my belongings, considerably more than what I had come with. When the crates were nailed shut in the courtyard of the shipper, I again felt the inconstancy and mobility of life. I was ready to travel. I spent the few weeks before I left in the apartment of friends, enjoying that transitory state when old cares seem to belong to the past and new ones to a distant future.

Almost a year after my emigration, I was unexpectedly confronted with an old problem. I was offered the direction of a museum in Germany. The museum was dedicated to the persecution and resistance during the Nazi period and was also marginally preoccupied with German-Jewish history. In the future, this aspect was to form the focus. The permanent exhibition, the core of a museum, had to be re-designed and there were plans for a complete reconstruction of the building. This job tempted me very much and I started holding discussions about the museum and my tasks. One single circumstance bothered me—for this job, I had to come back to Germany.

The difficulties of my life as a Jew in Germany had contributed a great deal to my move to Israel, and I now hesitated to expose myself to them again. During the last decade, I had regularly visited Germany and kept noticing that Jews and non-Jews were still grating on each other in public. "German" and "Jewish" were still separate, incompatible identities and provided explosives for heated debates. As director of an institution concerned with the Nazi period, I wouldn't be able to avoid these polemics. Many of these debates seemed directed not at understanding and eliminating prejudices, but rather at preserving group identities, and reinforcing wholesale judgments. But most of all, I was repelled by the nationalism that would be put on display on this occasion. I didn't want to expose myself to such situations again. Moreover, I got the impression that the rigid identification with Israel and the narrow boundaries of debate in Germany about the problems of the Middle East would soon exasperate me.

After my father's death, my mother was living alone in Düsseldorf at the time. She was excited by the prospect of her only son settling once again in Germany and often visiting her. She presented me with her experiences in Germany, which were so different from mine. She had meanwhile found a circle of friends, which consisted equally of Jews and non-Jews. She felt at home in Germany, maybe for the first time in her life anywhere. I was very happy for her, but couldn't trust that her recipe would work for me too. After long wandering and deprivations, she had reached the calm water of a stable and comfortable existence and could appreciate the achievement without being diverted by the unpleasant aspects of her surroundings. That was a perspective offered to her generation, but not to mine.

Meanwhile, I lived and worked in a country where neither my Jewish origin nor my opinions about Israel were in any special tension with my surroundings and I enjoyed it every day. Nobody seemed to find the subjects that had tormented me particularly explosive. Sometimes, when I fell back into the old habit of talking about "Germans" and "Jews," I encountered incomprehension. Weren't Jews who lived in Germany also Germans? That it cost me so much time and trouble to explain the long history of this construction was a good sign. Here, it was possible to remove the straitjacket of these identities that had emerged under the special conditions of the postwar period. Here there were no obstacles to acknowledging the immense cultural wealth given by my German-Jewish origin, without having to deny one or the other part of my identity. I decided to decline the German offer and to go on loving not only my homeland of Israel but also my homeland of Germany from afar.

I still participated fervently in political developments in Israel. The distance changed my perspectives and my feelings: I no longer experienced the conflict as a member of the Jewish community of Israel or out of "Jewish" sensibilities, and could now put myself more easily in the situation of the Palestinians and their sensibilities. No wonder that other feelings now began to plague me—impotence and rage—typical reactions to the hopelessly inferior situation in which this group has found itself for generations. The superiority Israel enjoys as an occupier and as a regional super power, the support it receives from Europe and the U.S., and the position of moral indisputability it still held despite thirty years of progressive colonization of conquered areas, must sooner or later drive an outsider to despair. Palestinians have hardly any prospect of fleeing their long nightmare. The chances are infinitesimal that the Jewish society of Israel will find the strength to give up the territories occupied in 1967 and the settlements. Even the most favorable prognosis—a settlement on the basis of the territorial compromise of 2000—would give the Palestinians a state divided into several unconnected territories without reserves for growth and without the economic bases necessary to absorb the millions of people still in refugee camps. Like many critics of Israeli policy before me, I came to the conviction that only one thing could change the situation: a drastic change in public opinion in Israel and the Western world.

In the early 1990s, I began to make my own modest contribution to this process. Because speakers from governments and parties in Israel and many Jewish journalists abroad constantly dismiss criticism of the settlements and the Apartheid regime in the occupied territories as one-sided or biased, Jews like me had an especially important role—to attack and disarm the many myths and justifications based directly or indirectly on the Holocaust or anti-Semitism. As I saw it, the horrible events of the millions of Jews murdered in Europe did not entitle the State of Israel to anything, certainly not to excuse the catastrophic results of the Zionist enterprise for the Palestinians. Only one group of people had special rights—the families of the victims and the survivors. A sharper awareness of the dangers of racism, anti-Semitism, and other social prejudices has led to a special consideration for the Jews as a minority, but that did not give Jews carte blanche. Consideration of minorities is a duty that obliges everyone, also Jews.

Ever since the failure of the Oslo talks, discourse about the conflict has been determined by the violence of the Palestinians and the Israeli countermeasures. The Intifada, a wretched struggle for independence, helped the maximalists on the Israeli side to portray the Palestinians as not ready for peace in principle. The indiscriminate violence against Israeli civilians was produced as proof that the Palestinians still wanted the destruction of the entire state of the Jews, a conviction shared by almost 70 percent of the Israeli population. Continuing the state of siege in the occupied territories—either by direct occupation or by sealing off Palestinian areas—appeared only reasonable. Every step Israel took in the West Bank and the Gaza Strip was justified as a defensive measure to save human lives.

The steps that could really end the bloodshed and open the prospect of an end to the conflict are hardly discussed anymore. First of all, that would be removing the true causes of the violence, the permanent settlement of the territories conquered in 1967 and the suppression of the population. What seems equally important to me is a real dialogue between Jews and the Arabs of Palestine and the adjacent countries. This will be successful only when the Jewish side also shoulders responsibility for the results of its actions—destroying the Arab society of Palestine, devastating its economic and cultural life—and acknowledges the injustice it committed. This is predicated on a political maturity of the Jewish society of Israel that is not yet in evidence. A prospect of peace and reconciliation within the state itself will exist only when Israel changes into an open society in which the rights and development of the individual citizen are protected and promoted regardless of race and religion, where freedom and human rights stand in the foreground rather than the dogmas of Zionism. Then Israel would finally be a country that acknowledges the most important Jewish tradition—justice.

"On three things does the world stand: on justice, on truth, and on peace" (Talmud, Abot 1:18).

* BIBLIOGRAPHY *

Preface

Scholem, G. *Von Berlin nach Jerusalem*. Frankfurt/M: Suhrkamp 1977, p. 73.

Chapter 1 - War

Ariel Sharon's remark about the PLO. In Friedman, T. *From Beirut to Jerusalem*. London: HarperCollins 1998, p. 143.

Chapter 2 - A Good Fence

Brynen, R. *Sanctuary and Survival: The PLO in Lebanon*. Boulder, CO: Westview 1990.

Davis, M. T. *Lebanon 1982: The Imbalance of Political Ends and Military Means*. Quantico, VA: Marine Corps Command and Staff College 1985.

——— *Operation Peace for Galilee—the 1982 Israeli Invasion of Lebanon. A Case Study*. Quantico, VA: Marine Corps Command and Staff College 1994.

Schulze, K. E. Perceptions and misperceptions: influences on Israeli intelligence estimates during the 1982 Lebanon war. *Journal of Conflict Studies* 16(1), Spring 1996.

Solley, G. C. *The Israeli Experience in Lebanon, 1982–1985.* Quantico, VA: Marine Corps Command and Staff College 1987.

Chapter 3 - Education of an Israeli

Bar-On, D. *Die "Anderen" in uns. Dialog als Modell interkultureller Konfliktbewältigung.* Hamburg: Edition Körber-Stiftung 2001.

Benvenisti, M. *Jerusalem. The Torn City.* Jerusalem: Isratypeset 1976.

Kimmerling, B. *The Invention and Decline of Israeliness. State, Society, and the Military.* Berkeley: University of California Press 2001.

Wilhelm II, Herzl Quotations. In Bein, A. *Theodor Herzl.* Vienna: Fieba-Verlag 1934, p. 549.

Chapter 4 - To Each His Own

Menachem Begin's Jerusalem speech of January 1952. In Segev, T. *The Seventh Million. The Israelis and the Holocaust.* New York: Henry Holt 2000, p. 216.

Brodesser, H.-J., Fehn, B. J., Franosch, T., and Wirth, W. *Wiedergutmachung und Kriegsfolgenliquidation. Geschichte, Regelungen, Zahlungen.* Munich: C. H. Beck 2000.

Central Bureau of Statistics. *Statistical Abstracts of Israel.* Main series. Jerusalem 1949ff.

Galinski, H. Jüdisches Gemeindeleben nach 1945. In *Vom Schicksal Geprägt. Freundesgabe zum 60. Geburtstag von Karl Marx*, ed. M. W. Gärtner, H. Lamm, and E. G. Lowenthal. Düsseldorf: Kalima-Druck 1957, p. 41ff.

Rabbi Robert Geis's speech. In Schoeps, H. J. *Jüdische Geisteswelt. Zeugnisse aus zwei Jahrtausenden.* Cologne: Joseph Melzer Verlag 1960, p. 319.

Grossmann, K. R. *Die Ehrenschuld. Kurzgeschichte der Wiedergutmachung.* Frankfurt/M: Ullstein 1967.

Oppenheimer, W. W. J. *Über die Jüdische Jugend im heutigen Deutschland. Eine sozialpsychologische Studie.* Munich: Juventa Verlag 1967.

Rosenberg, L. Gewerkschaften im Nachkriegsdeutschland. In *Vom Schicksal Geprägt. Freundesgabe zum 60. Geburtstag von Karl Marx*, ed. M. W. Gartner, H. Lamm, and E. G. Lowenthal. Düsseldorf: Kalima-Druck 1957, p. 87.

Chapter 6 - Even a Strong Nation Is Sometimes Sad

Brecher, D. C. *The First Af-Al-Pi Convoy* (Hebr.). Tel Aviv: Army Education Branch 1982.

President Jimmy Carter's announcement. In Brog, M. Seeking salvation at this museum. *Haaretz*, May 9, 2003.

Hausner, G. Foreword. In Shabbetai, K. *As Sheep to the Slaughter.* Bet Dagan: Keshev 1962, p. 5f.

Haycraft, Sir T. *Report of the Commission of Inquiry into the Palestine Disturbances of May 1921.* Résumé. London 1921. Available: http://domino.un.org/UNISPAL.NSF.

Jabotinsky, V. *The Ethics of the Iron Wall* (Russ.) 1923. Available: www.jabotinsky.org/jabhom_h.htm.

——— The iron wall. *Jewish Herald*, November 28, 1937. Available: www.jabotinsky.org/jabhom_h.htm.

League of Nations. *Mandate for Palestine*. Geneva 1922. Available: http://domino.un.org/UNISPAL.NSF.

Quotations from the air force ceremony at Auschwitz. In O'Sullivan, A. IDF to honor Auschwitz with flyover. *Jerusalem Post*, August 28, 2003; *Yad Vashem Press Release*, September 3, 2003: Israeli Air Force pilots flying over Auschwitz-Birkenau will carry "Pages of Testimony" from Yad Vashem of Jews who were killed on the same day 60 years ago; Barkat, A. Auschwitz museum opposes plans for IAF fly-over at camp. *Haaretz*, September 4, 2003; *New York Times*, September 4, 2003: "The museum at the former Auschwitz death camp today criticized a planned flyover by Israeli F-15 fighter jets during this week's ceremony in remembrance of victims."

Shabbetai, K. *As Sheep to the Slaughter*. Bet Dagan: Keshev 1962.

Chapter 7 - A Rest Stop in the Countryside

Central Bureau of Statistics. *Statistical Abstracts of Israel*, no. 29. Localities and Population. Jerusalem 1978, p. 41f.

International Committee of the Red Cross. *Report Concerning ICRC activity in the action at Deir Yassin (Jerusalem)*, April 14, 1948. Available: www.icrc.org/web/fre/sitefre0.nsf/iwpList575/B6A9183086F4997FC1256D8700564AEC.

Interviews with Mansur, Gilad, Toubassi, Geday, Monayer, Yassen, and Pundak. In Brecher, D. C. *Al Nakba. Die Katastrophe*.

DeutschlandRadio Berlin 1997; and unpublished interviews in the possession of the author.

Jabotinsky, V. *The Ethics of the Iron Wall* (Russ.), 1923. Available: www.jabotinsky.org/jabhom_h.htm.

——— The iron wall. *Jewish Herald*, November 28, 1937. Available: www.jabotinsky.org/jabhom_h.htm.

Krolik, S., ed. *Arthur Ruppin. Tagebücher, Erinnerungen, Briefe*. Königstein/Ts: Athenäum 1985, pp. 313, 322f.

A Place-Guide to Israel (Hebr.). Publications of the Ministry of Defense. Jerusalem: Carta 1979.

Pappé, I. *The Making of the Arab–Israeli Conflict, 1947–1951*. London: I.B. Tauris 1992.

Quotations of Ben Gurion, Shertok, Weitz. In Morris, B. *The Birth of the Palestinian Refugee Problem, 1947–1949*. Cambridge, UK: Cambridge University Press 1989, pp. 24f, 28, 31, 52, 55, 63, 116f, 140–43, 222f, 282.

Chapter 8 - An End, a Beginning

Davidson, I. Tension, pessimism and shame. *Financial Times*, September 30, 1982, p. 18.

Davis, M. T. *Operation Peace for Galilee—the 1982 Israeli Invasion of Lebanon. A Case Study*. Quantico, VA: Marine Corps Command and Staff College 1994.

Kahan, Y., et al. *Report of the Commission of Inquiry into the Events at the Refugee Camps in Beirut*. Jerusalem 1983. Available: www.jewishvirtuallibrary.org/jsource/History/Kahan.html

Epilogue

Israel Ministry of Foreign Affairs. *Four Years of Conflict. Israel's War Against Terrorism.* October 3, 2004. Available: www.mfa.gov.il/MFA/Terrorism-+Obstacle+to+Peace/Terrorism+and+Islamic+Fundamentalism-/Four+Years+of+Conflict+3-Oct-2004.htm.

Palestinian Red Crescent Society. *Total daily numbers of death and injuries—West Bank and Gaza during period Sept. 29 2000–Sept. 25 2004.* Available: www.palestinercs.org/Database. Date: September 27, 2004.

United Nations Economic and Social Council. *Economic and social repercussions of the Israeli occupation on the living conditions of the Palestinian people in the occupied Palestinian territory, including Jerusalem, and of the Arab population in the occupied Syrian Golan.* June 2004. Available: www.un.org/docs/ecosoc/documents.asp?id=699.

United Nations Office for the Coordination of Humanitarian Affairs. *Humanitarian Impact of the West Bank Barrier. Update,* No. 6. January 2006. Available: www.humanitarianinfo.org/opt/docs/UN/OCHA/OCHABarRprt-Updt6-En.pdf.

The World Bank Group. *West Bank and Gaza. Update.* March 2004, April 2006. Available: www.worldbank.org/reference/.